The
Reforming
of General
Education

The
Reforming
of General
Education

The Columbia Experience in Its National Setting

Daniel
Bell

Foreword by David B. Truman

With a new introduction by the author

Transaction Publishers
New Brunswick (U.S.A.) and London (U.K.)

Library of Congress Catalog Number: 2010024330
ISBN: 978-1-4128-1113-2
Printed in the United States of America

Library of Congress Cataloging-in-Publication Data

Bell, Daniel, 1919-
    The reforming of general education : the Columbia experience in its national setting / Daniel Bell.
        p. cm.
    Originally published: New York : Columbia University Press, 1966.
    Includes bibliographical references and index.
    ISBN 978-1-4128-1113-2 (alk. paper)
      1. Columbia College (Columbia University)--Curricula. 2. General education--New York (State)--New York. I. Title.

LD1269.5.C6B45 2010
378.1'99097471--dc22

                                    2010024330

FOR LIONEL TRILLING, COLUMBIA '25,

WHO HAS

"THE SCHOLAR'S CAUTION AND THE SCHOLAR'S COURAGE."

CONTENTS

INTRODUCTION TO THE TRANSACTION EDITION

THE RECONSTRUCTION OF LIBERAL EDUCATION*

A FOUNDATIONAL SYLLABUS

Daniel Bell

"Nothing at all has remained theory, everything has become a story."

—Gershom Scholem

A story: "When the Baal Shem [The Master of the Name] had a difficult task before him, he would go to a certain place in the woods, light a fire and meditate in prayer—and what he had set out to perform was done. When, a generation later, the "Maggid" of Meseritz was faced with the same task, he would go to the same place in the woods and say: "We can no longer light the fire, but we can still speak the prayers"—and what he wanted done became reality. Again, a generation later, Rabbi Moshe Leib of Sassov had to perform the task. And he too went into the woods and said: We can no longer light a fire, nor do we know the secret meditations belonging to the prayer, but we do know the place in the woods to which it all belongs—and that must be sufficient.... But when another generation had passed and Rabbi Israel of Rishin was called upon to perform the task he sat down ... and said: We cannot light the fire, we cannot speak the prayers, we do not know the place, but we can tell the story.

—Hassidic Tale, as retold by S.Y. Agnon

About thirty or so years ago, I wrote a book, *The Reforming of General Education*. In the older reckoning, as Comte put it, thirty years was the life span of a generation. Today, as historical time has collapsed into decades, "theoretical paradigms"—structuralism, post-structuralism, deconstructionism, and post-modernism—spin dizzily through the revolving doors of intellectual fashion, my book, I suspect, if someone stumbles across it in the stacks of a college library, would have an archaic echo and a musky smell. Or, in the high-tech mode, if the book is beamed up from a microdisk or CD-ROM, the language (but one would have to say, the discourse), with its emphasis on "conceptual inquiry," or the "nature of explanation," would surely seem to be dated, if not "irrelevant."

And yet, apart from an author's pride in the products of one's youth, the book might have some standing in a contemporary discussion of the "crisis" of liberal education (crisis being the only invariant term perhaps in the history of discourse) as a benchmark from the past and as a starting point in the effort presented to offer a "reconstruction" of liberal learning.

My book was an effort to defend the value of liberal learning against the centrifugal spin of intellectual fragmentation, and the whirlpools of specialization, which were turning a college curriculum into a cafeteria for many and a training diet for a few. It was an effort to defend the existence of the college as a distinctive intellectual experience or grounding in the logic of inquiry, rather than as a "corridor" of remedial learning; or as preparation for a career between the secondary school and the graduate or professional school.

Any venture into education (besides being an experiment in autobiography) requires an explicit relationship of philosophy, and a commitment to a particular philosophical point to justify the point of view. The traditional idea of general education was based, implicitly or otherwise, on one or another of two premises: one, that there were invariant truths about human behavior, and natural ends (*telos*) to which moral action should be shaped, as established by human reason; the other that there was a common body of knowledge (or books) that every educated person ought to know, under the pain of being judged uncultivated.

Both grounds, I would argue, remain as normative ideals. Yet neither, I argued, prepares a student to deal with structures of disciplines and the ways knowledge is revised. I was not concerned with the multiplication of knowledge, which was the belief behind the thought of the fragmentation of knowledge. Let me say here, as a necessary aside, that the argument about the exponential increase in the "amount" of knowledge (based either on the increase in the number of scientific journals or the "doubling rates" of library holdings) is completely misleading. The statements confuse data, information, and knowledge. To illustrate the distinctions, let me take the index of a book, through whose classifications we are given the necessary clues to what one finds in the book. *Data* (statistics, birth records, crop totals, minerals mined, etc.) is like a *name* index; it is easily ordered and usually alphabetized by name or ordinal amounts. *Information* (historical events, scientific results, concepts, such as democracy or equality) is grouped under the *subject index*; these are combinations of materials into some thematic form.

Knowledge is the *judgment* about the organization and groupings of information under different subject rubrics. Judgment derives from purpose, which allows the author and reader to revise and re-arrange the subjects for the purposes of one's own research.

Intellectual judgment, in this vein, derives from theory, and how the information fits into or disconfirms a theory. This means that knowledge is the construct of an "analytical index," which unfortunately few students or readers use when grappling with a book. To that extent, there has been no "exponential increase in knowledge (though in some fields, as in physics, we have the elaboration of theory, as when electricity and magnetism, though disparate in their original conceptions, are now understood as being a single unified force).

All of this points to the philosophy that underlay my book, the power of the single lexical phoneme in providing different ways of re-organizing, re-ordering, and re-arranging aesthetic forms and knowledge. To understand the nature of "re," one must know the history of the previous forms whose spatial planes in art or sound patterns in music or topographical knots in mathematics or the logic which sets forth "transformational rules," in physics or anthropology. The theme of "re" is central of course to the thinking of John Dewey, and finds marvelous exposition in his *Art in Experience*.

I did not insist that there is one and only one orderly structure, a trivium and a quadrivium, which all must follow. But whatever curriculum one stipulates, it is incumbent that the sequences one selects and relates be articulated into a coherent intellectual structure that is rationally defensible. Without that it is not education.

The Reforming of General Education opened with a detailed presentation and historical development of the three models of general education that had been followed by many American colleges, that of Columbia,

Chicago, and Harvard. It remains, I believe, the only such comparison in the educational literature. It outlined the structural changes emerging in the society, principally that of a "post-industrial society" (a theme I elaborated ten years later in a comprehensive book on that subject) and a new intellectual technology that needs to be embodied in the curriculum. And it dealt with the break up of two intellectual hopes upon which much of the philosophy of general education had been predicated: the idea of the "unity of knowledge," and more sharply, the "unity of science."[1]

The ground of the book was the experience of Columbia College, and the major influence was my colleague, Lionel Trilling, to whom the book was dedicated, as much in intellectual temper as his reflective mode. It was the confrontation of modernity with tradition that was the issue to be mastered. As I wrote then:

> Is it the task of the university to be a clerisy, self-consciously guarding the past and seeking assertively to challenge the new? Or is it just a bazaar, offering Coleridge and Blake, Burckhardt and Nietzsche, Weber, and Marx, as anti-tona prophets, each with his own call? No consensual answer is possible, perhaps "because the university is no longer the citadel of the traditional mode—only the simple-minded can believe it is—but an arena in which the critics once outside the Academy have, like Blake's the tiger (or Tyger) once outside the gates of society, found a place—deservedly—within. And the tension between past and future, mind and sensibility, tradition and experience, for all its strains and discomfitures, is the only source for maintaining the independence of inquiry itself.

And yet, there was a question. Again:

> [Art] is the freest activity of the human imagination ... the least dependent on social constraints ... and for this reason the first signs of changes in collective sensibility become noticeable in art. It is, one can say (in the phase of De Quincy) the realm of proleptic wisdom. Just as the agonized fantasies of a Rimbaud a hundred years ago prefigured the cruder cult of adolescence today, so the writhing of a Burroughs, or the anti-art of some modernist cults, may foreshadow the vulgate language and destructive impulses of thousands more tomorrow.

The anomaly of all this is that the thrust of modernity—what Professor Trilling has called the "adversary culture"—has itself become an established force, nowhere more so than in the university, while retaining its adversary stance.[2] These were cautions.[3] The courage lay in proposing a new rationale, the stipulation of the patterns of knowledge, and a set of proposals within the three as to how these patterns would be embodied in a curriculum. Curiously, each was a set of triads.[4]

The normative commitment was comprised of three objectives: *self-consciousness*, the forces that impel an individual from within and constrict him from without, the questions derived from Rameau's Nephew of authenticity; *historical consciousness*, beyond fact and chronology, necessary as these are, to provide a "vocabulary of reference" for the historical imagination and the nature of comparison for historical explanation; logic and *methodological consciousness*, the logic of conceptual inquiry and the relation of the knower to the known.

The patterns of knowledge, I argued, are fundamentally triadic in that different principles govern the acquisition of knowledge in the <u>sciences,</u> the <u>social sciences</u> and the <u>humanities</u>. In the sciences, learning is *sequential* in that specified steps are necessarily defined and have to be mastered before one proceeds to the next ones. In the social sciences, the pattern is one of *linkages* in that the kinds of an economy (market or command) are dependent on different political orders, and this, in turn, on the social structures of State and civil society, and that the understanding of one, necessarily involves, the understanding of its relation to the others. And the humanities are *concentric*, in that one explores the meanings of experience as a *ricorsi*, albeit within different contexts and hermeneutic levels, such as the understanding of tragedy and comedy. (As Groucho Marx once said: It is much harder to do comedy than tragedy, for while everyone cries at the same things, they laugh at different things.)

The curriculum would be structured in three steps. The first would be a grounding in history, the second, the acquisition of a discipline, and "the third-tier" courses that would apply the history and discipline to broad, synoptic problems, moral and practical. The history I proposed was Western history for (as I shall argue again), the matrix of our intellectual schemes, particularly the very idea of *concepts*, originates and develops in the West, and the roles of science and technology derive primarily from the new thinking developed in the Renaissance, as the idea of conscience and faith are redefined in the Reformation. I do not believe in the idea of "inter-disciplinary" schemes, for a discipline is an internally coherent, integrated body of concepts (such as neo-classical economics) that are applied to subjects (such as an economy). The third-tier allows for the knowledge gained in the two previous steps to come to bear on issues such as city planning to values and rights.[5]

A "Coda—about the future," is a reprise of the cultural theme sounded earlier. "A great and troubling task remains—to humanize technocracy and

to 'tame' the apocalypse. It will be easier to do the first than the second."
The technocratic mode, to which the university is increasingly committed, stresses professionalism and technique. In reaction, the apocalyptic
mode, as expressed in the humanities, becomes nihilistic or estranged
from the society. "One lives," I concluded, "in that painful alienation
which is the continuing knowledge of doubt, not certainty. And yet this,
too, is a state of grace, for as Dante said, 'Doubting pleases me no less
than knowing.'"

The Reforming of General Education, though later appreciated elsewhere, had little or no impact at Columbia, the place for whom the study
was undertaken. There was the resistance from an older faculty that did
not wish to be disturbed, and from the career-oriented or research-involved
faculty whose rewards came not from teaching, but from "the production
of new knowledge," as it was called, and whose advancement comes from
specialization and graduate teaching and research. Intellectual challenges
fall badly on the deaf ears of the educational theorists who are concerned,
usually, with classroom pedagogical problems (I mean no disparagement)
or on the indifferent minds of the research-oriented professors who are
committed to their own professional concerns.

Besides, this was a report of a "committee of one," which, by definition,
has no constituency other than himself and some fellow teachers.[6]

But the main reason why the report sank without much of a trace at
Columbia was the "storming of the citadel" by the student radicals who,
in the contagion of revolution thought that by challenging the University,
they were challenging (might even overthrow) the society. In the festival
of May 1968, in Columbia, as in Paris, the heady cry was that Imagination
would come to Power. Imagination came to earth at the end of police clubs
and many of the student leaders went underground (to surface briefly in
Chicago that year at the Democratic convention, in the "day of rage,")
and to live out their fantasies of revolution as Weathermen or in a spate
of bombings (which in one tragic instance blew up a house in Greenwich
Village in New York and killed some of the Columbia students making
the bombs).

Revolution, as tragedy or farce is not the setting for the "rational
reconstruction" of conceptual inquiry. As some students cried, as they
organized "belly-dancing" on the Columbia greensward: "Who are you
to tell me what to take as courses." To which I could only reply: "Because

you don't know what you don't know. If you did, you would not need me. As it is, you do."[7]

Notes

* I thank Irving Louis Horowitz for editorial advice with this new introduction.

1. The "unity of knowledge" was the theme of a symposium organized by the Smithsonian Institution on the occasion of the 200th anniversary of its founding, with essays by Jerome Bruner, Herbert Butterfield, Kenneth Clark, Claude Levi-Strauss, Stephen Toulmin, Fred Whipple, and others. The difficulty with the essays is that none of them could point to the ways the new developments in physics, art, psychology, et al. had any common foundations, but only, and largely through metaphor, how they had influenced one another. It was not convincing. For the collection, see *Knowledge among Men*, edited by Webster True (New York: Simon and Schuster, 1966).

The "unity of science," was a comprehensive and heroic effort by the philosophers of the "Vienna Circle," principally Otto Neurath and Rudolf Carnap, to outline the "unifying principles of science," centered, as they thought, on the principles of logical positivism which had been developed in the 1930s. Eventually, nineteen monographs appeared, first published separately and eventually collected in two volumes, *Foundations of the Unity of Science*, edited by Otto Neurath, Rudolf Carnap, and Charles Morris (University of Chicago Press, Volume 1, 1955; Volume 2, 1970).

One major irony is that one of the extended essays was the monograph by Thomas S. Kuhn, *The Structure of Scientific Revolutions*, a work, more singularly than any other, perhaps, which undermined the idea of the "unity of science." Kuhn's monograph, the second edition and enlarged, appears in Volume 2 of the *Foundations*, pp. 53-272.

2. The quotations are from the Doubleday Anchor edition, pp. 151, 149-150. The reference to Trilling is from his *Beyond Culture* (New York: Viking, 1965) pp. ix-xviii.

3. The dedication of the book was to Lionel Trilling, who has "The Scholar's Caution and the Scholar's Courage."

4. I leave it to a new Hermes Trismegistus (Hermes thrice great,) author of magical, astrological and alchemical doctrines, to explain the attraction of the triad.

For Plato, the parts of the soul, and the corresponding classes of the City, were the rational, the spirited, and the appetitive. For Fichte and Hegel, knowledge proceeded through thesis, antithesis, and synthesis (though there is a question whether Hegel employed this so mechanically). And for Freud, the personality was comprised of the id, the ego, and the super-ego. And the Gnostic symbol of all this is the triskelion.

5. The book suggests a large number of different third-tier courses in the sciences, social sciences, and humanities (see pp. 262-279).

6. I should point out that this inquiry was my one and only foray into the field of "education." The study was undertaken at the request of David B. Truman who was then the dean of Columbia College. David Truman, a thoughtful man was quietly aware that Columbia University, a great institution, was in danger of faltering. In the course of events, David Truman was destined to become president of Columbia University. By 1967, he had already become the provost and, because of the confusions of Grayson Kirk, the president, was in the command post during the student disturbances of 1968. Professor Truman made a mistake, I believe, in calling in the police when negotiations

with the adamant student radicals, encouraged by some middle-aged romantics, such as Dwight Macdonald and Norman Mailer, failed. This is still a disputed issue, but the outcome was that the college community was so divided that it became impossible for Mr. Truman to accede to the presidency of Columbia. Though I was one of those who strongly opposed Mr. Truman (who had been my mentor at Columbia) and who Mr. Truman may feel that he had been betrayed, none of this diminishes the respect in which I held him and the commitment he had to the University.

7. One admires, in these instances, the prescience of Trilling. For as he pointed out, in a wry reflection on the advance of the "adversary culture," when an intellectual institution fails to offer resistance to the new, especially that of the adversary stance "has developed the power to overturn old canons and establish new categories of its own," they will "fall into the inertness and weariness of all conventionalities, the conventionality of an outworn radical mode" (Op. cit.).

On Columbia, see my essay. "Columbia and the New Left," for a detailed account of these events, see *Confrontation*, edited by Daniel Bell and Irving Kristol, Basic Books, 1969.

FOREWORD

In ordinary circumstances a report to the faculty of Columbia College would not be distributed beyond Morningside Heights until it had become, through debate and amendment, a report from the faculty. The circumstances in which colleges such as Columbia are currently working are not ordinary, however, and Professor Bell's essay is not the usual sort of faculty report. To all but the least attentive it is apparent that liberal education, in general, and what is loosely called general education, in particular, confront a complex challenge. If this challenge is to be met, it will require close examination of unexpressed assumptions and prevailing practices, aiming toward reforming both, to use Bell's carefully chosen term.

Professor Bell's important contribution to meeting that challenge takes the form of a report that is unusual in at least two respects. First, it is intentionally the work of a committee of one. Although Professor Bell necessarily has drawn upon many sources in and out of Columbia for information and insights, the statement of the problem is his and the proposals for change at Columbia his alone. The solo performance is not a device for speeding the process of faculty legislation, nor was it so intended in this instance. It is rather a means of provoking discussion and wide-ranging deliberation, with compromises deferred until those often turbulent and uncertain processes have had their full day. No one, least of all the Dean of the College, can predict what action the Columbia faculty will take or when, but one can be confident that discussion will be animated and that the scope of the debate will be appropriate to the significance of the issues to which the study was directed.

The range and depth of Professor Bell's reflections constitute the second distinctive aspect of the report. This also was a deliberate intention, expressed hopefully when the commission was offered and fulfilled admirably by the result.

The conception of the project, from the outset, was not merely to suggest what changes might be made in Columbia's evolving program of general education. This was part of the purpose, to be sure, for that program over the years has had great strengths. One of these, by no means minor, has been its "shock value." Whatever else the Columbia freshman may have felt after joining the College, he could be in no doubt that he was exposed to an intellectual experience and was subject to demands qualitatively different from those of secondary school.

A second strength has been the subtle but discernible way in which the effects of these courses have permeated the whole of the student's experience in and after college and have in significant degree set the tone of undergraduate life. The educational importance of such stimulation is so fundamental that one phase of the study had to inquire whether, in consequence of actual or impending developments in the secondary schools, the program could be expected to have this impact in the days ahead. Professor Bell was asked to suggest modifications that might be made in order to assure its continuing vitality.

Favored in the past by a general education program that has proved itself both distinguished and effective, Columbia College nevertheless cannot for the future complacently and without reflection persist in an undertaking that may conceivably be out of date, and not merely out of fashion. It would be at least equally foolish, however, without full examination and without careful discussion of the implications, to change the fundamentals of an enterprise of demonstrated educational value. Professor Bell's endorsement of the basic purposes of Columbia's program will be welcomed by many members of the faculty and by large numbers of students and alumni of the College. His proposals for alteration deserve, and I am sure will receive, their most careful consideration.

But the problems of general education in relation to developments in the secondary schools are only a part of the current challenge to liberal education. Structural and attitudinal changes in the American society, functional changes in the American college and university, and spectacular additions to the quantity of what can be known confront education in the liberal arts with a set of issues whose range and difficulty extend to the fundamentals of the whole enterprise, fundamentals on which the long-term welfare of the society may well depend. In an age increasingly reliant upon specialists it is altogether too easy to leap to the conclusion that training in the skills that lie at the core of a specialty is all there is to the matter and to ignore the point that this is not the only or, surely, the most responsible way to educate the kinds of specialists that society will need.

The issue, as Professor Bell effectively argues, is not the specious one of "breadth" versus "depth," which implies a nonsensical choice between superficiality and competence. The central problem is rather relevant breadth versus a limited and dangerously irresponsible competence. Such personal competence may be equivalent to social incompetence; it may either ignore the moral and political consequences of what the specialist does or may permit him to make decisions on behalf of the society for which he is in fact unequipped.

A society, such as ours, that puts its talented young people under incredibly heavy and sustained pressures to compete, to choose, to excel, to make commitments—often less for their own good than for the gratification of parents and friends—may well be in danger of undervaluing the maturing, humanizing, liberating experience that can be found through a liberal education worthy of the name. Such an experience requires time, a challenging program, plus an awareness of and respect for the liberating of the mind and the imagination as a process inherently important, whatever its short-run market value. Yet the essential integrity of this experience and its enormous relevance for the future of the society may easily be sacrificed to senseless and unplanned pressures to get on with something apparently more utilitarian.

In such circumstances liberal education may be misconceived and misguided, but its potential relevance for the student and his society has never been greater.

Because Professor Bell's report tackles such problems as these, in a setting that extends beyond Morningside Heights and in a fashion certain to provoke comment, the faculty of Columbia College has given its consent to publishing the document before its own deliberations have more than begun. It does so not only in the hope rhar it will thus contribute to discussions on other campuses but also in the expectation that those discussions will assist its own. Sharing in this way the results of Professor Bell's reflections and inquiries is in keeping with the purposes of the Carnegie Corporation of New York in granting the funds that made the study possible. The Corporation, of course, bears no responsibility for the content of the report. The grant, however, is one of many that reflect the continuing concern of the trustees and officers of the Corporation for the problems of American education. It is a privilege to express gratitude for that concern in all its phases as well as in connection with this study.

The liberal arts college, whose imminent demise has been announced repeatedly for nearly a century, has as frequently confounded the forecasters. This hardiness may be a source of confidence, but it provides no guarantee that in the face of a new kind of challenge the usefulness and vigor of this distinctively American institution will continue undiminished. That guarantee will be won by a response to change that is purposeful and not merely adaptive, that retains relevance without abandoning inherited validities—objectives more easily put into words than into practice.

At least some changes that are beginning to appear raise doubts that they constitute responses of the requisite sort, and general education offers examples of particular pertinence. The term, of course, has never referred to a single set of courses offered uniformly by all colleges subscribing to the idea. Rather it has indicated acceptance of the policy of providing a common, if not always uniform, intellectual experience for all students for at least a portion of their undergraduate years, that experience not being bound by the conventional limits of particular disciplines. General education programs, whatever their individual form and content, have in consequence indicated acceptance by the colleges of a responsibility for setting priorities among types of knowledge. They have also implied a responsibility for exploring at least some of the persistent and changing relations among modes of human thinking, a responsibility whose effective discharge alone warrants the label "liberal" education.

These programs have been threatened from a number of directions: changed commitments by and demands upon faculties; a decline in the confidence necessary to discharging the responsibility of establishing priorities that is implied by the program; an increasing proportion of students pursuing their studies beyond the bachelor's degree and a consequent demand—sometimes encouraged by the graduate schools but as often created by the student's own desire for a head start—for more time in specialized work; changes in the preparation provided by the secondary schools, acclaimed but largely unassessed; and, in a number of disciplines, quantitative changes that allegedly require in consequence more time for an adequate undergraduate major.

Current responses to these threats include reducing or removing restraints on premature specialization and abandoning the policy of a common intellectual experience or substituting for it a loose distribution requirement that may amount to abandonment without acknowledgment. These and similar policies bear too often the mark of reacting to the new set of circumstances rather than the badge that is earned by coming to grips with them. They appear to rest on assumptions about the college and about liberal education that should not go unquestioned.

Stated in the boldest terms, these assumptions might include such propositions as the following three. First, college faculties are not, for various reasons, prepared to set the priorities that should define an appropriate common intellectual experience, but the secondary schools are able or can be equipped to do so, and this should be their task. Second, given the expansion of knowledge in all fields and the increasing difficulties involved in achieving mastery of any one of them, in order to prepare the kind of specialist that the society will need in the future, the years after secondary school must give an exclusive priority to accomplishing such mastery, whatever the costs in other directions. Third, the rate and quality of psychological and characterological development between the ages of seventeen or eighteen and twenty-one or twenty-two are not so marked as to make those years particularly valuable for exploring the forms of human thought and feeling and for establishing the habit of searching for relations, conflicting and compatible, among them; in consequence, the liberal arts college has no distinctive educational function to perform.

Not many in the college world, even among those who are ready to abandon the goals of general education and thus to withdraw from what might be a new flowering of liberal education, would acknowledge that they are working from such assumptions. But if the results of their efforts are not to rest upon these or similarly deceptive grounds, a reforming of liberal education is called for, one that meets the changed circumstances of the modern scene without forsaking goals that are no less valid for being ancient. The analyses and suggestions of Professor Bell move boldly and imaginatively in this direction, even though they may not find complete acceptance either in the faculty of Columbia College or among those outside Columbia who are concerned with the problems he examines. Both groups, however, will find themselves in his debt for confronting them with a set of difficult and profoundly important questions that must be faced even if they cannot be answered easily or with finality.

February, 1966

DAVID B. TRUMAN
DEAN OF COLUMBIA COLLEGE

A PREFACE,

BY WAY OF ACKNOWLEDGMENT

Any reflection on education is a venture in autobiography: In setting
forth a path for others, one retraces, first, the steps one has taken oneself. Where a "committee of several" Kas been set up to chart a
course, such explorations become a collective experiment in which—if
all agree upon the objective—each matches his own experience
with others in order to find common ground, While such a procedure
may lead to a consensus, it also runs the risk, in the effort to reach
agreement, of bypassing some rocky roads that could lead to larger
vistas. (And with rocks off the road, there are fewer to be thrown—or
suffered.) Though I serve here, in the designation of Dean David
Truman, as a "committee of one," I have not sought to anticipate
the final consensus or compromises that this report may evoke. It is
an individual exploration.

The solitary experiment in autobiography necessarily begins with
prejudices. I undertook this study with a prior set of convictions—it
would be less than honest not to say so. In fact, I accepted the assignment because I had strong prejudices about what ought to be done
in college education. I have sought, by butting my head against the
walls of other "prejudices," to test these experiences and convictions.
Thanks to the grace of many colleagues at Columbia, and friends
at Chicago and Harvard, I have rehearsed these ideas, at times inter-
minably, and listened to the conflicting criticisms. These have been
so persuasive that at times I have felt like the rabbi in the talmudic

story who, after listening to the first of two complainants, said to Her, "You are absolutely right"; at which the second one cried, "But wait, you haven't heard my side," After listening to her, he said, *"You* are absolutely right"; to which the rabbi's wife countered, "But how can they both be absolutely right?" And the rabbi in despair retorted, "You are right too."

I have tried—with what success I do not know—to convert my prejudices into opinions, and my opinions into knowledge. And yet, in the end it may be that the original prejudices remain. That result is something hardly novel, although the explanation is candid.

Acknowledgments are the discharge of private debts in a public place. I make them gladly.

I have three kinds of debts—intellectual, personal, and the one I owe my colleagues. The intellectual debts are often the most difficult to pay, for it is sometimes in a fugitive place or a stray conversation that an idea is suggested, and only after long and discursive reading does it fall into place. I am lucky in that, while working on this study, I found two books that gave an intellectual substance to my prejudices and whose ideas I have used in formulating some criteria for an adequate college curriculum. One is Ernest Nagel's *The Structure of Science,* which lays out a "logic of explanation" in dealing with the nature of inquiry. The other is Joseph J. Schwab's *The Teaching of Science as Enquiry,* which discusses in a wonderfully lucid way the dependence of science upon conceptual innovation, and applies these ideas to the problems of teaching.

The debts to my colleagues are many. In the course of a year's research, I spoke to over a hundred persons whose comments seemed sufficiently important to me ro take some notes which I was able to use in writing this book, and the recitation of all these names could only burden these pages. I do want to single out, because of their special courtesy to me as a guest, Edward Levi, Joseph J. Schwab, Edward Shils, Milton Singer, and Warner Wick at the University of Chicago, and Paul Doty, John H. Finley, Stephen Graubard, and Gerald Holton at Harvard. At Columbia, I spent considerable time with the chairman of each College department and further imposed on them several inquiries and questionnaires, and I thank them collectively. The members of the Committee on Instruction, the policy body of the College, spent considerable time in discussion of chapters 4 and 5 of this book, and each one generously undertook to write detailed annotations and comments on the first draft; I thank them individually: George Fraenkel, Carl Hovde, Leon Lederman, Bert Leefmans, Walter Metzger, and Robert Murphy. Much of my time, as well as much of this discussion, was devoted to the general education courses at Columbia and here I had the cooperation of Quentin Anderson, Robert Belknap, and Howard Porter on the Humanities; and of Dwight Miner, Orest Ranum, and Robert K, Webb on the Contemporary Civilization courses. A previous report on the Humanities course, completed two years earlier by a committee that Fritz Stern headed, provided some important assessments and useful cautions for my own procedures.

My personal debts are fewer but more intense. During the course of research, in 1963-64, I conducted two surveys of the senior and freshman classes in which about 225 students were interviewed, each for over an hour. The results, which were useful in evaluating the courses, are too bulky to be reported here, while the discussion of other aspects of student life would be too wide-ranging and would distort the essential purpose of this book, which is to present a critique of curriculum. I hope that the results of these surveys will find publication in some sociological journals. But I do want to express my appreciation here for the cooperation of Professor Renee Fox of Barnard, who helped in the preparation of the schedules, and her research class at Barnard, who conducted the interviews of the Columbia freshmen; and I want to thank, too, the Senior Society of Sachems for undertaking as their year's project the interviewing of the senior class. Jill Jordan, working with the Bureau of Applied Social Research, was responsible for the coding of the results, the preparation of the computer program, and the preliminary analysis of the results. In the assessment of the secondary school programs, two of my former students were especially helpful—Richard M. Andrews and Richard A. Epstein.

On the manuscript itself, besides the comments of the members of the Committee on Instruction, I have an obligation to a number of persons, but especially to George Keller, the editor of *Columbia*

College Today, who read two drafts with a scrutiny that bespeaks his fierce devotion to Columbia College and a gentleness of expression that made acceptable some ferocious exceptions to my formulations. Thomas Colahan, now associate dean in charge of curricular affairs, provided invaluable enlightenment about many aspects of College life, and also read the manuscript with care. Family obligations, while intrinsic to any work, have special relevance here because of the professional editorial reading of the manuscript by my wife, Pearl Kazin Bell, and because of the experiences and acute suggestions of my daughter, Jordy Bell, a recent student at the College of the University of Chicago, Class of '65. Barbara Rubenstein and Carol Berkin provided secretarial help.

Several more general obligations are part of the personal debt. The Carnegie Corporation of New York provided the funds for a year's work and for the research studies and travel. But a simple acknowledgment would fail to express my gratitude for the informal manner, the friendly counsel, and the unobtrusive support that mark the procedures of this foundation; I wish to thank John Gardner and Alan Pifer of the Carnegie Corporation for their confidence.

Dean David Truman of Columbia College suggested this inquiry, and these pages, in many instances, have been an unspoken dialogue with him. His importance to Columbia, at this juncture, derives only in part from his defense of "the Idea of the college" today.

This book is dedicated to Lionel Trilling. Of him, one can only resurrect an older and more eloquent meaning of the word "charism"—the grace which befits a man for the life, office, and work to which he is called.

February, 1966   DANIEL BELL

THE REFORMING OF
GENERAL EDUCATION

The intentions of a book are often defined by its epigraph, for an epigraph is an extended metaphor with an implicit moral.

> When . . . that adorable genius William James . . . was finishing his great treatise on the *Principles of Psychology,* he wrote to his brother Henry, "I have to forge every sentence in the teeth of irreducible and stubborn facts."
>
> This new tinge to modern minds is a vehement and passionate interest in the relation of general principles to irreducible and stubborn facts. All the world over and at all times there have been practical men, absorbed in "irreducible and stubborn facts"; all the world over and at all times there have been men of philosophic temperaments who have been absorbed in the weaving of general principles. It is this union of passionate interest in the detailed facts with equal devotion to abstract generalization which forms the novelty in our present society. Previously it had appeared sporadically and as if by chance. This balance infects cultivated thought. It is the salt which keeps life sweet. The main business of universities is to transmit this tradition as a widespread inheritance from generation to generation.
>
> —*Alfred North Whitehead,* SCIENCE AND THE MODERN WORLD

Chapter One

INTENTIONS

This book is not a study of *the* American college, or an assessment of "general education" in the higher learning. It is an essay on a single institution, Columbia College, and its problems. To save one life, says the Talmud, is to save a world. Columbia College is a life for thousands of its students and faculty, a continuing partnership of its past, the living, and the future. Yet to study one life may also be a way of studying a whole world, for what the psychologist Henry A. Murray has said about a single person may also be said of an institution: in some ways it is like *everybody* else, in some ways like *somebody* else, in some ways like *nobody* else. This felicitous observation can be applied to Columbia College.

Like *all* other colleges, Columbia is bounded by the American culture and entwined in that culture's paradoxical assumptions: a desire for cultivation along with a utilitarian purpose to education; a populist spirit in the classroom (are students ever deferential to professors?) and a respect for learning; a training for citizenship, yet a skepticism about laws; a deference to *humanitas* and an emphasis on the acquisition of technique and training for the purposes of a career. To call attention to these antinomies is not necessarily to mock them; rather, it is to point up the difficulties that any educator faces when, in translating values into curriculum, he seeks to realize the purposes of American society. One knows from logic, if not from experience, that one cannot maximize two functions at the same time, though American society, with its Benthamite temper, persists in seeking the greatest good for the greatest number.

Like *some,* but unlike others, Columbia College is a private institution and therefore less subject to the overt political and vocational demands made upon the large state colleges. It is an urban college, housed within a large university strongly oriented to graduate work, and able to call upon extraordinary resources of subject matter (more foreign languages, about thirty to thirty-four, are taught at Columbia than at any other university in the world) and some of the best minds in the world for its classrooms. It draws its student body, nationally, from the top 5 percent of the intellectually ranked young people of this country, and self-consciously prepares that group to assume a place within the upper middle class of American society. Its students are strongly motivated to professional and academic careers, evidenced by the fact that 85 percent of its recent graduating classes have gone on to postgraduate or professional schools, the highest such percentage of any college in the country. It is small, admitting about 650 men a year into its freshman class, and, unlike the record of many large public colleges where more than 50 percent of an entering class fails to finish, Columbia graduates 82 percent of its freshman class in the regular four years, and over 90 percent after an additional year—a tribute to selection procedures, the persistence of the students, and the close concern of the College administration. In these respects, and in its fundamental concern with the liberal arts and general education, Columbia is most like Harvard and Chicago, though it probably shares many attributes with other Ivy League colleges, and much of what I say may have some relevance to the programs of these schools as well. In the limited time I had, however, I made direct comparison only with Harvard and Chicago, though I pass no judgment on them or their programs.

Finally, in the combination of its traditions, its institutional structure, and the character of the student body, Columbia College is uniquely itself.[1] Institutionally, the College is framed by a departmental structure which is, in most cases, rooted in the graduate school. These departments pick their faculty on the basis of a continuing contribution to scholarship, and a tenure position is held in the department, rather than in any particular school, though in prac-

---

[1] Columbia University also contains three other distinct undergraduate colleges (Barnard, for women; Engineering and Applied Science, coed; and General Studies, for adults over twenty-one, coed), plus a loosely affiliated College of Pharmacy.

tice (varying somewhat with the department) a man may spend most of his teaching rime in the College, in the School of General Studies, or in the graduate school.

The student body, heterogeneous in composition, has a cosmopolitan flavor rather than a unified character. Before the turn of the century, the Columbia College student body was drawn heavily from the professional and upper middle class of New York society. In the 1900s, the College began to draw the intellectually ambitious and professionally oriented children of New York's immigrant families, particularly the Jewish group (about 40 percent of each graduating class starts out for medicine or law), but since the end of World War II the College, in its geographical and social representation, has come to have a distinct national character, though the weight of ethnic group composition remains.

This variegated background manifests itself in the three broad social types characteristic of the student body: a group for whom Columbia College is primarily an Ivy League school—a place to achieve some prestige and some social polish, and make contacts for future career; a group whose ambitions are fiercely scholastic and professional; and a minority group of campus iconoclasts, political and esthetic, who in classic fashion react to the orthodoxies of university life by emphasizing individual temperament—in the past, this last group has included people as diverse as the underground man Whittaker Chambers, the monk Thomas Merton, and the poet Allen Ginsberg.

To identify the three groups in this fashion is not to make invidious distinctions among them. Each has had a positive and a negative component. The first has produced men who attained redoubtable political and professional distinction as well as those who have been lounge lizards and social spongers; the second has had its dry pedants and narrow professional practitioners as well as some of the most distinguished minds of their generation; and the third has had its share of intellectual fakes and poseurs as well as some of the most sensitive and interesting personalities of their time.

In its traditions and public character, Columbia has ambitiously sought to be the great university in the great city, though never wholly succeeding in that task. (What single institution can dominate this city?) The College itself bears a distinctive imprint, fashioned in large measure by its English faculty ("the imagination must be moral"—not an unfair characterization of its consistent instruction to its pupils?) and by the pragmatic orientation of its professors of philosophy ("the consequences of a statement are constitutive of its truth"). These departments, along with the history faculty, have been responsible for the formulation of the famed Contemporary Civilization and Humanities courses, the two sequences which have given Columbia College its distinction in general education, and which have been the core of its identity. This distinctiveness of outlook has been maintained by a strong inbreeding of faculty, especially in the humanities—men like James Guttman, John Herman Randall, Jr., Lionel Trilling, Jacques Barzun, Meyer Schapiro, Dwight Miner, Andrew Chiappe, Quentin Anderson, Theodore de Eary, Fritz Stern, Herbert Deane, and Steven Marcus,[2] who were students at Columbia College, and there acquired its commitment to "mind" and, as teachers, have given it a continuity of purpose.

Columbia College has had a long tradition of self-scrutiny. These reports, whether on the College as a whole, such as the Carman Committee's, or on special subjects, such as the committees headed by Ernest Nagel on Science, Justus Buchler on college expansion, David Truman on Contemporary Civilization, or Fritz Stern on the Humanities, have guided the present investigation and given me the sense of participating in a continuing inquiry.

This study began when Dean David Truman asked me in the spring of 1963 to spend a year reviewing the Columbia College curriculum, with particular reference to the program in general education. There was, I think, a double intention to his request. As a new Dean, he wanted an independent observer to provide an overall picture of the College. There had been no such general inquiry since 1946, when the committee headed by Dean Harry Carman produced, in a report written by Jacques Barzun (Class of 1927), the famed *A College Program in Action.* More important, perhaps, was the task of self-scrutiny for the College—as for all American colleges—in the light of the evident or assumed changes that have been taking place

[2] In 1964 about half the tenure faculty of the English and philosophy departments of Columbia College had been students in the College.

in American society: in the character of secondary education; the expanding functions of the university, with its shifting emphasis on research rather than teaching; the rapidity with which new knowledge and new disciplines are forming; and the transformation of this country's social and class structure.

A sense of these changes has led to much speculation that the traditional liberal arts college is being eroded, that it is no longer a "transforming experience" for a youth coming into a wide world of humane learning, but a way station between secondary school and graduate education. Presumably, its first function of general education is being diminished or taken over by the secondary schools, while at the same time early specialization, in order to accelerate a student's course through graduate education, is making the college simply a pendant to a superior school. Further, with the rise of "advanced placement" programs in the secondary schools, and the expanding number of students who take graduate courses in their senior year, the question has even been raised of the validity of the four-year college. There has been talk of reducing college to three years, or of combining the college courses with sufficient advanced graduate work to give qualified students a master's degree at the end of four years. These possibilities have taken on the status of experiments, and some schools have begun to reorganize their curricula with these aims in mind.

At Columbia College, these general questions have become manifest in specific ways. Ten years ago, the College adopted a "major and concentration" system which requires all students to take a minimum number of courses (as designated by each department) in a single subject, in addition to the "core courses" in Humanities and Contemporary Civilization which are taken in the first two years. The adoption of this requirement has in many instances encouraged early specialization, particularly in the sciences, where the sequential organization of courses leads a student to begin a major in his freshman year, and where the great amount of work to be covered often tempts a student to take as many as one-third of all his college courses in a single subject. Even outside the sciences, the students are now asked to take the introductory sequences in a major subject in their sophomore year, thus enabling them to take advanced courses and seminars in the two succeeding years. Often, this leads a student to postpone his required courses, and one consequence of these decisions is the disruption of the unity of the "lower college," which, with its emphasis on the Humanities and Contemporary Civilization sequences, was intended as a common core experience.

These changes, combined with the intellectual challenges to the formulation of these core courses, plus the problems of staffing that have occurred in the last half-dozen years, create grave difficulties for a program that, as the Columbia College catalogue states on its opening page, "still dominates the curriculum" and has been the source of the College's traditional identification. As a result the question is now asked: does general education still dominate the College curriculum? If so, how much longer can it do so? Should it, in fact, do so? In these very formulations, the purpose of the liberal arts college is called into question.

However, the fact that a question has been raised does not mean that it has to be answered in its own terms. It may not have been well stated, and may even be misleading. The first task is to scrutinize the questions. Have the changes in the secondary schools been of such decisive character and magnitude as to force a wholesale revision in the liberal arts curriculum? Do the pressures for early career specialization really undercut the need for broad general education?

One is reminded of the fact that when the initial expansion of the medical schools and law schools took place at the turn of the century, there was a strong demand for a reduction in the number of years of college preparation, so as to allow a young man to begin professional training at an earlier age. Nicholas Murray Butler, in fact, saw the university as a system of two-year junior colleges feeding students into the professional and graduate schools at the end of that period of study. (Bard College, for many years an affiliate of Columbia, was in fact "bought" for this purpose.) For many years schools of medicine and law admitted college students on a professional option plan after two or three years of preparation—sometimes awarding a college degree at the completion of the first year of professional training. Only after World War II, actually, was the system abandoned, when the professional schools decided after long experience that a full four-year preparation was indeed valuable and necessary.

May not this experience point to a conclusion that the present pressures to "speed up" college work as a preparation for graduate school reflect an unwarranted anxiety, nurtured in part by ignorance of the past? And if these questions are less relevant to the activities of the college, which others *are* to the point?

My second charge was to assess general education in the light of changes in the nature of new knowledge and scholarship. Was Columbia College adequately preparing its students not just to interpret the past but to understand the future, and giving them a means—call it sophistication, conceptual comprehension, or a disciplined mode of handling ideas—of coping with new kinds of knowledge as they arise? Thus, the biology that was taught in college twenty-five years ago is largely obsolete, as the biology taught today may be twenty-five years hence. Is there a way of teaching a student to comprehend biological phenomena so that he does not feel helpless when new models and ideas are developed, even though, years after college, he may no longer be able to grasp the specific data the new biology discovers?

In short, to broaden the two general questions: if general education is to remain the foundation of a college education, does it necessarily have to be the same kind of general education that has been taught in the last twenty years?

I have tried to be faithful to both charges, I have not sought to be "original" for the sake of novelty, or to discard the old simply because it is old. There are as many dangers in being modish as there are in holding stubbornly to old traditions just because they have been sanctioned by time, and because a faculty has a vested interest in an established way.

In short, my intentions are not to write a completely new college curriculum—this I could not do—but to indicate problematic areas, particularly as they cut across departmental lines, and to propose alternative modes of intellectual organization. In this fashion, I hope in this report to give the faculty and the academic community a sense of the college enterprise as a whole.

Beyond this reporting and analysis there is a third, personal intention: to argue that in the next decade Columbia College—like all colleges—must take radical steps to emphasize a distinctive new function. *My* belief arises less from the immediate changes in secondary education (whose effects, even in the stronger schools, have been exaggerated) than from changes in the way knowledge is acquired and utilized.

What I shall argue in these pages—the principle is simple, the applications are never so—is that in this day and age, and even more in the coming day and age, the distinctive function of the college must be to teach modes of conceptualization, explanation, and verification of knowledge. As between the secondary school, with its emphasis on primary skills and factual data, and the graduate or professional school, whose necessary concern is with specialization and technique, the distinctive function of the college is to deal with the grounds of knowledge: not *what* one knows but *how* one knows. The college can be the unique place where students acquire self-consciousness, historical consciousness, and methodological consciousness.

Liberal education, for me, is more than the cultivation of the humanities, although it is certainly that. It is an emphasis on the grounds of knowledge. For this reason I reject the commonly made distinction between general education as dealing with broad relationships, and specialized instruction as presenting detailed material within an organized discipline. The relevant distinction, I feel, lies in the way a subject is introduced. When a subject is presented as received doctrine or fact, it becomes an aspect of specialization and technique. When it is introduced with an awareness of its contingency and of the conceptual frame that guides its organization, the student can then proceed with the necessary self-consciousness that keeps his mind open to possibility and to reorientation. All knowledge, thus, is liberal (that is, it enlarges and liberates the mind) when it is committed to continuing inquiry.

But such necessarily sketchy formulations can only be hortatory, not persuasive. Moreover, the emphasis on conceptual analysis as the central task of a college education runs the risk of being interpreted as narrow scientism or as a belief in structural analysis alone. These are very far from my intention, for I strongly believe that historical consciousness is the foundation of any education and that the patterns of organizing and acquiring knowledge are different for the sciences, the social sciences, and the humanities; these differences make necessary a complex approach to the creation of a curriculum, I leave these bald statements as part of my stated intentions; the arguments are presented at appropriate points in the chapters that follow.

It may be useful to the reader if I seek here, in concluding my statement of intentions, to explicate the design of the essay. (Evelyn Waugh once said that a writer must never tell a reader where he is going, for he may never get there; this is a risk I shall have to take.)

The original assumptions of general education are examined in chapter 2. The first section sketches the history of general education at Columbia, Harvard, and Chicago. These three schools have provided the three basic "models" of general education which hundreds of other colleges, with varying modifications, have adopted, and a history of their programs is essential not only to the understanding of the development of general education in the United States, but to the debate today about the future of the American college itself. The second section reformulates the questions that have been raised about the efficacy of general education and about the position of the college as a whole in the scheme of higher learning, and uses these questions as the point of departure for the sections that follow.

Chapter 3 deals with those changes in American society that challenge existing college preparation. The first section discusses the emergence of a new national polity and its effects on the way social problems are defined in this country, and the changes in various disciplines that have occurred as a result of the so-called "exponential growth[1]" of knowledge. The second deals with the changes in the structure of the American university that have resulted from the federal government's new role in education, the rise of "research and development," the changing nature of the research function, and the "market" for university scholars. The third examines the changes in secondary education, particularly the role of advanced placement programs, and the new curriculum changes in physics, mathematics, biology, and American history. It also reviews briefly some changes that have been made by a number of specific secondary schools.

My own presuppositions are spelled out in chapter 4, No person, especially in such an inquiry, is exempt from specifying his values and his philosophical standpoint. Though not a formal statement of philosophy, these presuppositions may clarify the criteria that guide both my notion of what is important about the social changes taking place in American society and my reasons for suggesting the changes I do in the curriculum of Columbia College.

The college curriculum, with special reference to Columbia, is discussed in chapter 5. After indicating the changes that have taken place in the practice of general education at Columbia, Harvard, and Chicago, I then examine in detail the Contemporary Civilization, Humanities, and Science requirements at Columbia College, and the way the "major" system operates. In this section, I have made a number of detailed proposals for changes in the curriculum in the light of the social changes discussed in chapter 3 and of my own presuppositions. These proposals add up to a distinct change in the nature and pattern of general education, and represent for me the heart of the inquiry.

Chapter 6, a reprise, is a review of the proposals and an attempt to relate them to the problem of curriculum as a whole.

There are two omissions I am acutely aware of, and it would be remiss not to mention them. One is the analysis of organizational contexts and institutional change; the other, the changing concerns of the student body and the character of their demands.

Any discussion of curriculum eventually has to come to grips with institutional realities. As a sociologist, I believe that much human behavior is shaped by the structures in and through "which an individual lives and works. These structures set forth the formal lines of authority, the legal or bureaucratic rules of operation, the norms and sanctions that prescribe or constrain behavior, and the values or traditions that legitimate the exercise of power. A university is unlike a business corporation, a government bureaucracy, a prison, or a hospital in its values, its hierarchies, and its capacity for tolerating differences; yet it is also subject to some common rules of organizational analysis. These rules allow us to see which parts of the organization are the most resistant to change and which parts facilitate change. Further, one can distinguish between changes that only modify a structure and those that transform it. Any proposal to change the curriculum also proposes to change the structure, and some of my proposals would result in significant transformations. The faculty needs to be deeply aware of this.

Equally, any discussion of curriculum must take into account not only what students should learn, but how the students' own needs and puzzlements affect them. The events at the University of California at Berkeley in 1964-65, and the nascent radicalism of a small but articulate group at Columbia, have made us all aware of the dissatisfactions and disorientations of the students about the character of their educational experience. Any judgment about a curriculum is a judgment of what a student's intellectual experience ought to be; these are explicit in the text and are reviewed in chapter 6. But a student's world is more than an intellectual one, for it involves the relationship of intellectual study to other commitments—political, moral, aesthetic, and religious. I have tried to keep this in mind.

Yet within the confines of my time and task, I have undertaken only to deal with the intellectual problem—the content of curriculum—and to eschew the analysis of institutional structure and the character of student life. The redefinition of general education is what I have set as the agenda of debate.

Chapter Two

THE ORIGINAL ASSUMPTIONS

Historic Traditions

COLUMBIA COLLEGE[1]

Columbia College has always been proud of its role as the pioneer of general education in the United States. The Carman Committee report of 1946, reevaluating the College curriculum after World War II, indicated the magnitude of Columbia's innovation, as well as the working philosophy of this program:

> The introduction of orientation courses in Columbia College, with the establishment in 1919 of the course in Contemporary Civilization, was the beginning of a quiet and gradual revolution in undergraduate instruction throughout the United States. Although a number of colleges are still weighing the idea of requiring introductory courses so planned as to acquaint the student with the framework of Western culture, yet the dissemination of the idea has been very wide; and its use as a basic formula by many of our most important colleges and universities in the present re-examination of curricula is evidence of

[1] I have drawn freely in this section on the following sources: *Columbia,* by Frederick Keppel (New York, Oxford University Press, 1914); *Reminiscences of an American Scholar,* by John W. Burgess (Columbia University Press, 1934); *The Rise of a University,* Vol. II: *The University in Action,* From the Annual Reports, 1902-1935, of Nicholas Murray Butler, ed., by Edward C. Elliott (New York, Columbia University Press, 1937); *A College Program in Action,* by the Committee on Plans (New York, Columbia University Press, 1946), hereafter referred to as the "Carman Committee"; *A History of Columbia College on Morningside* (New York, Columbia University Press, 1954), especially the chapters "The Van Amringe and Keppel Eras," by Lionel Trilling, and "Reconstruction in the Liberal Arts," by Justus Buchler. While I have relied greatly on these sources, particularly the Trilling and Buchler essays, the inferences I hive made, as will be clear in the text, are my own.

the depth to which it has influenced higher education in this country.

[The] three two-year sequences in science, the social sciences, and the humanities have brought us, we believe, to the point at which the younger student is offered a comprehensive view of what goes to the making of an intelligent citizen of the world. The salutary influence of these courses upon the mental consciousness and capacities of our students has been accepted by all bur an almost negligible minority of the students themselves; and the merging of previously divided interests in the departments of our instruction, as well as the broadening effect of this merging upon the instructors who have conducted the courses, are probably results of no less importance to the well-being of college education,

(One should note, in dealing with the nature of this tradition, the key terms in the statement: "orientation courses," "the framework of Western culture," "three two-year sequences in science, the social sciences, and the humanities," "comprehensive view of what goes to the making of an intelligent citizen of the world," "the merging of previously divided interests in the departments of instruction." In the discussion that follows, I shall use these terms as a base line for describing the changes in general education in the present-day Columbia College, and I shall regard them as intentions against which my proposals for revision can be judged.)

For a program that has had such extraordinary influence, general education at Columbia was the result of a curious mixture of parochial, sociopolitical, and philosophical motives. Within Columbia College, if I have read the history correctly, there were three impulses: the College's struggle against the German tradition of the university, with its "professional" emphasis, which had been favored by Professor John W. Burgess and President Nicholas Alurray Butler; the abandonment of a sterile classicism symbolized by the Latin entrance requirement, which aped the English model; and the changing character of the student body, particularly as the children of immigrants began to predominate intellectually, if not in numbers, in Columbia College. These three elements were inherent in the proposal by John Erskine, in 1917, to set up a General Honors course that would read and discuss one classic a week. The intention in reading the "great books" was to inculcate in the student a humanistic rather than a professional orientation; to force him to confront a great work directly, rather than treat it with the awe reserved for a classic;[2] and, in the contemporary jargon, "to acculturate" a student whose background and upbringing had excluded him from the "great traditions."

Within the larger American society there were two important influences, more general in nature, upon the shape of the new education. One, which universities were struggling to assimilate, was the great rush of knowledge coming out of empirical investigations in recently developed disciplines like institutional economics and sociology. (In 1910, for example, Amherst College, then under the leadership of Alexander Meiklejohn, set up a general) course entitled "Social and Economic Institutions" to "unify" or "integrate" social studies.) The second influence, and perhaps the more important, was World War I. When the United States entered the war the country was divided in its feelings, and the government had set up some organizations to propagandize, indoctrinate, and educate the country about America's war aims. On behalf of the Students Army Training Corps, which had been established in colleges throughout the country, the government asked Columbia to prepare a course in "War Issues." A committee headed by Frederick J. E. Woodbridge, the famed philosopher—a colleague of John Dewey—who was then dean of the Graduate Faculties, drew up a syllabus. After it was approved in Washington, the course was given at Columbia and at all other Student Corps centers. While the "War Issues" course was in progress, various faculty members (including John J. Coss of the philosophy department and Harry J. Carman of the history department) felt that there should be a course devoted to "Peace Issues." These two influences resulted in a course, offered in the fall of 1917, entitled "Contemporary Civilization"; it was required of all freshmen and was conducted five days a week, at nine, ten, or eleven o'clock, on the fifth floor of Hamilton Hall. As Justus Buchler remarked, "The men

---

[2] "One opposition to the plan came from men who were concerned to protect what they conceived to be the scholarly integrity of their subject. To some scholars who had spent a lifetime in the study of certain authors or certain books, it seemed sacrilegious chat undergraduates should be presumed able to read them with understanding in a single week. Erskine replied that every book had to be read at some time for the first time, that there was a difference between a reading acquaintance with great authors and a scholarly investigation of them." Trilling in *History*.

in Washington whose responsibility it was to conduct American policy in World War I could hardly have contemplated a new departure in higher education. Yet they had a direct connection with it."

Thus the Erskine course on the "great books" and the Woodbridge course on War Issues shared in the ancestry of general education, both at Columbia and elsewhere. Yet the yoking of these two produced tensions and paradoxes that were not always evident to the practitioners of general education: The Erskine program, with its emphasis on the classics of Western thought, constituted, as Lionel Trilling has put it, "a fundamental criticism of American democratic education," while the Contemporary Civilization course was an open and frank acknowledgment of the direct responsibility of the College to the stated democratic needs of society.

One can see both parts of this paradox in the separate developments of general education at the other two institutions that in the last twenty-five years have been so strongly identified with it; Chicago and Harvard. General education at Chicago has always had the flavor of an aristocratic critique of the democratic—perhaps one should say populist—foundations of American education. What steered Harvard toward general education after World War II—at least as formulated in its famous Redbook (so named after its cover, but actually entitled *General Education in a Free Society*)—was a response to the obligation, assumed in the name of democracy, of providing for all citizens "some common and binding understanding of the society which they will possess in common." The program at Columbia College itself, as will be evident in these pages, has not been immune to the opposite stresses of this paradox.

"Never has a college been more frequently pulled up by the roots," Frederick Keppel remarks in his book, *Columbia.* Between 1763, when Myles Cooper revised the curriculum to make it correspond with that of his own Oxford college, and 1905, when a study based on Nicholas Murray Butler's first presidential report defined the function of the College as the training of students for professional work, the records show eleven revisions of Columbia's program. The uprooting was especially intense at the turn of the century.

John W. Burgess, who placed his large stamp on Columbia University during his tenure as professor of history, political science, and international law, had long been an admirer of the German academic tradition, having worked with some of the great German historians of his time. Burgess, who came to Morningside in 1876, setup Columbia's first graduate school, and became the dominant voice in the university for several decades. He sought to mold Columbia College into a university on the German model, devoted to scholarly research and the training of students in modern methods of scholarship. In this effort, he was supported by Frederick Barnard, the president of Columbia.

Columbia College—or the School of Arts, as it was called at the time—was, Burgess said, "a small old-fashioned college, or rather school, for teaching Latin, Greek, and mathematics and a little metaphysics and a very little natural science." The function of an undergraduate college, he argued, should be "gymnastic." That is to say, it was to do what the German *Gymnasium* did—give the students the tools of learning by means of drill and textbooks. These tools the student was to use in the higher schools of the university, which trained individuals for practical professions and for scholarship. The university teacher, Burgess added, was a different order of person from the college teacher—what he imparted in his lectures was always original with him, always the fruit of his own research and thought; the college teacher, by contrast, was but a schoolmaster of superior sort.[3]

---

[3] As Lionel Trilling has described the problems of Columbia in the period before Butler became president: "In many respects . . . Burgess's view of things was to prevail over Van Amringe's (the dean of the College], and, as we follow the dean's annual reports over the years, we see that their writer was required to engage in never-ending defense of the idea of liberal collegiate education. President Seth Low had no disposition, such as President Barnard [his predecessor] had had, to abolish the undergraduate school entirely, and Van Amringe could quote with approval Low's very sensible remarks in definition of the nature and function of such a school. And it was under Low that Van Amringe's proposal was accepted that the name of Columbia University should be applied to the whole community of schools and that the undergraduate school should be known not as the School of Arts but as Columbia College. But although it was something to have the official assurance of continued existence, and although it was something to have a name, the life of Columbia College was not to be untroubled or even, really, secure. Between Columbia College and its university there was not the same relation that obtained between certain undergraduate colleges of the eastern seaboard and the

Burgess' ideas about the college were adopted by Nicholas Murray Butler, the successor to Seth Low and Frederick Barnard, who sought, at least in the first decade of his tenure, to translate them into practice. In his report of 1902, President Butler expressed his belief that "four years is ... too long a time to devote to the College course as now constituted, especially for students who are to remain in university residence as technical or professional students." He looked to a time when the public high schools would tend "more and more to give the instruction now offered in the first year, or first two years, of the college course." In his next report he advocated the institution of a two-year course as an option to the usual four-year program. In 1905 he was pleased to report that arrangements had been made for the acceleration of undergraduate studies. Students would now be admitted in February as well as in September. They might complete the 124 points required for their degree in as few as three years by entering with advanced standing and by attending summer sessions. It was now possible for them to take all prescribed work and a considerable portion of their required hours of elective work in the first half of the undergraduate course.

In that same report of 1905, Butler went on to announce, with considerable pride, the plan of "professional option"—the "Columbia plan," as it was called—by which a student after two years of college might go on to one of the university's professional schools (with the exception of the School of Law, which required 94 points for admission). Dr. Butler summed up the meaning of the new arrangement in the following words: "The Faculty of Columbia College say explicitly that to prescribe graduation from a four-year college course as a *sine qua non* for the professional study of law, medicine, engineering, or teaching is not to do a good thing, but a bad thing." His own comment was: "Any culture that is worthy of the name and any effi-

great universities that developed from them, Columbia University did not, like Harvard, Yale, and Princeton, make the old undergraduate college of its original charter the center of its interest, the recipient of its first attention, the mainstay and first principle of its life, allowing other schools to grow up around it but never to dominate it. Indeed, at Columbia the contrary was true."

In this and the following several pages, I have, without always observing the punctilio of citation, made generous use of Professor Trilling's fine description of this period.

ciency that is worth having will be increased, not diminished, by bringing to an end the idling and dawdling that now characterize so much of American higher education."

Against Butler, the college ideal was defended by John Howard Van Amringe, the dean of the School of Arts and later of the College. The purpose of the College, he said, was not to make professional men and specialists but to "make men." The College, said Van Amringe in 1905, was close to being "degraded into a mere vestibule to a professional school," so that the student no longer had much to do with his own intellectual development, but was "pre-this" and "pre-that" profession.

In the curious political terminology of the day, Butler was considered to be a "progressive"' and Van Amringe a "conservative." After all, the German universities, which were Butler's ideal, could display triumph after triumph in every kind of scholarship, and serious men in the United States who looked for the same kind of academic progress took a dim view of the intellectual life available to undergraduates and those who taught undergraduates. And yet, as Professor Trilling sums it up, "it was not the progressives but the conservative party that was in the end to be proved right. The conservative fell back on the Renaissance ideal of the whole man, and on the ideal of the gentleman, of the honorable and responsible citizen of enlightened and gracious mind. It would have been difficult for Van Amringe and his group to demonstrate in just what way the College 'made men'; they could scarcely have shown how Greek and Latin and mathematics and a little metaphysics could have had the moral effect they were said to have. Van Amringe may have been speaking out of a prejudice which derived from the provinciality of Old New York and from the provinciality of the crusty classical tradition, for he had aspired to be professor of Latin and Greek before he became professor of mathematics. But the prejudice, if we are to call it that, was in entire accord with John Erskine's belief that humanistic studies were of the first importance in collegiate education, a belief which was to establish itself in the Columbia College of a later day and to have its decisive effect upon collegiate education all over the country."

The stand against professionalism, thus, was one of the shaping elements of what would become, in the post-World War I years, the new Columbia College. A second was the abandonment of an emphasis on the classics as the basis for the bachelor of arts degree. In 1897, the College had abolished the Greek entrance requirement, but retained Latin as a basic requirement for admission. Those who sought a bachelor of arts degree had to demonstrate proficiency in Greek or Latin. But the trustees, in order to maintain the emphasis on the classics, voted in 1905 to give a bachelor of science degree to those who preferred subjects alternative to the classics,

For a decade the College offered both the B.A. and the B.S. degrees, but in 1914 Dean Keppel, in his annual report, pointed out that a large number of the students who were candidates for the bachelor of arts degree found the Latin requirement burdensome and oppressive. In 1916 the faculty voted to discontinue the bachelor of science degree and to abolish the Latin requirement for those entering and seeking the B.A., and this decision was accepted by the trustees. No subsequent change in the entrance requirement was as basic as this one, as the former director of admissions, Frank Bowles, pointed out. "The abandonment of Latin as a requirement meant inevitably the abandonment of the entire system of education of which the classics were a symbol."

One of the chief consequences of this action—one that the College was mindful of in making the move—was to change the ethnic and social composition of the College. In the emphasis on Latin, students from the public high schools, where Latin often was either not taught or taught poorly, were at a disadvantage against those from private preparatory schools. The abolition of the Latin requirement made the public high school more important as a source of student supply. The result was that it helped to bring a new kind of student into Columbia.

The change in the character of the Columbia student body—the third parochial element that shaped the new college—was already evident before the war, and Dean Keppel's frank discussion of the question in his book *Columbia,* written in 1914, is instructive. "In view of the present rapid rate of growth," he wrote—and one should note that the registration in the College was about 900 while the total number of living alumni was then 2,800— "it is very possible that a limitation of numbers in the near future will enable the College to strike a more definite note. While doubtless the old New York stock will always be represented, Columbia is not likely ever again to be a fashionable college *per se,* and the temptation is lessening to make it too much like every other college in the details of its student life and interest. Efficient entrance machinery cuts out the hopeless incompetent. The different strains in the membership, particularly the boys of various foreign stocks, the influx of freshmen from out of town, and the students from other colleges, all unite in producing a social diversity which is a factor often unappreciated in college life."

"Social diversity," in this context, was a euphemism for Jews, and with his characteristic courage Keppel confronted the question directly. "One of the commonest references that one hears with regard to Columbia" he wrote, "is that its position at the gateway of European immigration makes it socially uninviting to students who come from homes of refinement. The form which the inquiry takes in these days of slowly dying race prejudice is, 'Isn't Columbia overrun with European Jews who are most unpleasant persons socially?'" Columbia, said Keppel, is not "overrun with Jews." But he defended their admission. Not only were the Jewish students intellectually stimulating, but Columbia, he said, had a public duty to aid the ambitious but socially maladroit child of immigrants. "What most people regard as a racial problem is really a social problem," he wrote, "The Jews who have had the advantages of decent social surroundings for a generation or two are entirely satisfactory companions. Their intellectual ability, and particularly their intellectual curiosity, are above the average, and the teachers are unanimous in saying that their presence in the classroom is distinctly desirable. There are, indeed, Jewish students of another type who have not had the social advantages of their more fortunate fellows. Often they come from an environment which in any stock less fired with ambition would have put the idea of higher education entirely out of the question. Some of these are not particularly pleasant companions, but the total number is not large, and every reputable institution aspiring to public service must stand ready to give to those of probity and good moral character the benefits which they are making great sacrifices to obtain."

It was this social diversity—not just the Jewish students but the transformation of Columbia from a genteel New York college to a national school—that was to give Columbia its cosmopolitanism and intellectual vigor in the two decades following World War I.

"The year 1919 can be justly regarded as marking the actual birth of the new Columbia College," Justus Buchler remarks in his admirable essay. The detailed evolution of the curriculum between 1919 and 1954 is recounted by Buchler and need not be rehearsed here.[4] What is important here is that the new Columbia College was dedicated firmly to the tradition of the liberal arts rather than to professionalism; that it sought for social diversity in its student body; and that, unlike some later schools, it was committed to no doctrinal philosophy of education other than exposing the student to major intellectual ideas and expanding his imagination. It is the combination of these three elements that gave general education at Columbia its distinctive stamp.

The tradition of the liberal arts at Columbia was embodied in the idea of three broad courses—Contemporary Civilization, the Humanities, and the Sciences—which would be required of all students. These courses evolved slowly. Contemporary Civilization, at the start a one-year course, in 1929 became a two-year sequence, the first year dealing primarily with the intellectual traditions and institutional development of Western society, and the second year, with changing emphases, focusing on contemporary socioeconomic problems. The two-year Humanities sequence (the first year was initiated in 1937, the second in 1947) concentrated in the first year on the masterpieces of literature and philosophy, from Homer to the nineteenth century, and in the second year on the masterpieces of music and the plastic arts. Though in principle the College was committed to a parallel organization in the Sciences (successive committees called for a "specially constructed and well-integrated two-year course in the natural sciences" and courses "to stress inclusive organizing princi-

[4] The histories of the Contemporary Civilization, Humanities, and Science courses are discussed, in a different context, in chapter 5.

ples of the sciences rather than special techniques for mastering specialized subject matters"), institutional and staffing difficulties confounded the various efforts to create such general education science courses. From 1934 to 1941, a two-year course, Science A and B, was offered as an option to the specialized science courses, but this ended during the war. Since World War II the Science requirement has remained simply two years of any science courses, a requirement that can be fulfilled by any selective combination of two one-year or one two-year course, in any of a half-dozen fields.[5]

This idea of a foundational "tripod" led logically to the conception, which was formalized in 1936, of a "lower college," where the commonality of work would be emphasized, and an "upper college," where students would be able to pursue their individual interests. The new curriculum, as Dean Herbert Hawkes, Keppels successor, put it, recognized the needs of three types of students: those who looked forward to a professional school, those who "by temperament and ambition" sought to be scholars, and those whom Hawkes called simply "the citizen to be," men who "wanted a broad and variegated development of mind and knowledge. The college rejected an orthodox "majoring system"—an 18-point sequence in each of two departments ("To demand of all students that they satisfy a stipulated minimum of work in one or two fields was to reduce them all tacitly to the second of three categories of students—the potential specialized scholar," wrote Buchler)—and introduced a system of "maturity credits." Courses of an advanced character carried maturity credits, and a student was required, in addition to completing a total of 124 points (126 after 1947), to pass courses carrying a minimum of 60 maturity credits. Thus, students usually took two years of common Lower-College work, and two years of Upper-College courses, though none of the latter were prescribed.

The interest in general education, which had emerged just before World War II, along with the reconsideration of curriculum made necessary by the social upheavals of the war, led Dean Harry Carman (Hawkes' successor) to appoint a Committee on College Plans, which in 1946 carried out a thoroughgoing review of the curriculum.

---

[5] These include astronomy, mathematics, physics, chemistry, botany, zoology, geology, and psychology.

The committee reaffirmed Columbia's original commitment to the liberal arts. "It is no lip service to tradition to declare once more that the liberal arts program should be the heart of our interests and aims as a college. In the meaning of liberal arts we include all studies that contribute to the art of living, as distinct from the channeled preparation for making a living." The committee found that "our objects with respect to the purpose of the first two years have now been realized through the courses in Contemporary Civilization, Humanities, and the Sciences. . . . [It] feels that the plan of the freshman and sophomore work has plainly demonstrated its fitness for contemporary needs. It feels quite as strongly, however, that the important effort of the next few years must be the working out of plans for upperclass instruction,"

The problem of upper-college instruction grew largely out of the "professional option" plan that had been instituted in 1905, whereby a student at the end of his third College year might enter one of the university's professional schools (or an approved medical or dental school) and after his first year there receive the A.B. degree from the College. Many students were preprofessional in their basic outlook, if not in their specific career choice, when they entered the College. The work in the lower college emphasized disinterested and liberal study. But competitive pressures for admission to professional school, the rising costs of education, and the likelihood of military service, all served to sharpen the undergraduates' vocational consciousness, and for a considerable number of students a year of professional study replaced the fourth year of college work. At a time when four years of college had become the norm before one could enter professional school, the Columbia system was serving as an inducement to accelerate college work.

Late in 1953, the College faculty voted to abolish both the professional option (except for pre-engineers) and the maturity credit system, replacing it with a "concentration" or "major" requirement of at least 24 points in a single department, plus 12 points of work in a related field (premedical students were required to take only 18 points of concentration) in the upper-college years.

The intention of the faculty was to provide a full four-year college program based on a rigorous liberal arts foundation. However, the unintended consequence of the major system (as we shall see in chapter 5), combined with the new societal pressures for early specialization and for acceleration into graduate work, as well as innovations like the "multitrack" system in the sciences, may have worked to weaken the unity of the lower college itself. With the "major" system—which has been the dominant feature of the College in the past decade—Columbia entered a new phase in general education, a story which is picked up again in chapter 5.

Columbia College has counted itself, justly, as the pioneer of general education among American colleges. But it is necessary to point out, in discussing the traditions of this idea, that Columbia College has never had a doctrinal commitment, like Chicago's and Harvard's (at least in theory, if not always in practice), to a *single* theory or substantive formulation of educational philosophy.

This has been due to three factors. One of them was the influence of John Dewey, with his emphasis on the *process* of learning and the *continuity* of experience, rather than on an unvarying curriculum based on a conception either of "eternal verities"—a hierarchy of knowledge, the specification of a major tradition of thought—or of a body of great or fundamental ideas or great books as the organizing conception of the courses. (As Buchler, reflecting the Dewey tradition, puts it: "To think of learning as a preparation for something beyond learning is a defeat of the process. The most important attitude that can be formed [as Dewey stated in *Experience and Education*] is that of desire to go on learning.") Thus the Columbia curriculum has been adaptable either to the specific needs of the existing student body (as in the implicit notion of "acculturating" the ethnic-group student to Western traditions), to the changing conceptions of what the central problems of society are (particularly in the Contemporary Civilization courses), or to the shifting states of knowledge in the several fields themselves.

The second factor was the proposition, enunciated specifically by Dean Herbert E. Hawkes in 1922, that "the student is the focus of the undergraduate college." It was Hawkes's theory that in the graduate school the subject is paramount; in the college it is the student.) Thus the College sought primarily to be aware of the individual person whose capacities it was trying to develop. At the most general level, the College has been aware of the student through its placement examination and its advisory system, which Columbia pioneered as unmistakably as it did the founding of the basic courses.[6] More specifically, the very diversity of the student body—its numerous geographical and ethnic backgrounds; the many different scholarly and vocational intentions—and the large number of upper-level elective courses that can be offered by a powerful university have encouraged a variety of pursuits and a variety of influences that have mitigated against a single doctrine.

Third (though the point is rarely made explicitly in the theoretical and philosophical discussions of the College and its curriculum) has been the institutional structure of the university itself, in which the locus of attention and power has come to be "the department," rather than any larger entity. Though the College has a distinct identity and ethos, the content of the courses—although less so in the basic lower-college courses—has been defined by the departments, and not by the College administration or the College faculty as a whole. Whether this is vice or virtue, the consequence has been that the interests, slants, and prejudices of the departments, rather than any central or unified source, have shaped the curriculum. This can be seen, to some extent, in the different histories and doctrines of the Humanities and Contemporary Civilization courses. While the College has sought to establish a common rationale for the two sequences, they have moved in somewhat different directions—the implications of which are discussed in detail in chapter 5.

It would be untrue to say that because it lacks a unified doctrine— the idea once expressed by Robert M. Hutchins that without some "theology or metaphysics a unified university cannot exist"—Co-

---

[6] "The essential fact about the placement examination is that it was given to the student *after* his admission to the College, in order to determine on what level he should pursue certain studies within the undergraduate program. The essential fact about the advisory system is that from the beginning it has been predominantly in the hands of the teaching staff rather than of a professional guidance staff; for the very meaning of an outlook that stressed attention to the individual student and the continuity of the educational process with the living process required the men who advised to be also the men who knew the students in the classroom and on the campus." Buchler, in *History.*
Both facts remain true of Columbia College today.

lumbia College has been subject to the winds of eclecticism. It would be fairer to say that within the broad rationale supplied by Dewey's ideas (a philosophy that was more explicit in the original construction of the general education courses than it has been in the last decade and a half) a number of diverse intellectual tendencies—Marxism, historicism, existentialism, analytic philosophy, the new criticism—have, in varying degree, subsequently influenced the successive formulation of the courses and are examples of the receptivity to experience and experiment which is the fundamental tradition of Columbia College. While in a sense, again because of the nature of institutional structure, this has served to make a virtue out of necessity, the sensitivity of the College to the nature of continuing inquiry has led not only to the acceptance of broad intellectual diversity as a practice, but to a willing endorsement of this diversity as a general principle of liberal education.

THE COLLEGE OF THE UNIVERSITY OF CHICAGO

Over the past twenty-five years the College of the University of Chicago has undergone the most thoroughgoing experiment in general education of any college In the United States. Many confusions about the purposes and curriculum of the Chicago College have arisen because of a loose identification of its curriculum with that of St. John's College of Annapolis or with the Great Books program, which has been conducted in the university extension. Actually, the Chicago College experiment resembled neither of these. Nor was the college completely the embodiment of the ideas of Robert M. Hutchins, the genie of the university. Though the general conception of the "Chicago plan" was outlined by President Hutchins in his 1936 Yale lectures (published as *The Higher Learning in America*), the character of the college was developed by its successive deans, Aaron J. Brumbaugh, Clarence Faust, and F. Champion Ward, and its curriculum by the college faculty; and the detailed program, in fact, was somewhat removed from Hutchins' ideas, most of which were embodied, rather, in the curriculum of St. John's.[7]

---

[7] Much of the confusion of the College of the University of Chicago with St. John's of Annapolis arises understandably out of the history of the two programs. In 1936-37, Mr. Hutchins invited Stringfellow Barr, a historian, and Scott

The detailed history of the Chicago experiment is a long and involved one, going back to 1937, when the innovation of a four-year program entirely devoted to general education was first accepted by the university."[8] In seeking to describe the college, it is difficult to find a long enough period of time when the curriculum was sufficiently "fixed" to allow one to say: this was the Chicago curriculum. Much of the difficulty stemmed from the radical tenor of the proposed innovations, the continual testing of ideas and programs, the resistance of the divisions[9] to the college program, and the complicated relationships with secondary schools and graduate schools which arose out of Hutchins' effort to reorganize drastically the pattern of educational sequence in the United States. What follows, then, is not a picture of general education at Chicago at any single point of time, but an "ideal type," which may serve to identify Chicago's essential conceptions and tradition.

There were, one can say, five basic intentions underlying the gen-

Buchanan, a philosopher, both at that time of the University of Virginia, to be visiting professors at Chicago in order to consider the place of the trivium and quadrivium—grammar, rhetoric, and logic; and arithmetic, geometry, music, and astronomy—in modern education, and, with a committee of their own choosing, to frame a curriculum based on a study of the "great books" of Western civilization. The project created a great furor at Chicago, uniting those who opposed Hutchins' educational views with those who felt that too many revisions of the college curriculum would be unsettling. As Scott Buchanan described the situation shortly afterward: "The University of Chicago saw red, and they almost burned our books so that we couldn't read. Our presence made [the] Dean of Humanities a great deal of trouble. It was a great relief for everybody but the donors of the money for this project when St. John's [College in Annapolis] called the members of the Liberal Arts Committee to put its program into operation."

[8] My main sources here are *The Idea and Practice of General Education: An Account of the College of the University of Chicago,* by Present and Former Members of the Faculty (Chicago, University of Chicago Press, 1950), and my own experiences as a faculty member of the college from 1945 to 1948.

[9] While the University of Chicago is organized by departments, its basic structural unit, introduced by Hutchins in 1930, is a fourfold divisional pattern of the social sciences, the humanities, the physical sciences, and the biological sciences, each headed by its own dean. Initially, the divisions were responsible for graduate and undergraduate education, but the college gradually recruited its own faculty. Complicating the organizational structure has been the existence of degree-granting committees, which, in the case of the Committee on Human Development, cut across divisional lines; the faculty of the Committee on Social Thought, on the other hand, usually has no departmental affiliations and is completely autonomous.

eral education program of the College of the University of Chicago. The most sweeping was the attempt to break the traditional lock-step pattern of American schools. In most areas the pattern is 8-4-4: eight years of elementary school, four years of high school, and four years of college. Less commonly, the introduction of a junior high school has created a 6-3-3-4 sequence. What Hutchins proposed, reviving an earlier suggestion of William Rainey Harper, the founding president of the University of Chicago, was to group the last two years of the secondary school with the first two years of college, and to form a new college devoted entirely to general education. At the end of that four-year period, the student would be given a regular B.A.

A number of disquieting features about the state of American education had led to this revolutionary proposal. One was the distrust of the high school as archaic in its program, unserious in its intentions, and largely a waste of time. Second, it was felt that two years of general courses were insufficient grounding for a liberal arts education—in most colleges, as at Chicago, the division between two years of general education and two years of electives or specialization was the rule. But the most important consideration was the theoretical effort to redefine the role of a college within a university framework.

In the thinking of the great pioneers of the American university— Gilman at Hopkins, Eliot at Harvard, Harper at Chicago, and Butler at Columbia—the major emphasis had been on the primary role of the graduate school with its encouragement of original scholarship, as central to the purpose of the university. Gilman had originally proposed to start Hopkins off without an undergraduate college. At Columbia, as we have seen, there had been repeated proposals to abolish the college. In his inaugural address at the University of Chicago, in November, 1929, Robert Hutchins saw in the college, and in general education, an end in itself; and it was in this light that the Chicago revisions were initially undertaken. "The emphasis on productive scholarship that has characterized the university from the beginning and must characterize it to the end," he said, "has naturally led us to repeated questions as to the place and future of our colleges. *They could not be regarded as training grounds for the graduate schools, for less than 20 percent of their graduates went on* [italics added]. . . . Nor did the argument that we should contribute good citizens . . . make much impression on distinguished scholars anxious to get ahead with their own researches. . . . At times, therefore, members of the Faculty have urged that we withdraw from undergraduate work, or at least the first two years of it. But we do not propose to abandon or dismember the college. . . . The whole question of the [relation of the] first two years of college to the high school on the one hand, and to the senior college on the other is one of the most baffling that is before us."

In effect, while the Chicago plan was seen in later years as being akin, say, to the French system, with the proposed four-year college (combining the last two years of high school and the first two years of college) analogous to the lycée, after which the student would go on to the university for work in a special faculty like letters or law, *the original Hutchins' intention was to provide a general education as the terminal school experience for most youths attending college.* It was an effort to provide a liberal arts education as an end in itself, without any notion of vocational or preprofessional training. The post-World War II situation, in which a rising percentage of students (80 percent of Chicago's graduates today) go on to graduate work, and in which the college itself has become a preparatory school, was not foreseen. Whether, given this fact, Mr. Hutchins would still have held to his conception of general education is an interesting point to consider.

The second basic conception of the Chicago plan was a completely prescribed curriculum for all students, no matter what their vocational plans, intellectual interests or capacities, and backgrounds. The intention was to define a common body of materials in the various fields of knowledge which should be mastered by any person who considers himself educated. Hence there were to be no electives or specializations. A student could "place out" or "achieve" courses by demonstrating a competence in certain subjects, and thus go through the college at his own pace, but the curriculum as a whole was fixed.

One of the practical difficulties, which was never resolved, was the difference in situation between those who entered the college after their second year of secondary school and those who entered after finishing high school. Although the new four-year college was first adopted in 1937 (alongside an existing two-year lower-college program), it was only in 1942 that the four-year program became *the* College at the University of Chicago. But the war years, and the returning rush of veterans after the war, wrought havoc with the program. Theoretically, the full program consisted of fourteen yearlong courses, designed for those students who entered the college after the second year of high school. Those who finished these courses received a B.A. But other colleges, particularly graduate schools, rarely recognized this as a true B.A. and often required the Chicago College graduate to take a year, and sometimes two, of additional courses before they admitted him to graduate work. For those entering the college with a regular high-school diploma, the prospect of having to spend three or even four years in general courses only to find that the degree was not completely acceptable for graduate work elsewhere was unpalatable.

In the postwar years the college was in a dilemma. On the one hand, few students in the secondary schools were taking advantage of the new college program. (At its peak it is doubtful whether the early high-school entrants ever constituted more than 20 percent of the college population.) On the other hand, veterans with high-school degrees were eagerly seeking admission to college. For a time the college toyed with the idea of reducing the number of required courses so as to allow the "regular" student (i.e., one with four years of high school) to complete his work in two years, and thus maintain the time equivalence with the early entrants. But this threatened to destroy the meaning of the B.A., and only underscored the contention of other colleges that the Chicago B.A. was only a two-year degree. The only solution, which Chicago took after the retirement of Chancellor Hutchins in 1950, was to abolish the radical idea of combining high school and the college years (though a certain number of places were kept for early admission of highly qualified students), and to create a full four-year general education B.A. for the students with high-school diplomas.[10] But even here, the factor unforeseen by Hutchins tended to vitiate this program, for more than

---

[10] Later, a bachelor of science degree was offered jointly by the college and the divisions of biological sciences and physical sciences.

80, rather than 20, percent of the college's graduates went on to graduate work, and the Chicago College was unable to maintain a system of four years of general courses without the introduction of specialization and concentrations.

It was once said that Hutchins' conception of the radical reorganization of the high-school and college years was basically sound, but that the timing was unfortunate. A closer reading of Hutchins' original conception—that general education would be the *terminal* experience for the college youth—indicates that even if the war and postwar years had not confounded the college, the rise in graduate education, and the consequent pressure for specialization, would have served to undercut the Chicago idea. One can say, in retrospect, that a reorganization of the national educational pattern, in which one would group together the last two years of high school and the first two years of college into a general education B.A., then a three-year specialization in a subject leading to a M.A., and finally a two- or three-year Ph.D., organized around a research investigation, would be a more rational schema than the present system. But this was not the original Chicago conception, and the current reorganization of the secondary schools, seeking to emphasize the new work in the sciences and in mathematics, makes it a remote possibility.

The heart of the Chicago plan—the third basic conception of the college—was the organization of all knowledge into a comprehensive number of fields which would give the student not the sum of factual knowledge in that field but its basic organizing principles. These were not survey courses. Nor were they—though the claim was made freely—training in or the understanding of a discipline. (Perhaps I construe the term too narrowly, but I understand the word "discipline" in this context to mean a group of analytical concepts ordered into a body of theory and applied to a subject matter. Thus, economics is a discipline, while international trade or national-income accounts are subjects. A group of many related subjects using a common discipline, or group of related disciplines, would be a field.) The Chicago plan sought to draw together the disciplines in three fields— the humanities, the social sciences, and the natural sciences—and to consider problems which, by their nature, could only be understood by applying concepts from different disciplines. (A typical problem in the social science course would be, for example, "freedom and order.")

These interdisciplinary efforts were never wholly successful because the discussion, say, of economic policy—for example, government policy on monopoly, business, and labor—required some basic knowledge of economics that was not always present; in consequence, weeks had to be devoted to the intensive explanation of economic concepts (e.g., elasticity and supply-and-demand) before one could discuss policy. At best, those courses and those topics were most successful which, by their nature (e.g., the relationship of culture to personality), enlisted materials from different disciplines that could genuinely be fused.

In the construction of the course sequences, the interests of the staff more often determined the content than did the intentions of the administration, and since the large staffs brought together persons of diverse backgrounds and trainings, the debates about the courses were lively and provocative. The courses, as I can testify from personal experience, were extraordinary intellectual adventures for the teaching staff; and perhaps this was its prize, if unintended, virtue, for what a teacher finds exciting he can communicate best to his students. Whether in the end the courses had the intellectual unity or theoretical clarity claimed for them is moot.

In the social sciences, the first-year course—largely an inheritance from the high-school program—dealt with American democracy, its philosophical presuppositions, and the "great issues" of American society. It was, in effect, a sophisticated course in American history. The second year—which for a long period was the introductory year for those students who had graduated from high school—was organized around the theme of society and culture, concentrating in large measure on the impact of industrial society on the individual. The third year considered the value problem of freedom and control, raising questions about the nature and limits of economic freedom, the relationship of economic freedom to the political order, the role of bureaucracy, and the like. Here, there was an explicit effort to indicate the relationship of social science inquiry to philosophical issues. In each of the courses there was a basic core of "great readings" appropriate to the questions, and *a* large, shifting body of current materials and arguments that exemplified either recent research or the issue under discussion. The social science courses did not carry a distinct "Hutchins" stamp or a "great books" flavor. They were principally sociological or anthropological in inspiration, drawing from the classical writers in these fields, and from contemporary empirical materials. What made them distinctive was the breadth of their coverage.

The humanities, and to a lesser extent the natural sciences sequence, reflected the distinctive "Aristotelianism" one associates with the Chicago approach. By Aristotelianism, I mean here little more than the effort to find the controlling principles of "classification" in the definition of subjects or of disciplines within fields. Thus, if one contrasts the Columbia and the Chicago approach to the humanities, in the Columbia program the emphasis is on the single great work, seen in its own terms, which reflects in itself qualitative values that are to be elicited by the student who confronts the work. The masterpiece is the "experience" for the student. There is little effort to group works on some related principle, or to read them in cultural or historical contexts. In the Chicago courses, on the other hand, the concern was with the classification and analysis (though not with the history) of kinds of books. The major emphasis was on the identification of genres, the principles of genre, the nature of rhetoric, and the theories of criticism which might or might not be relevant to different kinds of work. Curiously, there were fewer "great books" in the Chicago humanities sequence than in Columbia's, Nor was there an effort, as at Columbia, to keep works of literature, art, and music distinct; in the courses at Chicago these were mingled in order to establish contrasts in appreciation.

The natural science sequence was divided equally, over a three-year period, between the physical and biological sciences. Seen formally, on the basis of topics (e.g., motion, light, atomic structure, metabolism, genetics, learning), it somewhat resembled the conventional survey course. At Chicago, however, the emphasis was on the reading of original papers and on problems that were to be solved in the laboratory. (Two characteristic problems were: an investigation of floating and sinking, based on Archimedes' essay "On Floating

Bodies"; and a consideration of the pendulum, derived from Galileo's "Two New Sciences.") One can raise a variety of questions about such a course: that it was more the history of science than a discussion of contemporary scientific knowledge, that the integration was formal rather than substantive, and the like; and these are objections that are relevant. But the chief difficulty the Chicago College faced with this course, as with many of the others, was not intellectual but institutional—the problems of staffing, of relating them to old-line departments, and the like. And this difficulty runs like a thread through the three colleges we are discussing.

The capstone of the three general sequences was a course that bore the *joli-laide* title of "Observation, Interpretation, and Integration." In the Chicago vernacular the course was always called O.I.I., and by the students, predictably enough, "Oi, Oi, Oi"—to the bewilderment of outsiders who rarely understood what the initials or vocables stood for. The intention of the course was to provide an integrating schema for the general courses, establishing the principles of *their* organization. (It replaced an older course, given before 1942, called "Methods, Values, and Content.")

Though a cursory glance at the titles of the three sequences in the year-long course—the Organization, Methods, and Principles of the Sciences—might lead one to assume that it was a course in the philosophy of science, it was actually, in the light of the Chicago approach, a justification of philosophy, as antecedent to science. The first quarter, the best worked-out section of the course, dealt with the classification of the different sciences and their rationales. It dealt, in effect, with the alleged hierarchies of knowledge. Major readings were in Plato, Aristotle, Boethius, Aquinas, St. Augustine, Bacon, Comte, Kant, and Carnap. Typical problems concerned the definition of classification, the differentiation of the early fields of knowledge, and the question of which sciences presupposed which others. The second quarter, on the methods of the sciences, dealt with the nature of induction, the contrasting methods in the sciences and humanities, and the like. In addition to reading in traditional philosophy, there were selections from Mill, Durkheim, Poincaré, Dewey, and Einstein. The third quarter, on *principles* in the sciences, rarely had consistent definition. In an effort to demonstrate how different sets of principles are employed in the treatment of a philosophical issue, the course, in one of its characteristic years, presented four readings on the theme of "pleasure," as illustrated in the work of Plato, Aristotle, Hume, and Mill, and then treated of the categorical imperative in Kant as differentiating certain moral problems, e.g., distinguishing ethical duties from the duties of right.

Despite the reiterated use of the word "science," it can be quickly observed that the emphasis was more on the traditional questions in the history of philosophy rather than on the modern questions arising out of the theories of Hume and Kant such as the limits of empiricism; the nature of theory construction and verification; the nature of explanation and the status of general laws; the distinction between "cultural sciences" and the "natural sciences," between modes of relationships *meaningfully* and *logically* related to each other (as in German post-idealism) and modes of relationships *causally* or *functionally* related to each other, between normative theory and positivist theory; the relation of postulational systems and axiomatic theory to statistical and probabilistic models; and and so on.[11] I call attention to this difference not to argue (at least not at this point) the relevance of one or another emphasis as most adequate to general education, but because the O.I.I. course represented, to the extent that any single course can, the specific "ideological" commitments of the Chicago curriculum.[12]

Apart from the three broad divisions, and the integrative course in the "philosophy of science," the Chicago scheme also contained a course in the history of Western civilization. In the original pattern laid out in 1942, history as an organized study had been virtually eliminated by the new emphasis on analytical inquiry by fields. But a dissatisfaction with the lack of historical knowledge of the students

[11] For a comprehensive formulation of the central problems of the relation of traditional philosophy to science, see Morris R, Cohen, *Reason and Nature* (reprint ed,; Glencoe, Ill., Free Press, 1959), and for the relationship of scientific inquiry to the principles of explanation, Ernest Nagel, *The Structure of Science* (New York Harcourt, Brace, and World, 1961).

I have also found helpful, in this connection, the discussion by Talcott Parsons, *The Structure of Social Action* (New York, McGraw-Hill, 1937), especially chapters 13 and 14.

[12] The course, later called O.M.P,—the Organization, Methods, and Principles of the Sciences—was ended in 1963.

led, in 1948, to the introduction of this Western civilization course. The central thread was a set of topics along a chronological line: units on the Greek polis, the Roman empire, and Christianity; medieval society in the twelfth and thirteenth centuries; the Renaissance and Reformation; the French Revolution; Great Britain and nineteenth-century industrialism; and the Russian Revolution. But because the "Chicago philosophy" has usually been skeptical of or even hostile to the "historical approach" (seeing in it only a minor and, even then, an inadequate way to organize knowledge, and failing to provide philosophical integration), special cultural problems such as conceptions of space and time in Plato, Aristotle, Augustine, Leibnitz, and Kant, and the techniques of representing space in art, were inserted as pendants to the historical concentrations: thus, the unit on space and time followed the discussion of Christianity, and the representation of space in art followed the Renaissance.

The ironic fact is that in the tangled history of the Chicago curriculum, the most ambitious and representative course, that on "Observation, Interpretation, and Integration," was the first to be sacrificed when the college began to adapt to more traditional modes of instruction, while the "History of Western Civilization," which initially stood outside the Chicago scheme, has proved to be the most durable of the courses—perhaps because of its essential traditionalism.

The fourth element of the Chicago plan was the creation of an autonomous college faculty whose sole duty would be to teach the general courses. The purpose of this move was twofold: first, to find a faculty with the competence to teach broad undergraduate courses; and second, to give the college dean the authority to recruit such a faculty without having to negotiate with the departments or the divisions of the university. Appointments, even tenure appointments, were made in the college only, and in the general field, such as social science or humanities, since the college did not teach distinct disciplines.

The courses at Chicago were run as staff courses. Course hours, usually four a week, were divided between two lecture hours and two discussion hours. The lectures were given by the staff members to provide background material, each person taking responsibility for a unit of the course. The discussions, which concentrated on the syllabus readings, were led by the same staffs. Weekly staff meetings were held to review materials, to present coaching materials for staff members insufficiently acquainted with a topic, and to discuss questions that should be raised in class.

One might assume that there would be difficulty in finding a faculty with the broad competence and interests to teach such courses, especially since there were no graduate schools which prepared men for such jobs. Yet after the war, Chicago recruited a young faculty of undeniable brilliance and subsequent renown, whose lectures (given more to impress each other in the barnyard competition) were of extraordinarily high caliber. But the expanding market for college teachers in the 1950s, if not the system itself, proved the undoing of the college. Younger men, oriented to careers in their disciplines, were afraid of becoming the "superior schoolmasters" whom John W. Burgess had earlier described as the kind of person a college teacher ought to be. They wanted to do research, become involved in graduate teaching, and gain recognition in their own fields. Lacking joint appointments in the departments, the younger men began to move out of the college.

If the college could have institutionalized a system whereby younger men taught for five or so years in the general courses in order to broaden themselves, and then were able to move into the divisions, it would have had a more stable faculty. But a combination of ideological reasons (the idea of a separate college) and the hostility of the graduate divisions made this impossible. In recent years, the system of a separate college faculty has been abandoned, and the college has sought to integrate its permanent appointments with the graduate divisions.

The fifth element of the Chicago plan was the development of comprehensive examinations at the end of the year courses (although "advisory" quarterly grades were posted) by an independent examination staff. There were two reasons for independent examination: to test competence in a general field of knowledge on an objective basis, and to place the student in an easier relationship with the instructor, since the instructor was not the assigner of academic rewards and penalties. Since the instructor did not usually read examination papers (unless he held a joint appointment on the examination staff), the difficulty of testing six hundred or more students in a single course often led to undue reliance on multiple-choice, machine-graded examinations, rather than essays. And this has been a consistent criticism of the system.

The Chicago plan, as I have drawn this composite of the 1950s, was the most comprehensive experiment in general education in the history of American academic life. Its successes and failures, both intellectual and institutional, are worth careful study in the evaluation of general education today; I make a further effort along this line in chapter 5, in considering the more recent history of general education at Chicago, Columbia, and Harvard.

HARVARD COLLEGE

The movement toward general education in the United States received great impetus after World War II with the publication, in 1945, of the Harvard report entitled *General Education in a Free Society* (familiarly known, and hereafter referred to, as the Redbook).[13] In many places it quickly became the bible of general education, particularly in smaller colleges and state universities. (Like the Bible Itself, it was often either unread or sometimes read too literally.)

The purpose of the Harvard report, it should be noted, was not primarily to write a curriculum for Harvard College (indeed, only one of its six chapters dealt with Harvard) or even to propose a model program for all of higher education, but to formulate a complete educational philosophy for American society. Much of its discussion, in fact, was on secondary education. Its influence, however, was largely on the colleges.

---

[13] In this section, as in the discussions in chapter 5, I have relied greatly upon the Redbook; on the report of Professor Jerome Bruner, as chairman of a subcommittee of the Committee on Educational Policy, in February, 1949, on the problem of science in general education; on the "Report of the Special Committee to Review the Present Status and Problems of the General Education Program" (May, 1964), known informally as the Doty Committee (named for its chairman, Professor Paul M. Doty); and on interviews with various people in the Harvard program.

Just as the divisive experiences of World War I provided the impulse for the Contemporary Civilization course at Columbia College, similar troublesome problems confronting American schools during World War II prompted the establishment of the General Education Committee at Harvard. Such problems as "why we fight," the principles of a free society, the need to provide a consistent image of the American experience, the definition of democracy in a world of totalitarianism, the effort to fortify the heritage of Western civilization, and the need to provide a "common learning" for all Americans as a foundation of national unity, were the factors that shaped the thinking of the Redbook. Indeed, the Harvard report explicitly stated that the "supreme need of American education is for a unifying purpose and idea."

The need for a unifying purpose in American education was impressed upon the authors not only by the war and the changed relation of America to the rest of the world, but by the failure of the secondary school system, and the gulf, as the authors saw it at the time, between those Americans whose education stopped at the high-school level and the small minority who went on to college. In fact, almost the entire orientation of the Harvard report is to the necessary changes that must take place in American education because of the failure of the high schools to provide, as they had in 1870, a common learning for all Americans. Interestingly enough, there is not a single reference in the Harvard report—one can take this as an indicator of the speed of change and the magnitude of the problem—to graduate education and its relation to the college curriculum. The entire emphasis is on the secondary school and the college.

The necessary movement to general education, according to the Redbook, derived primarily from the change in the character of the high school. In 1870, the base line chosen by the authors, those who went to high school were the children of the well-to-do. The function of the high school was clear: it was to prepare the student for college. The high-school curriculum, narrow and rigid, perhaps, by modern standards, yet was compact and clear in its intentions. One taught the young citizen logic by mathematics, taste by the Greek and Latin classics, speech by rhetoric, and ideals by Christian ethics. The teachers were college men, the student body was homogeneous, the society had a unified character in that the educated elite had a common training and ideal—the Christian ethic.

In 1945, the authors of the Redbook could write: "Except for a small minority, the high school has. . . ceased to be a preparatory school in the old sense of the word. Insofar as it is preparatory, it prepares not for college, but for life," Seeing America thus, as being constituted of a small college elite and a large high-school mass, the authors asked, "How can these two groups"—those who go only to high school and those who go on to college—"how can these two groups, despite their different interests, achieve from their education some common and binding understanding of the society which they will possess in common?"

The answer, to the extent that one could be given, was expressed in the twin themes of democracy and heritage. The function of the schools, beginning mos: explicitly at the secondary level, was to inculate common standards by expressing "the best and fullest truth that can be known" (while recognizing that "truth is not fully known") and in embracing "as fully as possible the mainsprings of our culture."[14]

The authors of the Redbook laid out a program for general education in the high schools without prescribing in detail what the high schools should teach. In the humanities, for example, they proposed that the secondary schools concentrate on great works. "The root argument for using. . .great works in literature courses is briefly this: ours *is* at present a centrifugal culture in extreme need of unifying forces. . . . Therefore the books which have been the great meeting points and have most influenced the men who in turn have influenced others are those we can least afford to neglect. . . . It is a safe assumption that a work which has delighted and instructed many

---

[14] The authors say further, in remarks I can construe only as implicit rebukes to the Hutch ins and Dewey philosophies, "Neither do we think this culture [is] wholly reflected in any one list of great books, which, important as they may be in setting forth standards, necessarily neglect the relevance of these standards to the present. But we are equally suspicious of those empiricists who believe the truth is to be found only in experiment, a position that finally implies the denial of any stable truth. Without denying a partial value of any of these views, we believe rather that the main task of education is to interpret at all stages both the general and the particular—both the common sphere of truth and the particular avenues of change."

generations of ordinary readers and been to them a common possession
. . . is to be preferred to a product which is on its way to limbo and
will not link together even two school generations."

In the social studies the authors recommended a concentration on
history in order "to set forth the main tendencies in the development
of modern civilization," and stressed the importance of work in
American history. Pointing out that in some school systems pupils
"are exposed to American history three, four, even five or six times,"
the authors questioned this repetition and urged a single one-year
course in the high school, "strongly factual in nature," emphasizing
"the careful and even detailed study of many of the principal events,
movements, personalities, and institutional developments in American
history." The aim of such a course, they said, "is to provide a basis
for. . . participation in the work of citizenship."

In the sciences, the Redbook argued that "a course in a particular
science does not really fulfill the aims of a general education. There
is a place for a rigorous and highly integrated introduction to the
sciences as a whole" that would include something of the history of
scientific discoveries and some discussion of major scientific concepts
and hypotheses. Such a course "might not only be the ideal offering
for the terminal student but the best possible introduction for those
who will go on to the individual sciences." As a second course in science, the authors proposed a course in general biology, because the
subject matter "can be dealt with largely in a descriptive way, and
because the content of this course is more intimately related to his
daily experience and educational needs. Such a course should, for
example, provide informative and emotionally neutral approaches to
such subjects as personal and community hygiene, nutrition, and sexual
reproduction."

The section on the role of mathematics in the secondary school
curriculum divided into a discussion of the subject as it should be
presented to the mathematically inept student, and to those who
would have to use mathematics in college work. For the former, the
authors advocated stimulating their interest in the "number relations
of arithmetic and in the elementary principles of geometry by presenting mathematics in various disguises—such as shop mathematics,
business arithmetic, mathematics of the farm, and so on. . . . If fur-

ther mathematics is to be given these pupils, informal geometry and mechanical drawing offer the greatest chance of success because of their concreteness." For students going on to college who have mathematical aptitudes above the median, the Harvard group proposed work in algebra and geometry, although for students "who by the tenth or eleventh grade have decided that their interest in science and mathematics will not extend beyond a general education in these areas, no further work in mathematics can probably be prescribed." Instead "it might be more valuable to give them in the senior year, just preparatory to entering college, an introductory survey of elementary trigonometry, statistics, precision of measurement, and the use of graphs."

I have gone at length into this exposition for two reasons. First, because the proposals for the secondary schools are in miniature the proposals for the colleges, and, second, to illustrate the gulf in thought that has opened up within two decades. In the last five years a veritable revolution has begun in the secondary schools in the teaching of mathematics, biology, physics, and social studies and the humanities. These innovations (described in chapter 3) are a far cry from the recommendations of the Harvard book. I have no intention, at least for the moment, of arguing the validity of one or another approach; I am merely pointing up the contrasts. These can be focused on two values. In the Harvard report, the emphasis is on broadening the subjects. The more recent approaches, particularly those initiated under the influence of Jerrold Zacharias of M.I.T. and Jerome Bruner of Harvard, seek to emphasize the structure of the subject matter itself. In the earlier instance, the emphasis was on the needs of the student and the commitment to democracy; in the later one, it has been on the changing nature of the subject matter and the needs of a scientific or technological society.

The Harvard report, prepared between 1943 and 1945, had the benefit of twenty years of the Columbia experience and an acquaintance with the theory, if not the practice, of the Chicago plan. Surprisingly, except for one flattering reference to the Columbia Contemporary Civilization course in its own proposals for Harvard College, neither Columbia nor Chicago is mentioned, nor is there an assessment of their experience or theory. The closest the authors come to an attempt to "give perspective to our discussion of Harvard College" is a cursory two-page discussion of "five major approaches to the problems of general education" none of which fits either the Columbia or the Chicago plan.[15]

Why there should have been such parochialism is difficult to understand. The interesting fact is that the proposed humanities and social science courses for Harvard were remarkably close to the spirit, if not the actual texts, of the Columbia College courses. And in the insistence that every Harvard and Radcliffe student be required to take the same first-year courses, so that general education should involve the students in a common or shared experience, they were clearly echoing the Columbia and Chicago philosophy.

The overall theme which the authors of the Harvard report set forth to guide the common general education program was the "heritage" of Western civilization. The emphasis on history was central. "Even in the natural sciences a sense of the historic was to be preserved," a successor committee reports, in summing up the intentions of twenty years before. "The authors of the Redbook," writes the Doty Committee, "hoped that, in both the physical sciences and biological science courses, serious attention would be given to the earlier

[15]"It may be said," write the authors, "that there are now five major approaches to the problem of general education in these colleges: 1) distribution requirements, 2) comprehensive survey courses, 3) functional courses, 4) the great books curriculum, and 5) individual guidance."

The first of these—and the most widely used, as the authors note—Is simply a limitation on complete elective choice, requiring the student to distribute a flexible portion of his courses among various areas. The second type, largely self-evident from the term, comprises survey courses organized, usually, in the four fields of the humanities, social sciences, physical, and biological sciences. The term *functional,* the authors note, has been given to courses which prepare a student for immediate problems of life. The recent report of the American Council on Education, entitled *Design for General Education,* describes four such courses: personal and community health, problems of social adjustment, marriage and family adjustment, and vocational orientation. The Great Books program, which the authors identify with St. John's College, involves four prescribed years in the study of approximately one hundred great books of the Western tradition, supplemented by ancient and modern languages, mathematics, and laboratory science. Individual guidance describes the programs of such schools as Bennington, Sarah Lawrence, and Black Mountain, where, after the student has explored a number of different fields for two years, a reading and tutorial program is planned around a central interest that the student pursues for the remaining two years.

developments of the subject and to the great scientific writers of the past. Thus, the emphasis on the historic 'classic' achievements of our civilization was not limited to any particular area; it was, in fact, the informing spirit of the program as a whole."

If one looks at the specific proposals of the Harvard report, the rationale is strikingly that of the Columbia Humanities and Contemporary Civilization courses. In the social sciences, it was proposed that all students take a course that might be called "Western Thought and Institutions." "In a single course," the authors argued, "it would be folly to attempt the comprehensive survey of the entire range of European institutional development and social thinking from the time of the Greeks to the present day, and no such project is proposed. . . . We may suggest, however, that in the writings of Aquinas, Machiavelli, Luther, Bodin, Locke, Montesquieu, Rousseau, Adam Smith, Bentham, and Mill, to mention no others, one can find materials admirably suited to serve the purpose of such a course. These writings will be best understood and most valuable to the student when read in the economic, social, and political context of their times. They should, that is to say, be studied not simply as great books, but as great expressions of ideas which emanated from certain historical backgrounds. . . . The course is not unlike the very successful introductory course, 'Contemporary Civilization,' which has been given at Columbia during the past twenty-six years, although we suggest that it would be preferable to deal with fewer topics and to read longer portions of fewer books than has been customary in that admirable course. In a formal sense, 'Western Thought and Institutions' would be a new course, but it would be building upon the experience derived from courses which have been successfully taken by freshmen at both Harvard and Columbia."

In regard to humanities: "It is proposed that the course in the area of the humanities which will be required of all students be one which might be called 'Great Texts of Literature.' The aim of such a course would be the fullest understanding of the work read rather than of men or periods represented, craftsmanship evinced, historic or literary development shown, or anything else. These other matters would be admitted only insofar as they are necessary to allow the work to speak for itself. Otherwise they should be left for special, not general education." In dealing with the mode of treatment, the authors wrote: "There is not one best way of introducing people to Homer or Plato or Dante. Or, if there is, which it is not known. Freedom for the instructor is essential. He only teaches, in this field, by letting his students watch the play of a mind with a mind that their minds may play in turn. The play he shows them must be representative of 'the all in each of all minds,' to use Coleridge's phrase, but it cannot be tied down to another man's notion of what is educative. And yet if a course in literature deserves to be compulsory, there must be wide agreement both as to what it is attempting and how it will attempt that." Because reading a great work requires time for reflection, the Harvard report suggests concentrating on a few major texts "since the best commentary on an author is frequently some more of his writing, and since great books are great in part through the power of their design, the amount for single authors cannot be cut beyond a point. . . . Each [book] must be read completely enough for its parts to help one another to the full. Probably, therefore, a course which chose eight great books would be trying to do too much. A list from which a selection would be made might include Homer, one or two of the Greek tragedies, Plato, the Bible, Virgil, Dante, Shakespeare, Milton, Tolstoy."[16]

These lengthy citations are not given to advance the sterile claims of priority for Columbia or to reinforce local pride, but to point up the high degree of congruence, both in the motives that shaped these proposals and in the agreement on approach and subjects—a consensus all the more important as a point of departure for analysis today, since the subsequent practice at Harvard was somewhat at variance with the original proposals, and the adequacy of the Columbia courses has come under question.

In the sciences, the Redbook proposed two general education courses in the physical and biological sciences; neither would be a factual survey, but would emphasize principles and methods. In the first of the courses, the core would be physical concepts, with mate-

---

[16] The Columbia faculty members who participated in the debates (during 1963-64) of the Stern Committee on the Humanities at Columbia will recognize with a wry smile the selfsame arguments that took place in the making of that report.

rial from other sciences—chemistry, astronomy, and geology—introduced only to the degree that they are pertinent to the problems under discussion. The organization would emphasize historical development in order to foster a sense of science as part of the total intellectual and historical processes. In a note, presciently interesting for the developments that have taken place in recent years, the authors comment: "It is expected that this course will he given in two versions adapted to the wide differences in mathematical achievement of entering students. Both editions of the course should have precisely the same educational objectives and fundamental structure. They would differ only in rate and rigor of presentation."

The course in biological science "should lay constant emphasis upon general concepts and upon modes of scientific approach to biological organisms. It should convey not only knowledge concerning organisms, but how this knowledge was acquired and how it impinges upon other areas of interest and learning." The authors suggest a review of classic experiments in the history of biology and an effort to introduce the student to the classic literature of biology such as Harvey's *Circulation of the Blood,* Darwin's *Origin of Species,* Claude Bernard's *Introduction to Experimental Medicine,* Beaumont's *Observations on the Physiology of Digestion,* and Mendel's first paper on plant hybridization, (Again, the proposal's similarities to Columbia Science A and B, and particularly to the Chicago course, are striking.)

The program proposed for Harvard was radically different from what existed up and to that time. "Before 1945," as the Doty Committee summarizes it, "Harvard operated with a rather complex 'distribution' requirement. Departmental courses were divided into three areas: I) natural sciences; 2) social sciences; 3) arts, letters, and philosophy. These areas were then subdivided so that eight sections emerged, and the student was required to have a minimum of one full course in each of the four sections, representing all three areas. The requirement was both difficult to understand and easy to evade. The sections were heterogeneous units and the system was so loose that almost any collection of courses would meet the requirement."

In place of the distribution requirement the Redbook proposed that every Harvard and Radcliffe student would take the same lower-level humanities course, the same lower-level social science course, and one of two lower- level natural science courses. In addition, each student would also take three upper-level general education courses, all of which were to be designated from a list approved by the Committee on General Education, These courses were to be sharply distinguished from departmental courses and could not be counted for departmental concentration. To quote the Doty Committee again: "There was an evident concern that, unless they were carefully guarded, general education courses might drift back into old-fashioned 'survey' courses for particular departments. And however difficult it might have been to say exactly what a general education course was, it is clear that the authors of the Redbook hoped for something far more meaningful and dramatic than this. Indeed, they clearly hoped that their proposed program would offer a major counterwave to the tides of specialization which, in their view, were beginning to engulf not only students and scholars but the foundations of a free society."

The Redbook proposals, which I have outlined in detail, were, never actually adopted at Harvard even though the book was widely read and discussed elsewhere. Shortly after the appearance of the report, the Harvard faculty voted, on October 30, 1945, to approve "the principle and program of general education" as recommended in the Redbook, but by the rime the program was made compulsory on March 8, 1949, a number of significant changes had been made which modified the proposals so radically as to make any recognition of the original program difficult,

The hope of providing a shared, common experience was never realized. For example, the proposal that students take the same humanities, social science, and (one of two) natural science courses at the elementary level was superseded by an offering of four or five alternative courses in each area.[17] These introductory general education courses were offered by the great luminaries of Harvard, but

[17] "One side effect of offering several elementary alternatives in each Area," comments the Doty Committee, "has been to make it impractical for General Education Ahf, the course in composition that replaced English A, to keep any direct contact with the general education program. In point of fact, the proposal of the Redbook on this matter has never been implemented."

when these professors were away, or decided not to teach in a particular year, the course was not offered; or, if the course title was kept, it often had a vastly different content when given by another man. Thus the emphasis on general education at Harvard was not on a common course, a basic theme and its coverage, but on varied treatments of a subject by an outstanding figure. Not a "great ideas" or "great books" course, the Harvard program, in effect, became a "great man" course. As one of the "great men" at Harvard explained the system: "We expose the students to a great mind and hope, then, that they will educate each other." Given the high caliber of the Harvard freshmen, they undoubtedly do.

The change from the original intention was sharpest in the sciences. In 1949, a faculty committee headed by Jerome Bruner repudiated the idea that the teaching of science could be done through the history of science or by a case-method approach. Instead of a historical emphasis, the Bruner Committee proposed that a student be given a "knowledge of the fundamental principles of a special science," and an "idea of the methods of science as they are known today." The difference between a general education and a departmental course in science would consist, then, only in the selection and coverage of topics, not in approach. The Bruner Committee went further to virtually nullify a compulsory requirement in a general education course in the natural sciences entirely. When the general education program was initiated in 1949, students were permitted to substitute three departmental courses for one natural science general education course in that area (presumably for students majoring in the field). The Bruner Committee proposed to reduce the number of departmental courses from three to either two middle-level or one "advanced" departmental course. All its proposals were adopted by the Harvard faculty.

Nor was the intention that the general education courses deal with "classic works" and historic themes—an intention that did shape the early courses—completely maintained. In the last decade a number of courses primarily analytical in character were introduced into the social sciences and the humanities, and the historical emphasis has almost entirely disappeared (except in physics) from the natural sciences.

In a different sense, the multiplicity of courses—each of varied character, and few congruent with each other either in scope or in type of treatment—raised questions about the "equivalences" of one course to another. Of the five social science courses offered in 1963-64, for example, three were historical, overlapping to some extent in topic and in treatment of episodes in Western history; one dealt with constitutionalism in America; and one with psychological conceptions of man. In what sense could one say that the student who had chosen one or another of the courses had received a "general" education? Was it in the type of approach offered by the course (e.g., a synoptic inquiry drawing upon several disciplines), the historical or analytical range of the courses (i.e., the breadth of the subject matter), or something else? The principles or criteria guiding the general education committee in approving the course was never wholly clear. And just how the students would be able to use the courses "to educate each other" by talking over their experiences in the common freshman dormitory was never wholly apparent.[18]

Another important area of general education proposed by the Redbook has also been vitiated. The authors originally proposed that in addition to three compulsory first-level general education courses, students would also be required to take three full upper-level general education courses to be created by the faculty. In practice, this requirement became virtually nonexistent. While there are a large number of upper-level general education courses, which stand outside existing departments (such as David Riesman's "Character and Social Structure in America" and Erik Erikson's "The Human Life Cycle"), the departments also offer courses that are eligible for ful-

---

[18] The advanced standing program has wreaked its own havoc on the elementary general education program. Under a rule adopted in 1954, students entering with sophomore standing would be exempted from two of three elementary general education courses. In 1963, almost 20 percent of the class was eligible for sophomore standing.

As the Doty Committee comments: "Interestingly, no effective changes were made in the rules pertaining to their concentration requirements. If taken seriously, this disparity would seem to suggest chat general education was regarded as something that, after a certain minimum achievement, could be dispensed with, whereas special or departmental education should be taken at the highest level of which the student was capable. An alternative view, of course, would be to hope that better prepared students would do *both* their departmental and their general education work at a higher level."

fillment of the upper-level general education requirement, and for career reasons students are more likely to take these as a means of doing additional work in their chosen subject. (Thus, 35 percent of the Harvard students and 18 percent of the Radcliffe students in a recent class took *no* such second-group general education course, while other students, on the average, took only one.) The Doty Review Committee concluded: "The concept of upper-level general education, which was emphasized in the Redbook and was a unique feature of the Harvard scheme, has proved less important in practice than in the original theory."

The crucial problem at the upper, as at the elementary, level is that the original effort to differentiate between general education and departmental courses, and thus to distinguish between a concern with heritage or relationships and with the introduction to a discipline, has deteriorated. In its review, the Doty Committee points up this problem: "In the case of the lower-level alternatives, the line that separates general education from departmental courses has lost much of its original sharpness. Thus, for example, of the fifteen elementary general education courses offered in the 1963-1964 catalogue, four counted for departmental concentrations and were listed as prerequisites for further departmental work. In a few other cases, the committee could find no particular reason why the courses involved should not be counted by departments."

To point to these erosions (and some modifications, which are discussed in the pages on more recent developments in chapter 5) is not to say that Harvard has forfeited its commitment to general education. But the character of that commitment, and the scope and content of the work in general education, have altered sharply. One has to distinguish clearly the traditions and original intentions of general education from its subsequent practice and philosophy. What is true of Harvard has been the case at Chicago and Columbia as well.

THE COMMON QUEST AND THE DISPARITIES

The general education programs at Columbia, Chicago, and Harvard have been the chief instrumentalities for the realization of the liberal arts intentions of these colleges: to free a student from provincialism and to lead him to self-discovery through an awareness of tradition, to confront him with the persistent issues of morals and politics, and to give him an understanding of the interconnectedness of knowledge.

If one can summarize the working principles and commitments that, in varying degrees, have shaped the individual programs at the three schools, they would be:

1. Ideological. The initial impulses were the unifying needs of American society and the desirability of instilling in students a sense of common tasks, though not necessarily a single purpose. The key word here would be *consensus*.[19]

2. Tradition. In all three schools, the main effort has been directed at making the student aware of the history of Western civilization in order to broaden his vistas, to make him aware of the recurrent moral and political problems of man in society, and to chart the travails of the idea of freedom. If there is a single conclusion to which the programs point, it would be that of instilling the idea of *civility*.

3. Contra-specialism. The American university, as it emerged in the latter decades of the nineteenth century, brought with it a new religion of research. Even scholarship in the traditional disciplines was conceived, within that purview, as being concerned with detailed and specialized problems. The reaction of the liberal arts college was to strike out against specialism. The rallying cry, in this respect, was *humanitas*.

4. Integration. The multiplication of knowledge, the rise of many new subfields and subspecialties, the crosscutting of fields, all led to a desire for courses that emphasized the broad relationships of knowl edge, rather than the single discipline. This integration was to be achieved through a survey of fields, the elucidation of fundamental principles of disciplines, the centrality of method, or a combination of all of these. Whatever the varying emphases, the underlying as sumption was of the need for an *interdisciplinary* approach; and this

---

[19] In self-defense, perhaps, I should say the word "consensus" was used before it became employed so profusely by the Johnson administration. Consensus was an explicit term in the Chicago courses, as an intention; it clearly underlay the purposes of the Harvard report; and it represents what Columbia initially sought to do, forty-five years ago, as a result of the War Issues and the Peace Issue course ideas.

became one of the key terms in the language of general education.[20]

While there was, I believe, a set of common intentions that defined the purposes of general education at the three colleges, there have also been large disparities in the institutional and pedagogical arrangements—elements which subtly influence a student's experience. These are more recalcitrant to exposition than the discussion of formal intellectual content.

At Columbia and Chicago, all students take a common general education course, organized around a syllabus, and presumably share a common intellectual apperception, if not experience. At Harvard, within each field there are a number of individual courses, each presumably in some intellectual sense equivalent to each other; and the common experience for the student derives from the exchange of ideas among friends, cliques, or roommates taking the different courses.

At Columbia, the mystique is the course. At Harvard, the central experience of the student is in a large lecture hall, along with two or three hundred other classmen, listening to a polished lecture by the "great man," and then engaging in a discussion of the readings in a small group under the leadership of a "section man," a graduate student who has received his directives on what to evoke in discussion, in a seminar with other section men led by the "great man." The course is thus a pyramidal hierarchy in which the student, at the base, has no direct contact with the "great man" other than through the mediation of the section man.

At Chicago, the students in the common course, often numbering as many as six hundred, typically listen to one lecture and engage in three discussions a week. (Earlier, this had been two lectures and two discussions.) There is a formal equality of the staff in the course (the chairman is an administrative head): the lectures are shared by the staff, and each man also conducts one or two discussion classes.

---

[20] The Harvard Redbook summarized the problem in this fashion: "Why has this concern [with general education] become so strong in late years? Among many reasons three stand out: the staggering expansion of knowledge produced largely by specialism and certainly conducting to it; the concurrent and hardly less staggering growth of our educational system with its maze of stages, functions, and kinds of institutions; and not least, the ever-growing complexity of society itself."

Each member of the staff holds a regular faculty rank. A student may find his discussion section led by a professor or by an instructor, but during the term he will have had a chance to hear all or most of the men in the course.

Columbia has consistently opposed the use of large lecture performances in the introductory courses.[21] Each class is limited to twenty-five students and is taught by a regular member of the staff. The course, unified by the syllabus but decentralized in its operation, becomes for many students a "lottery," in that some students will have an experienced and sometimes a well-known professor, while others will have a young, beginning instructor whose credentials are little known. (Neither attribute, it should be pointed out, is a guarantee of good teaching: the professor may be tired and stale, the instructor enthusiastic; or the professor may be wise and subtle, the tyro awkward and heavy-handed.) Here the emphasis has been most completely on the course.

In all three colleges the general education program has been in difficulty both for intellectual and institutional reasons. In the nature of my inquiry, I can discuss only the *intellectual* questions that apply to the three programs and, by extension, to the practice of general education as a whole. It is to the more general questions that have been raised about general education that I now turn.

---

[21] As the Carman Committee tartly observed: "The test of experience in teaching these orientation courses in Columbia College strengthens our belief that they are not the place for the display of personality in the form of lectures to student audiences large enough to fill a theater. For many years we have given in Columbia College no required courses of the pontifical type, in part because the students know the defects of the type, but principally because the man-to-man effectiveness of a proved instructor, young or old, with a small group—usually twenty or twenty-five—has had much to do with active undergraduate interest in the introductory work, and with the easy and steady improvement of the courses themselves."

Some Current Questions

THE EROSION OF THE COLLEGE IDEA

What is a question? A question, said Felix Cohen, is really an ambiguous proposition; the answer is its determination.[22] In this section I shall set down some straightforward questions; the ambiguous answers are reserved for later discussion.

The general assumption seems to be that the American college is losing its traditional function. A number of writers, in varying tones of dismay, have voiced this fear in recent years. Perhaps the most forthright and unequivocal diagnosis of this condition—verging almost onto prophecy—was made by Columbia's provost, Jacques Barzun, in a speech at the convocation of Hofstra University, on December 12, 1963, which received nationwide attention."[23] Since a direct confrontation with a single argument can highlight a problem more directly than a discussion of diffuse ideas, I have taken Professor Barzun's point of view, extremely perhaps, as prototypical, and treated it as such.

With his characteristic ironic brilliance and merry bravura, Professor Barzun said the following. (I have rearranged somewhat the order of his statements in order to schematize the argument and I have bridged these with some interpolations.)

> If we stand off and look at the silhouette of the American college—I speak of the solid and serious ones, not the shaky imitations—what we see is the thinning and flattening out of its once distinctive curriculum under pressure from above and below; the high school taking away the lower years, the graduate and professional schools the upper.

General education itself, Professor Barzun points out, has in forty years transformed our entire precollegiate schooling.

---

[22] The talmudic parable reverses the order of events; A man runs down the street shouting, "I've got an answer! Who has a question?" In the more esoteric versions, the parable reads; If God is the answer, what is the question?

Which is the most difficult to find: the right question, or the right answer? In this—also a question—lies the heart of the educational inquiry.

[23] The speech, entitled "College to University—and After," is reprinted in *The American Scholar* XXXIII, No. 2 (Spring 1964), 212-20.

The good high school now gives the historical surveys, the introductions to social science, the great books, that formed the substance of general education. What is more, the Advanced Placement System has managed to fill in the old vacuum of the eleventh and twelfth grades with real work, so that more and more freshmen—even without Advanced Placement-find the first year of college feeble and repetitious. They've had the calculus, they've had a grown-up course in American history, they've read Homer and Tolstoy. College holds for them no further revelations; it no longer marks the passage from pupil to student, from make-believe exercises to real thought.

The colleges, he writes, are being transformed by the driving spirits of specialization.

The reality is that the best colleges today are being invaded, not to say dispossessed, by the advance agents of the professions, by men who want to seize upon the young recruit as soon as may be and train him in a "tangible skill."

This, at any rate, is true in the colleges attached to universities. Consider the forces at work. First, it seems desirable to have the great scholar teach undergraduates, and he naturally teaches them as if they were future scholars in his own line, as professionals. Then, the young themselves want to get on as quickly as possible, and in the last two years of college they elect a major which relates directly to the future profession. . . . An even stronger influence is that of the young teachers, all Ph.D.'s who need to establish themselves. This they can do only in one way: by showing productivity in research. . . . Accordingly, these junior scholars decline to teach anything not related to their own specialties. As one of them said to me, they "do not want to teach secondhand subjects." Firsthand subjects are necessarily narrow, and what is worse, they are treated as if everyone in the class were to become a professional, a duplicate of his own teacher.

The different courses in the colleges, he points out, no longer have liberal content, but each repeats a professional intention, so that the student has no interest in these.

No undergraduate can believe that he is going to be at the same time and anthropologist, a Milton scholar, an historian, and a chemist. Yet that is what modern teaching assumes about him in successive hours of the college day. . . . The motive to study is inevitably lacking in at least three out of four classes when so conducted, that is, when the listener is not addressed as a person or a citizen, but only as that dreadful model of our age: the useful member of society who must be clothed in qualifications and armed with licenses to practice.

The consequence of all this is clear.

In short, both teachers and students are responding to the spirit of the times. They are impatient with everything that is not directed at the development of talent into competence. . . .The meaning of this is plain: the liberal arts tradition is dead or dying . . . . sooner or later the college as we know it will find that it has no proper place in the scheme of things. . . The trend seems to me so clear that to object would be like trying to sweep back the ocean. It would be foolish to repine or try to prolong a tradition which has run its course.[24]

Is there then to be, as Max Weber once warned, the world of "specialists without spirit, sensualists without heart"? Or is it that Professor Barzun's style has carried us away? One feels that Barzun, in his temperamental reaction to the pedant's "gray on gray," works his canvas in a bold chiaroscuro, but that the picture is not so black-and-white as he makes it out to be. Let me convert some of his determinate answers to ambiguous questions.

Has not Professor Barzun overdrawn the picture of the advanced work in the secondary schools? Do they teach the materials which

---

[24] Professor Barzun, it should be emphasized, does not welcome this course. He is not, despite the Cassandra-like tone, Jacques le Fataliste, but Jacques le Moraliste; and in his skecch of what he thinks may follow, he is engaging in the irony characteristic of his wit; "If this happens—and I ask you to remember that I shall do nothing to bring it about, but on the contrary everything to retard it; if this happens—I say, *IF:* then the students and the professions and the universities and the nation will benefit in a number of ways. The cost will be emotionally great: we all feel an attachment to that unique institution, the American college. On the strength of this feeling millions 'want to go to college' without quite knowing what they may expect from it. In the past, their innocent hopes were not disappointed; now it is the best colleges that disappoint the most, for the reasons I mentioned. So the first benefit of the change will be that students' natural desire for exploring the world of ideas will be fed by secondary school teachers, who still believe and practice general education, instead of deserting their charges to indulge in research.

"Next, the professions and the university which trains for them will benefit in having their students' exclusive attention. Finally, the concentrated training can begin a few years earlier than now; therefore the country will benefit through a fresher and larger supply of professionals. Acceleration may then become normal and cairn, instead of being special and frantic. All this will occur if—I say again, if—the colleges follow consciously or unconsciously, the tendency evident in their actions for the last dozen years."

are to be found in the colleges—Homer and Tolstoy? This is an empirical question, and subject to verification.

Can the secondary schools teach the kind of materials that one finds in a college? Is knowledge all of one piece, so that the humanities and the social sciences can find a place in the high-school curriculum in the way that the ordered and precise contents of the sciences are now doing? Take as a single question, the nature of the Humanities. As Barzun describes them in his book *Science: The Glorious Entertainment,* "The humanities draw all their substance and most of their meaning from the inhumanity of man's life; they wallow in blood and strife and disaster." Can the secondary schools make such a picture intelligible to teen-agers—without turning the best of them into Rimbaud caricatures (which the hipsters already are). These are evaluative questions that can be answered only with critical judgment.

Is it really so clear that the graduate schools in the future will welcome early specialization and not prefer to have their students receive a more diverse preparation? Professor Barzun comments: "Oddly enough, while the liberal arts college, abetted by the graduate school, is squeezing out the old liberal education, the chief professional schools still ask for it in their candidates for admission. The law schools want students who know some history and can read English; the medical schools want well-rounded men." Yet, as he well knows, only thirty years ago these selfsame professional schools sought to foreshorten liberal arts education and admit students into professional schools after only two years of college. Can one assume that the pressures for early specialization—an aspect, perhaps, of competitive pressure for the, at present, limited number of places in schools, a number that is bound to expand—will continue? This is an indeterminate question, answerable only in time.

Finally, can one define general education as being largely the survey of the past, of great books? These did provide, at one time, a level of sophistication that can now be achieved more readily by students than their parents could. But is this the only kind of sophistication that is meant by the phrase "general education"? This is a debatable question, and I carry this debate over into the next section.

In sum, Professor Barzun seems to be saying that the college is on a local track, and will soon be quickly overtaken by the express train of history. But does he have the timetable aright? And are his sights correctly filed? These are necessarily rhetorical questions, and serve only to close a section.

THE ANTINOMY OF IDEAS

Professor Barzun's apprehensions about the future of the American college derive from the impact of broad social changes taking place in industrial society (and these form the basis of additional questions that will be considered in chapter 3). But he does retain, as does Columbia College, the belief in the validity of a liberal arts education. And if this tradition is to be maintained, and embodied, as it has been in the past, in a general education program, a different set of questions about the meaning of a liberal education arises. These are questions which do not deal with the "structural position" of the college in the educational ladder, but intellectual questions about the scope—and emphasis—of the liberal arts today. These questions may be divided into three sections; the relation of East to West; the relation of Past to Present; and relation of Analysis to History.

On the relation of East to West. To overcome the parochialism of the contemporary, the major innovation of the general education program, going back to Columbia's Contemporary Civilization course in 1919, was the introduction of a course in Western civilization. The intention was to demonstrate the nature of a heritage, of diverse traditions, of political complexities and moral dilemmas. Since the end of World War II, and the enlargement of the world as a new, great *oikumené,* the major universities have offered diverse courses in the cultures of other civilizations. Columbia College has a program in Oriental Civilizations which a student may offer in fulfillment of the second-year requirement in Contemporary Civilization. Harvard offers a first-year course in the "Traditions of East Asia," which is one of the regular options in the general education offerings. Chicago had sequences in Russian, Indian, and Islamic civilizations and required a student to take one of these in fulfillment of his undergraduate requirements in the social sciences.

These courses have produced a rich assemblage of literature as source readings for these students.[25] The courses seem to be popular and to attract students not Just for the exotic reasons of learning about a strange way of life but as a means of broadening the imagination. And these may be sufficient justification unto themselves.

But if other cultures or civilizations are to be included within the scope of general education or liberal arts programs, a number of intellectual questions suggest themselves. What is the unit to be delimited: is it the territorial-political unit, defined through time, such as Chinese civilization or the Ottoman empire? Or is it to be a cultural-religious tradition such as Muslim civilization (from North Africa to Indonesia) and Buddhism in its many different forms? Is the criterion of selection to be the present political or cultural importance of an area (China, India, sub-Sahara Africa)? Or some broader cultural principle that illustrates diffusion, culture contact, or patterns of expansion and contraction (e.g., the spread of Islam)? What does one mean by a "civilization"? Is there some inner form, ethos, or eidos, some entelechy or pattern, that defines a civilization over a certain expanse of time? In studying a civilization, does one concentrate on a temporal sequence, marking off periods or happenings peculiar to the civilization, or does one emphasize styles (such as art forms), or institutional structures (such as family and stratification systems), in order to study either successive cultural changes within the system or the comparative institutions among systems? Can we, in effect, have an anthropology of civilizations? (It is only recently that anthropologists such as Alfred Kroeber, Robert Redfield and Milton Singer have begun to again discuss these questions— and with the deaths of Redfield and Kroeber we have lost two of the

---

[25] The Columbia materials are to be found in the three volumes: *Sources of Japanese Tradition, Sources of Chinese Tradition* and *Sources of Indian Tradition,* 1958-60, under the general editorship of Wm. Theodore de Bary (New York, Columbia University Press). The Harvard course uses the volume *East Asia the Great Tradition, by* Edwin O. Reischauer and John K. Fairbank (Boston, Houghton Mifflin, 1958 and 1960). The Chicago materials are collected in diverse syllabi, published by the University of Chicago Press. The "Introduction to the Civilization of India" has gone through several different editions, the most recent being two volumes of selected reading edited by Myron Wiener (April, 1961). The Russian readings have been edited by Thomas Riha, completed in 1963, and the Islamic readings by Marshall G. S. Hodgson were published in 1964.

most distinguished students of the subject—in terms that are manageable for inquiry.[26]) In short, should the general education programs still concentrate largely on Western civilization; and if others are to be included what is the definition of the unit?

In an analogous sense we can pose the question, in the development of general education programs, of an emphasis on Past or Present. In the Carman Report of 1946, there occurs (in response to a proposal to extend Humanities A into a third term to cover the nineteenth and twentieth centuries) the following: "The question was settled by recognizing that the readings for Humanities A should be books of established eminence. *There is for us no question as to the place in the history of European culture of Sophocles, of Dame, or of Voltaire, We have not yet a similar perspective for Carlyle or Nietzsche or Freud.*"

Twenty years have brought about a different perspective, and the judgment about the three latter figures, however valid in 1946, surely by now strikes us as odd. But the recurring question remains: How much of the contemporary—in the humanities and in social thought-belongs in an introductory program, or in the college program as a whole?

One radical critic, Paul Goodman, has argued that the contemporary, and, in particular, a discussion of the avant-garde, should have no place in the university. For him it is not that the university is the guardian of the past, but that its role should be a conservative one precisely in order to encourage the student to be radical. The college, thus, is the arena in which the classic confrontation of fathers and sons is played out in its own way: the confrontation of past and present, of tradition and modernity, find their expression in the confrontation of teacher versus student in the classroom. The avant-garde and the new, Mr. Goodman claims, should be searched out by the student on his own in order to enhance the sense of discovery; if

---

[26] See, for example, Robert Redfield, "Thinking About a Civilization," in Milton Singer, ed., *Introducing India in Liberal Education* (Chicago, University of Chicago Press); Alfred Kroeber, *An Anthropologist Looks At History* (Berkeley, University of California Press, 1963).

the new were presented for discussion in the classroom, it would diminish the necessary shock of recognition.

From a different perspective, and applying his argument to the social sciences, David Riesman has argued that in the introductory contemporary civilization or social science courses, the concentration on historically removed societies, such as Greece and Rome, or the Middle Ages, creates too much of a rupture for the new kind of student entering the colleges, particularly the children of working-class and disadvantaged ethnic groups. In a study of Montieth, a small new liberal arts college in Detroit that is an autonomous division of Wayne State University, and of Oakland, a similar experiment of Michigan State, Riesman found that at the latter, where a modified version of the Columbia College Contemporary Civilization course is taught, students from working-class families who take the course feel themselves to be cut off from their parents, have no universe of discourse at home, and find themselves estranged socially and culturally from their roots, while at Montieth, where the introductory social science course is devoted in large measure to contemporary politics, and where students undertake empirical polling studies, the sense of relatedness to life is high, and the family is brought into the orbit of the student's own expanding horizons. Riesman, it might be said, takes a populist view of culture, feeling that the traditional liberal arts program encourages snobbery and false aristocratic judgments. His criteria for the liberal arts are their relevance to the present and the extent to which they involve the students in contemporary pursuits, including popular culture. In Riesman's view, therefore, the college is the agency of innovation and exploration rather than the guardian of tradition.

I do not mean to counterpose Goodman and Riesman as polarities. It could be argued, for example, that one can combine the two by emphasizing tradition in the humanities and the contemporary in the social sciences, without a necessary contradiction in ideology. But Goodman and Riesman do remain, each in his own way, expressions of sharp, individualized contemporary responses in a milieu where balance and blandness have predominated. And one can gain a good deal that is valuable in setting up both viewpoints as signposts to follow or to ignore; at lease one then knows where one is *not* going. That, too, is sometimes a gain. (For the impatient reader let me say, briefly, that I repudiate both views, but this is reserved for its place in chapter 4.)

The third intellectual division is that of History versus Analysis. I should note, immediately, that by "history" I do not mean factual chronology. Surely one wants a student to know when and where crucial events or turning points took place. One wants him to know the time and the outcome of the Thirty Years War and the Treaty of Westphalia, or the relationship, say, of Hobbes to Descartes. But the knowledge of chronology and relationships finds meaning only in some further intellectual scheme. In the broadest sense—and we are talking here of general education programs, not of an entire university curriculum—the question is whether one wants to emphasize historicism, with its doctrine that the understanding of an event can be found only in its unique context, or the analytical approach, which finds meaning in a phenomenon as one of a type-class, and seeks, further, a sense of invariant relationships. As we have seen in the case of the Harvard curriculum, a similar kind of issue—even put as crudely as this—has had crucial relevance for the teaching of science. Does one teach science through its history, or by analysis of its models of inquiry? This is both a pedagogical and an intellectual question, But if, say, one argues that science is best comprehended by an analytical approach, does the argument hold for the social sciences as well? Does one look at society largely as a succession of social stages, or does one seek to identify certain processes (rationalization, universalism, circulation of elites) as underlying elements of such successions?

It is obviously impossible, in this brief compass, to establish, merely by a statement of polarities, the range of intellectual issues. My intention here has been only to set forth a framework for the discussion of the intellectual problems encountered in any reorganization of the liberal arts program.

To this inventory can be added one other question that reaches to the heart of a general education program: the future of interdisciplinary studies. The surge of general education after the war coincided with the intellectual blossoming of a new approach—the attempted cross of disciplines in order to case light on broad problems; e.g., the fusion of anthropology, psychology, and sociology in order to deal with the interaction of personality and culture. This interdisciplinary approach, in the social sciences at least, seems to have faded, and one finds once again a renewed emphasis on the specific discipline itself. Yet in the sciences, one finds the multiplication of cross-disciplines such as biophysics and biochemistry, which emerge out of the disciplines themselves. Is there a lesson for the interdisciplinary approach to be found in its history in the sciences? In the broadest sense, however, how dependent is general education on an interdisciplinary approach and, at what level—the introductory or advanced—can such an approach be best utilized?

THE STRUCTURE OF THE UNIVERSITY

The first group of questions, using Professor Barzun's essay as the talking point, might be called sociological: they derive from the judgments of changes taking place in American society and call into question the historic role of the American college. The second group of questions is intellectual: they deal with the organization of knowledge, and the principles of selection. Finally, there is a broad group of questions that we might call, narrowly, institutional: they deal with the organizational structure of the university and the way this structure shapes the activities of the college. For any single institution, the crucial questions about structure derive from the specific allocation of decision-making and authority: the centralization or decentralization of power, the budget-making process, the locus of decision over appointments and-tenure, the autonomy or dependancy of the departments, etc. Three general questions about collegiate structure can be raised.

The first is the "balance" of the college in relation to the graduate school. Does the university see one or the other as its predominant concern? What degree of staff separation should exist between the two? At Harvard, almost all the major figures of the university teach in the college and, at least until recently, the bulk of their teaching assignment was in the college, or in joint college and first-year graduate courses, rather than in the graduate school. At Chicago, in the

1950s, the college and divisional faculties were entirely separate, and only a few faculty members held joint appointments. Only now are the two being merged.

At Columbia, there has been a mixed pattern. While all tenure appointments are made to a unified university department, in a number of instances, particularly in the social science and English departments, separate faculties for the College and the graduate school do in fact exist. In the Humanities, partly because of tradition and partly because graduate students can become an onerous load to carry, some of the major figures in the university have preferred to do most of their teaching in the College. In the social sciences, the reverse has been the rule. There has been an unwritten but unmistakable status distinction between membership in the Graduate Faculty and in the College, and moving from Hamilton, the College hall, to Fayerweather, the Graduate Faculty social science office building, has indicated a promotion important not only for one's position in the university but for recognition in the wider professional field as well. In some measure, this distinction arises from the fact that membership in the Graduate Faculties in the social sciences signifies concentration in the more prestigious activity of research than in teaching, and research allows one to command government and foundation money and to build small fiefdoms in economics, political science, and the like. Yet curiously, in the sciences, where research prestige is highest, the major figures in all the universities, Columbia as well as Harvard and Chicago, take turns at teaching in the College. One reason may be that in the sciences there are fewer graduate courses than in the social sciences, since much of a student's further training after the first year or two of graduate work, consists of an apprenticeship in research projects rather than lecture courses and seminars. Another may be that in the sciences there is a proud tradition of transmitting one's advanced knowledge into undergraduate courses and initiating the bright students into the newer mysteries of the field.

In recent years, the pattern at Columbia has been changing. In the economics and sociology departments, where a marked division between the College and graduate departments had existed, there is now a freer intermingling of tenure personnel, and a greater interest on the part of the Graduate Faculties in the College. The sense of separation between the College and the Graduate Faculty, except for a few departments marked by old feuds and vested interests, has been reduced. Yet for Columbia, as for many other schools, two developments arising out of the changing nature of the educational "market" pose an important problem for the College, One is the reduction of teaching loads as professors turn increasingly to research and as the competitive market allows professors to "buy" reduced time as a condition of their jobs. The second is the expansion—which will be even greater in the next few years—of junior teaching personnel in both divisions.

At Columbia, for example, the normal teaching load is three courses per semester. To this is added, in the graduate school, the reading of masters essays, membership in Ph.D. oral examination committees, supervision of doctoral theses, and participation in the defenses of doctoral theses. In many schools—and sometimes, though inconsistently, at Columbia—the graduate teaching load is reduced to two courses. But since a professor will usually give a graduate lecture course and a research seminar in his subject, he may thus have no time for College teaching. Or, if he sometimes does give a third course or alternates a teaching year in the College, he prefers to teach an upper-level College course in his subject, rather than an introductory or a general education course.

In the expansion of faculty, the influx of a larger number of junior teachers and a greater reliance on course assistants and preceptors— a practice that until now has been resisted at Columbia, but one that has spread in many schools, particularly the large state universities- has exposed students increasingly to inadequate or inexperienced in- structors, particularly since many of these younger men have detailed knowledge of a particular specialty acquired in recent graduate work but are less qualified for the broader general education courses, since their preparation for these courses interferes with their professional concerns. More often it is the student who is shortchanged. What can one do about this situation?

Problems of intellectual organization are susceptible to theoretical solution and continual reexamination. But the problems of staffing are more recalcitrant of solution, especially when the supply of outstanding teachers and scholars is limited, and the demands on their time multiply. In the last decade, the general education courses at Columbia, Harvard, and Chicago have come into crisis as much as from staffing difficulties as from intellectual dilemmas. But it is much easier, and more the academic habit, to deal with ideological questions than with organizational difficulties, and many of the problems of the general education courses, which are actually rooted in institutional dilemmas, have been masked by argument about intellectual content. In the coming years, the staffing difficulties of the colleges will be the most crucial that any university administration will have to face.

A second order of questions about institutional arrangements, which to some extent overlaps analytically with the first, is the relationship of research to teaching, especially in general education. The presumption has at times been apparent, and this underlay the creation of two separate faculties at Chicago, that the college should primarily be the place for teachers while the graduate school is the place for scholars or researchers. This has led—particularly in recent years when research has become such an overpowering source of prestige—to sharp complaints about the subordination of teaching as such, or a sense of injustice when superior teachers have failed to obtain proper recognition (and salary and promotion) because of their inability or unwillingness to do research or to contribute to scholarly publications.

While one can point to a number of outstanding teachers and scholars in any university who publish very little, the more general question can be raised whether, in the light of the rapid advances going on in every field, the distinction between research and teaching is tenable in a university context. In the sciences, for example, where the changing content of each field is inextricably linked with the experimental processes of discovery and verification, can one have superior instruction except by those who are themselves involved in the research process—and who are capable of translating, not necessarily their findings, which may be quite limited, but their modes of procedure into an adventure for the student? Is it possible in the social sciences, particularly in economics, sociology, and anthropology, where the disciplines are now achieving some measure of agreement about conceptual frameworks and research techniques, to simply accept secondhand the formulations and findings of others without taking some part in the research work of the field, or having some form of continuing education in the newer methods that are being made available? If, in the broadest sense, a university is a community of scholars, can one truly separate research (or scholarly investigation, or critical and reflective inquiry as represented in publication) from teaching? And if one cannot, what institutional arrangements are necessary, other than the sabbatical year, for the interplay of the two functions?

Closely tied to the question of the "balance" of research and teaching is the third question of the "organizational units" of instruction, the departments. The college is the stronghold, perhaps the last, of the unity of knowledge. A student, it is hoped, should get a sense of the relatedness of fields, of the relatedness of problems, the dependencies of subjects upon one another, and the common procedures of inquiry and verification that underlie the disciplined acquisition of knowledge. Yet not only is knowledge itself becoming more fragmented, but departments in the university exist in inglorious isolation from each other, intellectually as well as organizationally. One sees that the loyalty and allegiance of a young scholar is increasingly to his department and to his discipline, often at the expense of his interest in the college or the university and its own institutional life. The intense need to stay abreast of work in the field, combined with greater job mobility as the intellectual market expands, lessens the attachment of a teacher to his university and even to his students. Are there, then, some institutional mechanisms that can overcome this fragmentation and facilitate the sense of common purpose which should unite a faculty not only in its own specializations but in the work of the institution as a whole?

Finally, to bring together these three areas of questions—sociological, intellectual, and institutional—into one broad frame: in the light of the changing structure of knowledge itself and the changing patterns of intellectual life—the rapid introduction of new conceptions (game theory, information theory, structural linguistics) and the imperative need of any person who pursues an intellectual or managerial career for continuing education, beyond college and graduate work—does the organization of the college by traditional disciplines, balancing general education with specialization, serve to best advantage? Should the college be primarily concerned with providing a coherent picture of the past and emphasizing the humanistic foundation of knowledge, concentrating thus on history, philosophy, and literature, and leaving to the graduate and professional school the more special training? Or rather, should the college be primarily a place concerned with the nature of analysis and the methodological foundation of knowledge? Or, to ask a different type of question, should the college assume that, since an individual necessarily will have to be involved in continuing education for the rest of his life, it need not, or should not, "cover everything," but concentrate for the particular individual on a single field in order to give him a sense of depth—as is the case in the English university system, where a man takes a degree in a field, rather than covering a whole spectrum of required courses? Or is there some way, still, of giving a student a conspectus of relevant knowledge as an intellectual whole?

These are not necessarily questions of an either/or nature, but of more-or-less. To state the questions this broadly is to restate the purpose of this inquiry.

Chapter Three

THE TABLEAU OF SOCIAL CHANGE-

TODAY AND TOMORROW

In the Society

The United States of America is, in the phrase of S. M. Lipset, "the first new nation." It "created itself" out of an act of will, and wrote a national constitution as an act of faith in its future. It was the first country to create a modern party system, and, strange as it seems, the Democratic Party is the oldest existing political party in the world.

Yet even more strange, perhaps, is the fact that only within recent decades has the United States passed from being a nation to becoming a *national society* in which there is not only a coherent national authority, but where the different sectors of the society, economy, polity, and culture are bound together in a cohesive way and where crucial political and economic decisions are now made at a "center." It is perhaps only by understanding this new state of affairs (rather than some stale notions about capitalism) that one can identify the sources of the social strains that are evident in contemporary America. Within the confines of this chapter, such an argument can be outlined only schematically.

The first, if not the most important fact is that we now have a national economy that is interdependent through government, rather than through the market, in a hitherto novel way. By its vast spending, particularly in the aerospace and electronic industries, the government has reworked the economic map of the country, creating large new industries in Texas, California, the Pacific Northwest, and sections of New England. More than that, the federal budget (amounting to about 15 percent of GNP) and government fiscal policy have become the main determinants of the general level of economic activity. But it is not just size alone that makes the role of government significant. It is the commitment to specific and conscious policy goals. It is now the stated intention of the United States government, going back twenty years to the passage of the bill that announced the theme in its title, to maintain full employment in the country. Toward that end, the Council of Economic Advisors was created. Out of historical experience and the development of economic sophistication, there has come the awareness that full employment is possible through continued economic expansion and the maintenance of a high enough level of "aggregate demand," or purchasing power, to keep the economic machine moving. As symbolized in the "great tax cut" of 1965, the responsibility for the maintenance of aggregate demand is a basic task of government. Quite obviously, this has become a managed economy. The impact of government fiscal policy is direct and pervasive; it is the binding cement of the national economy.

If there exists now, for the first time, a new kind of national economy, there exists equally, in the same perspective, a new national polity. The lines were first laid down by the New Deal in the 1930s, in the assumption by the federal government of many regulatory functions that had previously been exercised by the states. What began at that time, and has been extended in extraordinary fashion, is the conscious direction of social change by the federal government. This is most obvious in the area of civil rights, wherein the passage of federal antidiscrimination and voting legislation during 1964-65 broadened considerably the role of tKe national government as an agent of change. Other significant steps, less dramatic, but in the long run equally important, have been taken by the federal government in its large-scale support of education, medical care for the aged, subsidies for the disadvantaged, housing, transit, natural beauty, and the like. These add up not only to the beginnings of a comprehensive welfare state but, in such measures as rent subsidies for the poor or the extension of financial aid to education, to the beginnings of a conscious social policy to make equality a prime goal of government policy.

Several threads can be distinguished in this weaving of a national polity. Perhaps the most important, politically, is the "inclusion" of minority groups into the society. Until the 1920s, political power in the United States was largely in the hands of a small, relatively homogeneous middle-class population, whose base was primarily the small town and rural areas of the country, while on the national scene the dominant influence was the business community. This homogeneity of power was first challenged by the rise, in the large northern urban centers, of the various ethnic groups that had come to dominate the city political machines, and who had begun to demand a share of power in the states as well. The second challenge, during the New Deal, was the emergence of trade unions as an important power group, and the creation of a government-protected labor movement in American society. The civil-rights legislation and antipoverty programs of the Kennedy and Johnson administrations have marked the third step—this time including the Negro and the poor within the polity.

But the rise of a welfare state is not only a change in policy; it signifies larger structural changes as well, principally the decline of the state governments as effective fiscal agencies in the allocation of resources for welfare, education, housing, and other social-service needs. Many groups in the United States have contended for the distinction of electing John F. Kennedy President of the United States in 1960. But one important group, largely unnoticed, was made up of American mayors who realized that the success of the various urban programs being thrust upon them depended in considerable measure on federal aid. The magnitude of social services and the rising costs of welfare, housing, and educational programs could no longer be managed on the narrow, outmoded tax base of cities or states. Only the federal government could engage in the effective program of "reallocating" revenues to meet local needs. Thus it is not only the need to maintain the general level of economic activity, but the equal need to redistribute tax resources for welfare services, that reinforces the emerging structure of a national polity.

Clearly, however, domestic pressures alone do not create a new national polity. The effort to pull the nation together as one enormous productive and fighting machine during World War II, and the continuing need, because of the new role of the United States in world affairs, to maintain a "mobilized posture," have given the federal government a new, centralizing function. In many instances, in fact, it has not been domestic pressures but foreign policy that has been decisive in shaping the national polity. This new, continuing emphasis on the international arena as the place of decisive policy decisions has brought with it the creation, for the first time in American history, of a large permanent military establishment, while the changing needs of military technology, arising out of the revolutions in weapons systems that have occurred in the last decade, have also brought the federal government into scientific research and development in an unprecedented way.

In all this, beginning with the explosion of the atom bomb and in the growing awareness of the crucial role of science and research in national security and in the economy—plus the general need, stressed by the scientific community, to support basic research unrelated to any particular utilitarian purpose—the federal government has become the chief underwriter of science and research in the United States. In 1963, of the 2.5 million technical specialists in the country (including 1.25 million scientists, technicians, and engineers), *three out of five were engaged in projects supported or sponsored by the federal government or were employed directly in government.* Science itself has become a "political constituency," a claimant on the society, and a group with its own informal representation in the political process. Since so much science and research is located in universities, the university, too, has become a force in the creation of a new national polity.

Finally, a national culture has come into being. It was long the complaint, voiced with great resonance by Henry James, that America, with no aristocracy, no church, no clergy, no diplomatic service, no great universities, no political society, lacked the social texture that could give the country (to use present-day jargon) a national Establishment.

In the new national society there has been a burgeoning intellectual class, located primarily in the great universities; and the ease of mobility—social mobility into and out of Washington, professional mobility between universities, and the simple ease of travel that brings academics together more often in conferences and professional meetings—has created in the intelligentsia a "consciousness of kind," making the professional and technical classes a distinct stratum in society and giving its leaders both national importance and some moral authority.

Even more significant has been the rise of a broad national "popular culture" woven together by television; by the national news weeklies, with their simultaneous publication dates from coast to coast; and by the movies, which make all parts of the country visible to each other. In television today the popular entertainment and news programs command simultaneous audiences in the tens of millions, making for a psychological and emotional impact whose importance is as yet unexplored. The funeral of the late President Kennedy, for example, united an estimated 85 percent of the television audience of the nation into a common attention and a common mourning. The visual impact of snarling police dogs chasing Negro youths in Selma, Alabama, made that city an immediate national symbol of moral indignation, and thousands journeyed to Selma to join the protest against those outrages.

What all this adds up to is that with the formation of a national society the federal government has gained a greater awareness of social needs, of the importance of anticipating and directing social change, and it has obtained a centralization of power unique to the American system. Yet these responsibilities are inescapable, arising out of the common necessity of managing our common affairs for the common welfare. Only national agencies are capable of undertaking such formidable tasks.

In describing the broad social changes that have been refashioning the United States, one axis of change is the creation of a national society on a giant scale. The other, which has great implications for all modern industrial societies, is the new impact of "knowledge"— its organization through systematic research guided by theory, and its mass dissemination through schools, publishing houses, and mass media.

Where it concerns the educational system, the nature of this "knowledge revolution" can be explored from four angles; the "exponential growth" of knowledge, the "branching" of new fields of knowledge, the rise of a new intellectual technology, and the rapid expansion of research and development as an organized activity of government.

The "exponential growth" of knowledge is now a prosaic idea. Derek Price, who popularized it, has estimated (in *Science Since Babylon*) that the total research effort in Great Britain since the time of Newton has doubled every ten to fifteen years (or about three times during the working life of a scientist). A major indicator of this expansion has been the scientific journal. The learned paper and the scientific journal were innovations of the scientific revolution in the late seventeenth century. It allowed for the relatively rapid communication of new ideas to a growing circle of men interested in science. From the first few journals, beginning with the *Transactions of the Royal Society of London* in 1665, the number grew until by the beginning of the nineteenth century there were a hundred, by the middle of the nineteenth century a thousand, and by 1900 some ten thousand such journals.

Since 1750, when there were about ten scientific journals in the world, the number has increased by a factor of ten every half-century. By 1830, when about three hundred journals were being published in the world, it became obvious that the cultivated man of science could no longer keep abreast of new, knowledge, and a new device—the abstract journal—appeared. It summarized each article in many journals, and the interested individual could then decide what to read in full. But as Price points out, even the number of abstract journals increased, following the same logistic curve, by a factor of ten in every century. Thus by 1950 the number of abstract journals had attained a critical magnitude of about three hundred. Moreover, each abstract journal itself has sizably increased. A journal devoted to publishing the abstracts of new papers in the chemical sciences now runs to some 13,000 pages annually, exclusive of indexes and cross-references; ten years ago it was only half this size.

The output of sheer words today is staggering. In 1964, nearly 320,000 separate book titles—nearly 1,000 works every day—were published throughout the world. Columbia University's new acquisitions, for example, take up two miles of bookshelves a year. In a single field, medicine, it is estimated that some 200,000 journal articles and 10,000 monographs are published annually, while in the physical and life sciences the number of books add up to about 60,000 annually, the number of research reports ro about 100,000, and the number of articles in scientific and technical journals to about 1.2 million each year. Consider what will happen when writers, scholars, scientists, and professionals in the new states begin to produce in great number in these fields!

But it is not the prodigious accumulation alone that is creating a distinctive change in the structure of intellectual life. It is the fact that new discoveries bring their own differentiation, or "branching," so that as a field expands subdivisions and subspecialties multiply within each field. Contrary to the nineteenth-century notion of science as a bounded or exhaustible field of knowledge whose full dimensions can ultimately be explored, each advance opens up, in its own way, new fields that in turn sprout their own branches.

To give an example: the field of shock waves, initiated in 1848 by the British mathematician and physicist G. G. Stokes and the astronomer J. Challis (who set up theoretical equations of motion in gases), led not only to significant contributions in mathematics and physics along this general line (by Mach, Bethe, and von Neumann, among others) but to the branching off of shock tube, aerodynamics, detonations, and magnetohydrodynamics as four distinct fields. Or, Nobel Laureate I. I. Rabi's success at Columbia, in 1929, in sending molecular beams through a magnetic field—a breakthrough in pure physics—gave rise to branching in several different directions: optics, solid state masers, atomic structures, and half a dozen other fields.

Sometimes a stasis is reached, and then a field spurts ahead. In 1895, Roentgen seemed to have exhausted all the major aspects of X rays, but in 1912 the discovery of X-ray diffraction in crystals by von Laue, Friedrich, and Knipping transformed two separate fields—X-ray and crystallography. Similarly, the discovery in 1934 of artificial radioactivity by the Joliot-Curies created a qualitative change that gave rise at one branching point to the work of Hahn and Strassman, which Lise Meitner correctly interpreted as the splitting of the uranium atom, and to Fermi's work on the increased radioactivity of metals bombarded with "slow" neutrons—which led directly to controlled atomic fission and the bomb.[1]

One can see this extraordinary proliferation of fields in the specializations listed in the National Register of Scientific and Technical Personnel, a government-sponsored inventory of all competent persons engaged in scientific work.[2] The Register classifies over 900 distinct scientific and technical specializations (outside the social sciences and humanities), compared with 54 listed twenty years ago. Thus physics is broken down into 10 basic divisions—acoustics, atomic and molecular, electromagnetic waves and electron, mechanics, nuclear, optics, physics of fluids, solid state, theoretical, and thermal phenomena—and each of these has subspecialties, making a total of 81 distinct specializations in physics alone. The life sciences are divided into 17 fields (e.g., anatomy, pharmacology, nutrition and metabolism, genetics, phytopathology) and each of these contains at least 10 or more subdivisions. In the newer interdisciplinary subjects, biophysics has 18 subspecialties, biochemistry 17, physical chemistry 26, geochemistry 7, oceanography 13, and hydrology and hydrography 12, while computer technology already has 7 subspecialties and the "mathematics of resource use" (operations research, information theory, and the like) has 13.

To the proliferation and branching of knowledge one can add the creation in recent years of what might be called a new "intellectual technology": the development of game theory, decision theory, simulation, linear programing, cybernetics, and operations research, many of which are tooled, as it were, by the computer. What makes the burgeoning of these fields significant is the effort, through novel intellectual techniques, to provide new and comprehensive theories

[1] I have drawn these examples largely from Gerald Holton's "Scientific Research and Scholarship: Notes toward the Design of Proper Scales," *Daedalus* (Spring 1962), pp. 362-99.

[2] The National Register is a cooperative undertaking of the National Science Foundation and nine professional scientific societies which in turn work with about 200 specialized societies to produce full listings. Scientists are considered eligible for registration if they have attained the Ph.D. or an equivalent degree in a field of science, or have similar qualifications gained in professional experience. A review of the nation's scientific personnel in 1960 brought forth a listing of some 237,000 persons. See the National Science Foundation's *Scientific Manpower Bulletin,* No. 12, 1960; and the descriptive brochure on the National Register, NSF publication 61-46.

of "rational choice" and to transform the social sciences in an unprecedented way.

Paradoxically, though this new intellectual revolution seeks "perfect" information, it starts out in vast linguistic disorder. Any eruptive change makes for great confusion, the more so in the new intellectual technology, since its innovators and practitioners are a motley pack of mathematicians, physicists, engineers (of all varieties), statisticians, biologists, neurophysiologists, economists, management consultants, sociologists, and each man brings to the new field his own perspectives, terminology, and concepts.

Thus, operations research, linear programing, systems analysis, and decision theory often overlap in technique and subject matter; yet, depending upon the occupational origins of the practitioner, one or another label will be used insistently to designate a distinctive approach. Information theory, for some writers, is a technical set of propositions, enunciated originally by the electrical engineer Claude Shannon, on switching circuits and channel capacity; for others it is a general field covering all problems of interaction, and it is then called "communication theory." Cybernetics is regarded by some writers as the design of self-regulating control mechanisms (such as the automatic pilot on an airplane, which adjusts speed and direction in response to wind variation in order to stay on a plotted course); others call it the new "queen of science," embracing all self-regulating behavior from mechanical devices to biological organisms.

Whatever the final clarification of terminology will be, it is clear that the computer and these new techniques open up vast new possibilities for the social sciences. It is an equal corollary that all future work in the social sciences will require a high degree of mathematical training and sophistication. One area is the refinement of knowledge—the handling of many variables. Warren Weaver once said that an effective social science was almost impossible because as a mathematician he could handle a three-variable problem or, through statistical probability, a hundred-variable problem, but that most of the interesting questions in the social sciences fell between three and a hundred. Thus, in charting voting behavior one could say that the relevant determinants are age, sex, religion, occupation, education, and a dozen other variables; but it has been difficult to hold more than a few factors constant in order to see which combination of determinants was decisive in a voter's choice. With the computer, however, a matrix can be set up to handle a dozen or more variables.

One can go even further. With the computer, complex situations can be simulated, which might make possible "controlled" experiments in the social sciences. By "varying" the situations and introducing different "independent variables" one can see what new alignments and combinations of decisions might be made by groups in a simulated environment.

Simulation has been applied to a large variety of economic and sociological problems, such as simulating an entire economy, charting demographic changes, or predicting changes of attitudes in response to changed social environments. Professor Richard Stone, of Cambridge University, has created a simulation model of the British economy, and is thus in a position to state what changes in different sectors of the British economy are required to achieve different economic growth rates. A bold effort to simulate social environments through a computer program, and thus carry out a "controlled experiment" in the social sciences, has been made by James Coleman at Johns Hopkins. In his book *The Adolescent Society,* Coleman showed how students deliberately "choose" to stress popularity or scholastic achievement at the unspoken behest of the cliques they belong to, or by identifying with a teacher. To see how these students would alter their behavior, Coleman subsequently worked out a computer model in which the degree of identification of the adolescent with his clique (as expressed in the actual soclometric tests) was tested by varying the rewards from parents, teachers, or peer group influencing the adolescent. (Technically, Coleman established different "gambles" for the individual's "preference scales.") In this fashion he sought to specify, for example, at what exact points a student might be willing to sacrifice scholastic achievement for social popularity, and vice versa. While an experiment of this sort would normally be made with a small number of students, using only a few variables, Coleman was able, by creating "fictional" students (though using actual preference scales), to chart the different choices of thousands of "students" as they responded to a half-dozen or so different variables, in numerous manipulated environments.

In the field of economics, various aspects of "decision theory" and "game theory" have already changed its dimensions. Linear programing, primarily an "ordering" technique to achieve optimal solutions where many alternative combinations confront a decision maker, is already widely used in business.[3] Statistical decision theory, as pioneered by the late Abraham Wald of Columbia University, sets forth strategies in "games against nature"—i.e., in situations partly subject to chance and only partly controlled by the individual. With these techniques one can minimize risks and reduce uncertainty. And in the theory of games, initiated by the late John von Neumann, a revolution has begun in the definition of economics itself. An economic problem, as it is classically defined in general equilibrium theory, is one in which individuals and firms try to achieve "maximum" or optimal results. But the outcome of a man's actions depends not only on himself but on the actions of others as well. If two competitors follow a pure "maximizing" strategy it would lead, in the extreme, to a total victory or total defeat—the so-called zero-sum game. Von Neumann's theory of games, as Oskar Morgenstern has argued, signified a clear break in the development of economic thought, since under the conditions of competition or conflict the bent of "rational behavior" is to follow a so-called minimax strategy, which seeks to minimize losses, rather than the economic principle of seeking to maximize gains. "The structure of this theory," Morgenstern writes, "is, consequently, quite different from the current neoclassical one of general economic equilibrium. Lacking a new specific calculus, one has to fall back essentially on the fundamental, combinatorial elements of mathematical reasoning. Eventually, a new calculus may have to be invented or discovered, as specifically suited to economic-social problems as the differential calculus was to classical mechanics."[4]

[3] These are used principally in so-called "queuing" problems, such as the question, in a factory, whether to handle orders on a first-come first-served basis, or wait until different combinations of order will be built up; or the question of how to plot the best routes and combinations in the shipping of bulk commodities from a wide variety of sources to a large number of different destinations, etc.

[4] Oskar Morgenstern, "Limits to the Use of Mathematics in Economics," in *Mathematics and the Social Sciences,* edited by James C. Charlesworth, a symposium sponsored by the American Academy of Political and Social Science (Philadelphia, June, 1963).

If decision theory attempts to specify the best choices for a given premise, systems theory seeks to spell out the unified consequences of any choice for all the units in the system. The word "system" by now has the widest and most varied use of all the terms in the new intellectual vocabulary. It is used by engineers to denote complex devices like computing machines. ("Systems engineer" initially meant someone who can design or work on computers.) Military technologists talk about weapons systems, sociologists about kinship or social systems, and economists, of course, about the economic system. But despite this great diversity, the foundation for a common conceptual framework in what Norbert Wiener has called "organized complexity" does exist.

Now, the idea of a system is an obvious one. The human body is a system operating in homeostasis. The American economy, while not an "organism," is so interrelated that changes in a key variable (e.g., investment) will cause determinate changes in other variables (employment, consumption, etc.). Yet in most areas of our lives we do not think in "system" terms. In a city, for example, there will be considerable discussion of the traffic problem, with only the dimmest realization that changes in traffic patterns will have important effects on industry locations, residential densities, and the like—one instance of how rarely we try to scrutinize a problem as a whole.

The Air Force has in the last ten years, for example, had the chastening experience of learning to think not about the production of bombers but about "weapons systems," and the difference is much more than a simple matter of terminology. In deciding what kinds of planes to produce, for example, the Air Force had to take into account such questions as target distances, cruise and dash speeds, bomb loads and yields, alternative ground bases or air refueling, enemy defense performance, enemy offense capabilities, and feasible production schedules; under each of these development variables there were four alternatives, each of which would have affected other aspects of the weapon—the length of landing strips, the size of crews, and so on. Designing a bomber therefore meant having a sense of the entire system in which the weapon was involved.[5]

[5] I take my example from the study by Albert J. Wohlstetter for The RAND Corporation, Document P-1530 (October 1958).

In a similar way, one can think of transportation along the Eastern seaboard, from Boston to Washington, in "system" terms: instead of saving a dying railroad line or building more high-speed roads because more people have cars, the "system" approach calculates how many persons want to travel and how much freight has to be moved over what varying distances, and what combinations of rail, truck, bus, and air vehicles will best serve such diverse needs.

In short, behind all this is an ambitious revolution in conceptual thought. To put it most generally, we tend to think of *entities* but not of *relations; items* but not *contexts; dualities* rather than a *field*. Most of our vocabulary is rich in dualisms like "man and environment," "history and nature," "mind and body," "man and spirit," but we lack *process* terms, which see these relationships as interacting and interpenetrative. When we look at a problem in dualistic terms, we get questions like "How far does environment influence man?" or "How far does man modify his environment?" (the usual answer is "to some extent"), rather than an attempt to examine the question in the unified way of the ecologist—as a biotic community, or as a single analytical system that emphasizes inter dependencies and patterned interchanges. By emphasizing relation of events (and not just classes of events), one goes beyond "classical" social analysis, just as modern logic has gone beyond its Aristotelian foundations.

The final item in this catalogue of the changing importance of "knowledge" is the recent emphasis on research and development. A simple set of figures makes this clear: in 1940, $377 million was spent by government, business, and the universities on research and development; by 1960 the total had risen to $14 billion; by 1964 the sum was well over $18 billion.

One can, however, overstate the magnitude of the change. The phrase "research and development" bides many ambiguities, and the customary division into basic research, applied research, and development does not always give a picture of the distribution of money or the value of work done. Thus, the complexity of modern weaponry accounts for much of the stupendous rise in "development" expenditures; and development costs make up more than two-thirds of the total of all research-and-development moneys. A change in accounting methods has also given a new look to what already existed. Thus changes made in 1960 in the budgetary procedures of the Defense Department, the single biggest source of research-and-development funds, greatly expanded the number of things classified under research and development. And in considering simple dollar figures, one has to remember the price inflation from 1940 to the present. Taking all these points into account, David Novick, an economist of the RAND Corporation, has stated that the estimated growth in research-and-development funds, in dollar terms, a sixty-fold increase from 1930 to 1958, in real terms should be deflated by half. Even so, the sums are impressive. And so is the number of persons now engaged in research and development. In 1940, about 37,000 persons were engaged in research and development; by 1960, the number had risen to 387,000, a growth rate of more than 10 percent a year.

In the expansion of research and development, a number of new social trends are evident. Before World War II, most of the research in the United States was underwritten by private industry, but today the basic source of funds is the American government. Given the increasing cost of research—a single experiment by Leon Lederman and Melvin Schwartz, a Columbia University team, which confirmed the existence of the neutrino, cost a million dollars—only the government would undertake such expenditures. Another crucial point is that while most of the research-and-development money goes into defense, a substantial sum—more than a billion and a half dollars a year for basic research alone—is being spent by the universities, under government contract. This financial fact is transforming the character of the universities as well.

The far-reaching consequences of these social changes are clear: society is becoming "future-oriented," and it is becoming more planned. Planning, in this instance, does not mean the centralized direction of the economy from a single source; it is doubtful whether such centralization is even possible in a complex economy. But in simpler and more differentiated ways, planning has already taken hold and will do so increasingly—among individuals planning for careers, corporations and organizations planning future growth and changes, and in a government that tries to anticipate new social needs and to identify future problems.

In step with all this is the growing need for professional and technical skills—and for the expansion of education facilities that train individuals in these skills. The professional and technical employees —the most highly educated of all workers—are, in fact, the fastest-growing occupational group in the United States (Table 1). In 1950, almost 5 million persons were employed as professionals and technicians. By 1960, the number rose 50 percent to 7.5 million. And by 1975 they will number 12.3 million, an increase of almost 65 percent.

Table 1

Employment by Occupational Groups: 1960 (actual) and 1975 (projected)

	1960	1975	*Percent Change,* 1960-1975
Total	66,700,000	88,600,000	33 percent
Professional and technical	7,500,000	12,300,000	64
Managers and proprietors	7,100,000	9,600,000	35
Clerical	9,800,000	13,700,000	40
Sales	4,400,000	6,100,000	39
Craftsmen and foremen	8,600,000	11,900,000	38
Operatives (semiskilled)	12,000,000	15,500,000	29
Service workers	8,300,000	11,300,000	36
Laborers	3,700,000	3,800,000	3
Farmers and farm laborers	5,400,000	4,400,000	-18

These projections, given in absolute figures, mask some important changes. If we examine these figures for *relative proportions* (Table 2), some interesting perspectives emerge. For one, the semiskilled

Table 2

Occupational Distribution of Labor Force as Percent of Total

	1960	1975
Total	100 percent	100 percent
Professional and technical	10.8	13.8
Managers and proprietors	10.2	10.8
Clerical	14.5	15.2
Sales	6.5	6.6
Craftsmen and foremen	12.9	13.4
Operatives (semiskilled)	18.6	17.5
Service workers	12.6	12.7
Laborers	6.0	4.2
Farmers and farm laborers	7.9	4.9

group, which from 1900 to 1960 went from 12.8 to 18.6 percent to become the largest single group in the labor force, will begin a relative decline. The proportion of laborers will show a sharp decline. Almost all other groups will about hold their own or gain slightly, but as a proportion of the whole the professional and technical groups will show an appreciably sharp rise.

It is the professional and technical class, therefore, which becomes the base line for future needs—and educational demands—of che society, and the bulk of these are in the scientific, teaching, and health fields.

Table 3

The Make-Up of Professional and Technical Occupations, 1960

	Persons
Total	7,500,000
SCIENTIFIC AND TECHNICAL	1,860,000
Engineers	850,000
Technicians and draftsmen	675,000
Scientists	335,000
TEACHING	1,775,000
Elementary school	1,000,000
Secondary school	600,000
College and graduate	175,000
HEALTH	1,629,000
Nurses	504,000
Physicians	235,000
Pharmacists	117,000
Dentists	97,000
Health technicians	330,000
Others	350,000
GENERAL	1,160,000
Accountants	400,000
Clergymen	250,000
Lawyers	230,000
Musicians and music teachers	175,000
Editors, writers, social workers, designers, etc.	1,000,000

Given the direction of the economy and the weight of government policy, it is quite clear that in the coming decades the demand for professional and technical personnel will place a considerable burden on the educational system. Take, as one example, the need for scientists and engineers: while the rise of all professional employments will by 1975 be almost *double* the average increase of the labor force, the demand for scientists and engineers, as projected, is almost *triple* this average increase. It is estimated that by 1975 we may need as many as 650,000 scientists in the United States, or almost twice as many as in 1960; and over the same period perhaps as many as 2 million engineers, compared to the 850,000 in 1960.

And yet, startling as these projections may be, it is quite likely that by 1975—and perhaps by the year 2000—the need for scientists and engineers can be fancifully looked at in another way. Harrison Brown has sought to demonstrate this by plotting the changing ratio of scientists and engineers to the total population. At the beginning of the century there was one scientist-engineer to about 1,800 persons in the United States. By 1960, the ratio was 1 to 200. (In India, there is one engineer or scientist to every 30,000 persons!) If one extrapolates these trends, by 1980 the ratio would be 1 to every 90 persons, and by the year 2000, 1 to every 40. By comparing this estimate of demand to the curve of supply, Brown concludes that we will need twice as many scientists and engineers as will be available in the year 2000. Or one can take, independently, the computations of the National Science Foundation, They have estimated that there is a 1:2 ratio between the number of engineers and scientists and the expenditures for research-and-development (e.g., from 1954 to 1960, the number of scientists rose 70 percent while research-and-development funds rose 140 per cent). So far, according to the Gilliland panel of the Science Advisory Committee, we are meeting the needs of the next decade, but the "fit" is a tight one.

In the health field, there are staggering needs for more physicians, nurses, and other technical personnel. The additional need for more professionals derives from three major factors: the fact that there is an increasing use of medical and hospital services; the change in the patterns of medical practice, as a growing number of doctors devote the greater portion of their time to research rather than to ministering to the sick; and the growth and the changing age dis-tribution of the population. (Today, 17 million persons are between ages 55 and 65, and 18 million are 65 and over; by 1975, there will be 20 million persons between 55 and 65, and 21 million of 65 and over). There are today, in the United States, about 260,00 physicians, and we now graduate 7,500 physicians a year. But this number is not adequate to maintain the *present* physician-population ratio during the next fifteen years (in fact that ratio declined somewhat between 1950 and 19(55), and with the increased demand for medical services the number of doctors will have to be expanded.

These projected gaps in scientific manpower suggest a new and unique dimension in social affairs: the economic growth rate in the future will be less dependent on physical capital (money) than it will be on "human capital." And this poses new problems for the society.

In the past, societies moving up the ladder of industrialization required huge sums of money to develop the "infrastructure" (i.e., highways, railroads, canals) and the basic physical plant of heavy industry (steel, energy resources, metals) in order to grow. Today the long-range expansion of the modern economy is limited by the impending shortages of technical and scientific manpower. (One can see this in such a growth area as computer technology, which employs about one-fourth of the 25,000 professional mathematicians in the United States).

The point is obvious. Physical, money capital can be generated rather quickly (as the Soviet Union has shown) by restricting consumption and "sweating" a population. But the planning of human capital is a much more difficult and arduous process. We need to know more about the genetic distribution of brainpower, the means of identifying talent, the procedures for raising I.Q.'s by reshaping home environments, the process of maintaining motivation, and the guidance and husbanding of talent over the long educational process. It means—given the length of schooling—vocational planning on a twenty-five-year cycle.

All of this points up the fact that we are entering a "post-industrial" society in which intellectual achievement will be the premium and in which the "new men" will be the research scientists, mathematicians, economists, et al. To say that the basic institutions of the new society will be intellectual is not to say that all or a majority of persons will be intellectuals, engineers, technicians, or scientists. The majority of individuals in contemporary society are not businessmen, yet one can say that this is a "business civilization." The basic values of the society have been embodied in the business institutions; the largest rewards are paid in business.

To say that the major institutions of the new society will be predominantly intellectual is to say, primarily, that the basic *innovative* features of the society will derive not from business as we know it today, principally the "product corporation," but from the research corporations, the industrial laboratories, the experimental stations, and the universities. The skeleton structure of that new society is already visible.

In the Universities[6]

The American university—as a complex of undergraduate college, specialized professional schools, and graduate institutions—is less than a hundred years old. It emerged with the establishment of the first graduate school at Johns Hopkins in 1876. It spread in the next quarter century because of the strong leadership of a few outstanding educators—Gilman at Hopkins, White at Cornell, Harper at Chicago, Eliot at Harvard, and Butler at Columbia. By 1900, there were ISO schools offering graduate study, though less than a third gave doctoral degrees (5 universities—Harvard, Columbia, Johns Hopkins, Chicago, and California—conferred half of the 250 doctorates earned that year).

From 1900 to 1940, as Bernard Berelson points out in his study, *Graduate Education in the United States,* "everything in higher education was increasing in size, and far faster than the population of the age group most directly involved. The latter did not even double in these four decades, but institutions offering the doctorate more than tripled, college faculties became five times as large, college enrollments six times, baccalaureate degrees seven times, and graduate enrollments and degrees from thirteen to seventeen times."

[6] For the statistical information in this section, I have drawn largely from the reports of the National Science Foundation, principally "Federal Funds for Science X" and "Reviews of Data on Research and Development"; the report of Harold Orlans for the Brookings Institute, "The Effects of Federal Programs in Higher Education" 1962; and a memorandum by Diana Crane, "Financial Support for Academic Research," taken from her Ph.D. thesis, "The Environment of Discovery." Columbia University, 1964.

In less than seventy-five years, the modern university, with the graduate school at the center rather than the college (despite its overwhelmingly larger number of students), had come to dominate American higher education. The graduate school arose in response to several needs: the increase in knowledge, the emphasis on scholarship as against teaching, the corollary emphasis on research as a coequal function of the university professor, and the need to train teachers for the burgeoning number of colleges in the country. These needs remain and, in fact, are multiplied by the proliferation of new fields of knowledge and the extraordinary increase in college attendance in the country.[7]

What is new today, and constitutes the further transformation of the American universities, is the predominant concern with research, the creation of new research institutes, centers, and laboratories, as the major organizational feature of the university, and the role of the federal government in underwriting the costs of this development. The university today, whether private or state, has come to be a quasi-public institution in which the needs of public service, as defined by the role of the research endeavor (whether initiated by the government or by the faculties), becomes paramount in the activities of the university.

What is equally new is that the universities, like the economy and the polity, are becoming part of a national system. The leading universities, as Edward Shils points out, "are becoming the universities of the whole society and not merely a small plutoaristocracy of the major cities, such as the Ivy League universities and colleges were for a long time, and still are, to some extent." The unity of the

---

[7] For all the fashionable denunciation of the Ph.D., there is some eloquent testimony to its use—at least its unintended use. Paul Samuelson has written: "I must confess my own original predilections were against our Ph.D. until, under the impact of direct empirical observation, I was forced to the view that the absence of a comprehensive Ph.D. program may be the curse of economics abroad. This is not because our average doctoral dissertation is a substantial contribution to scholarship. . . To look at the thesis is to miss the point; it is only the submerged peak of an exposed iceberg. If the Ph.D. program had never existed, we would have to invent it—for the simple reason that *it gives us the excuse to carry on advanced instruction in economics"* Paul A. Samuelson, "Economic Thought and the New Industrialism," in *Paths of American Thought,* ed. by A. M. Schlesinger, Jr., and Morton White (Boston: Houghton Mifflin, 1963), p. 231.

university system is coming about from the unification of the country, due in part to the ease and speed of travel and communication, and in greater part to the enhanced authority of the central government. There is a national academic market for scientific and academic personnel. And there is a constant interchange between government and the universities, as academics are called to Washington for their special talents, or men in government return, after a "tour of duty," to the universities to teach.

The tradition of "practical service" is an old one in American colleges, going back, primarily, to the Morrill Act of 1862 and the establishment of the land-grant universities. But most of that service was restricted to agricultural and extension work. What is extraordinary since the end of World War II is the bewildering variety of such services and the involvement of universities with almost every branch of government.

The most dramatic innovations have been in the physical sciences, where the government and the universities have created a unique partnership. The first model was the Los Alamos laboratory, which produced the atom bomb. Under contract with the Army, the University of California set up and managed the laboratory, while the Army paid for all costs, including that of research. After the war the Los Alamos laboratory passed under the aegis of the Atomic Energy Commission. Since the war, the AEG has continued its arrangements with various universities. In some instances there are laboratories operated by a single university, such as the Argonne laboratory which was managed by the University of Chicago, or by a consortium, such as the Brookhaven National Laboratory on Long Island, which is managed by Associated Universities Inc., a group of a dozen schools including Columbia.

Because of the high cost of equipment, the AEC has become the single largest patron of the physical sciences, particularly in the construction of the proton accelerator, a "machine" which by bombarding atoms with high electrical energy releases streams of particles. The Cambridge-Electron Accelerator, completed in 1963 at the cost of $12 million, will be operated by Harvard and M.I.T. with a $5 million annual research budget supported by the AEC. The AEC will retain title to the accelerator for twenty-five years, and thereafter it will revert to the universities. A mile-long linear accelerator is being built at Stanford University for its physics department at the cost of $114 million!

The same pattern of facilities built by government but managed by a cooperative group of universities has been adopted by the National Science Foundation in the fields of radio astronomy, oceanography, and geology. Although by statute the National Science Foundation operates no laboratories of its own, three national research centers, for which scientists had long pleaded the need, have been built and managed by groups of universities under contract with the foundation. These include the National Radio Astronomy Observatory at Green Bank, West Virginia, the Kitt Peak National Observatory in the Quintan mountains of southern Arizona, and the National Center for Atmospheric Research on Table Mountain near Boulder, Colorado.

More directly, various university laboratories service specific government agencies. The Jet Propulsion Laboratory at the California Institute of Technology conducts research on rocket propulsion for the Air Force and designs space craft for the National Aeronautics and Space Administration. The Massachusetts Institute of Technology set up the Lincoln Laboratory, under contract with the Air Force, to design the distant early warning system for the continental air defense, and later the university set up MITRE (M.I.T. Research and Engineering) to conduct the development work on the system. After a time the university felt that the work of MITRE was no longer sufficiently theoretical to warrant the maintenance of a university connection, and MITRE was set up as an independent not-for-profit corporation.

Recent years have seen an important shift in the patterns of government research spending. Though the totals have risen in every field, the relative influence of defense spending has declined as newer agencies, particularly the National Institutes of Health, have entered the research field. In 1952, the Department of Defense contributed 70 percent of the total federal funds for the support of academic research. In 1962 it was contributing only 24 percent. The same proportion, 24 percent, was contributed by the Department of

Health, Education, and Welfare, while the single 'largest government source of research money was the Atomic Energy Commission, whose grants made up 27 percent of the total federal funds to educational institutions.

The shift into the "life sciences" has been one of the more remarkable aspects of the role of government, especially since these grants are not tied in any direct way to "defense." Over the years the size of the grants has increased while the kinds of research supported have become increasingly diverse, including allergy and immunology, biophysics and genetics, nutrition and tropical medicine, psychology and sociology, and, one of the largest areas, mental health. In the twelve years from 1947 to 1959, appropriations for the National Institutes of Health rose from $8.1 million to $285 million. In 1959, N.I.H. spent over $140 million in research grants to more than 10,000 projects in nearly 1,000 institutions. By 1965 the figures had risen to more than 15,000 grants, totaling more than $538 million.

The effect of government-sponsored research, which extends now through all fields of science, has been not only to establish giant research centers, but to transform the work of the individual scientist as well. Bentley Glass, the eminent biologist of Johns Hopkins, and now the provost of the State University of New York at Stony Brook, relates, in a thinly veiled autobiographical account, the changing conditions of munificence in one university. In 1940, an assistant professor of biology received $100 a year from the departmental budget for supplies. He had one moderately good compound microscope and one binocular dissecting microscope. He made all his own media, did his own sterilizing in a pressure cooker, and was grateful for any janitorial help in washing the glassware. Twenty years later, the professor is in charge of two research laboratories, both supported by the federal government; a senior research assistant operates one of these laboratories, and he has research assistants to wash bottles, prepare media, and keep the animals. The annual research budget for the scientist, not including his university salary, is $50,000; and none of this comes from the regular departmental budget. The departmental budget at the end of World War II was about $70,000 a year; fifteen years later it was close to $1 million, and the staff had doubled.

But the transforming effect of research spending has not been in the natural sciences alone. With the spread of new nations (forty-six since the end of World War II) and the intensified competition with the Soviet Union and China for influence in these areas, the social sciences— economics, sociology, anthropology, and political science —have received tremendous infusions of government and more especially foundation money,[8] in order to train specialists both for work in government and to develop research material for policy purposes.

Area studies, combining the social science disciplines, has emerged as a new form of research and teaching. In a leading International Affairs school such as Columbia's, one finds a Russian Institute, an East Central European Institute, a Middle East Institute, a European Institute, an African Institute, a Latin-American Institute, an East-Asian Institute, all involved in training graduate students as well as conducting research; and in other sections of the university there are centers specializing in particular problems: the Research Institute on Communist Affairs, an Institute of War and Peace Studies (to deal with civil-military relations), a Research Program on Men and Politics in China (to build biographical files on Chinese leaders), a Council on Atomic Age Studies (which has published studies on "space law," the political role of scientists, and similar concerns with the social science of science), a Conservation of Human Resources Project (which has published more than a dozen studies of manpower), plus such esoteric programs as training in Uralic and Altaic languages (for research on Central Asian peoples).

The area studies institutes in many instances have become, in effect, semiautonomous graduate "colleges," in which the interests, concerns, and discussions of both the faculty and the students are more to the "field," than to the separate disciplines. A faculty member or student in the Russian Institute necessarily tends to focus his

---

[8] The heavy concentration of government money in the physical sciences has led the foundations to concentrate their support on the life sciences and the social sciences. In 1960, some 270 foundations (accounting for 87 percent of the total spending by 12,000 philanthropic foundations) spent 3437 million in support of their programs, of which $76 million went for research projects. Of this latter sum, 10 percent was spent in the physical sciences, about 50 percent in the life sciences, and 40 percent in the social sciences and psychology.

concerns and contacts with others on the Russian field, rather than on other economists or political scientists in the university. These area institutes are able to raise their own money, and are in a position to expand the number of tenure positions of various departments outside the "normal" table of organization.

Foreign policy institutes are commonplace in a dozen universities, as are centers for the study of economic development, social development (e.g., world urbanization), political development, and the like. Dozens of universities have government contracts to supply technicians and specialists for programs in underdeveloped countries, from the teaching of new agricultural techniques in Iran to city planning in India or Venezuela. Individual universities, because of the presence of outstanding scholars in a field, become known for specific area specializations (such as U.C.L.A. and Boston for African studies, the University of Chicago for India, or Columbia for Russian, Chinese, and Japanese studies), or, as in the case of the Center for International Studies at M.I.T., and the Institute for International Studies at Berkeley, cut across areas studies to concentrate on economic or political development. This proliferation is a far cry from the old graduate school idea of training in a discipline; yet in many universities, the area studies programs or the problem-centered institutes have gained considerable weight.

The reason the government and the foundations have turned to the universities rather than to private profit corporations (as in the case of overseas engineering projects which have been handled by private firms) is that these problems are intellectual, the universities are disinterested, and most important, perhaps, because the university structure—with its emphasis on research accomplishment as a measure of achievement and promotion, because of its job mobility, and because of its provisions for leaves—provides the condition of "dispensability" which is so often necessary in these situations. Max Weber once remarked that the reason for the preponderance of lawyers in the legislatures of democratic countries, as against, say, businessmen, or engineers, or labor leaders, was not only that these occupations could exploit the post advantageously (a businessman could gain advantages, too), but the "dispensability" of the occupation. A business executive cannot take leave from his job easily, or if he does he may not get it back; lawyers can carry on a practice while acting as legislators, or resume one quite easily if defeated. In the same way, the newer relationship between the expanding executive arm of government and the university provides its own conditions of "dispensability."

With all these changes, the universities are now in the process of a great transformation, carrying out multivaried functions which educators never dreamed of twenty-five years ago. The old Veblenian fear was that the "higher learning" was becoming a business enterprise, dominated by the business community and taking over the values of the business civilization. Though the businessman may still be important as a donor of funds for buildings and endowments, the university has a new paymaster, the government, and in the performance of its many new roles the university has become overwhelmingly dependent upon the federal government for its continued existence. The overall figures are stupendous. In 1940, the universities spent about 831 million for scientific research, of which the government contributed half—and that mostly under the aegis of the Department of Agriculture. In 1962, the federal government was disbursing more than a billion dollars a year for research and development in American universities, or 70 times the amount before the war. Science and defense have brought the government and the university community together to such an extent that even before the passage of the Johnson administration measures to aid higher education, almost 25 percent of the total moneys spent each year in higher education came from federal sources.

Even such a richly endowed school as Harvard finds itself inextricably dependent upon federal funds for its operation. In 1959-1960, according to President Pusey's report, federal funds supplied one-fourth of the total Harvard budget. But this overall figure fails to show the weight of federal support, for most of the government money was conspicuous in the research portions of the university budget. For example, in the division of engineering and applied physics, federal money supported 95 percent of the research, and in the physics department, 63 percent of the total expenditures on research. But federal support was crucial in other areas as well. For example, it supplied about 55 percent of the budget of Harvard's School of Public Health, 57 percent of the medical school, and 30 percent of the school of arts and sciences (though of that figure, half came from the money for the Cambridge Electron Accelerator). By 1962, the federal government contributed nearly $14 million to the construction, modernization, and remodeling of research facilities which are owned and operated by the University. In all, Harvard was participating in at least thirty-four categories of programs managed by some two-score federal agencies, under the general supervision of a dozen congressional committees.[8]

Columbia University, according to the testimony of President Grayson Kirk before the House Committee on Government Research in March, 1963, has received more than $200 million in federal research support since the beginning of World War II—when Dean George Pegram was given $6,000 by the Navy to continue some experiments in the liberation of atomic energy from uranium, the start of the Manhattan Project. In the single year of 1962-63, Columbia received $40 million in federal support, about 40 percent of which was in the health field, at the Columbia-Presbyterian Medical Center. In all, federal money was supporting some 700 different projects at Columbia.

Perhaps the most staggering picture of change is that supplied by Clark Kerr in depicting the University of California as the embodiment of the new "multiversity." In his 1963 Godkin lectures at Harvard, published as *The Uses of the University,* President Kerr said:

> The University of California last year had operating expenses from all sources of nearly half a billion dollars, with almost another 100 million for construction; a total employment of 40,000 people, more than IBM and in a far greater variety of endeavors; operations in over a hundred locations, counting campuses, experiment stations, agricultural and urban extension centers, and projects abroad involving more than

[8] The question about the encroachment of government control, the freedom of the university, and the independence of the researcher under these conditions is an important one, but lies outside the scope of the present statement. From all the available evidence, and the problem is summed up in the inquiry by Harold Orlans for the Brookings Institute, the universities have been able to maintain a full autonomy, and few of the feats commonly voiced have materialized.

fifty countries; nearly 10,000 courses in its catalogues; some form of contact with nearly every industry, nearly every level of government, nearly every person in its region. Vast amounts of expensive equipment were serviced and maintained. Over 4,000 babies were born in its hospitals. It is the world's largest purveyor of white mice. It will soon have the world's largest primate colony. It will soon have 100,000 students—30,000 of them at the graduate level; yet much less than one third of its expenditures are directly related to teaching. It already has 200,000 students in extension courses—including one out of every three lawyers and one out of every six doctors in the state.

As Kerr asked, perhaps in self-wonderment: "How did the multiversity happen? No man created it; in fact no man visualized it. It has been a long time coming about and it has a long way to go."

But more than a sociological transformation of the university into a multiversity has been taking place in American higher learning, The universities are responsible for a new kind of status revolution as well—a revolution in the society, as well as within the world of higher learning.

Forty or so years ago, American education was dominated by the Eastern Ivy League colleges, because these schools, in the composition of their student body, *reflected* the existing status structure of the society. Today, with higher education as the chief route of social mobility, the elite universities *determine* the new status positions of the post-industrial society. The singular fact is that a small number of universities have become the channels to place and position in the society. A higher degree with creditable work from one of the elite universities has become the passport to a position in one of these universities, to a place in the major research laboratories, and to an administrative position in government.

About fourteen universities now dominate the academic scene.[10]

[10] Based upon a study by Haywood Kenniston in 1957, and one by Albert Bowker in 1964. The criterion of inclusion was principally the repute of the departments, though a composite weighting[1] often obscures the strength of a particular school either in the sciences or humanities. But by general consensus, these were the rankings: Harvard, California (Berkeley), Columbia, Yale, Michigan, Chicago, Princeton, Wisconsin, Cornell, Illinois, Pennsylvania, Minnesota, Stanford, and U.C.L.A. If technological institutions were included, M.I.T. and the California Institute of Technology would place high on the lists.

The faculties of these institutions are drawn largely from within the elite circle, and it is uncommon for individuals with degrees from other graduate schools to break into these ranks. The reasons are fairly simple. Most universities are subject to a form of "inbreeding," in that home-grown disciples and apprentices have an obvious advantage over outsiders, ("We should not forget," writes Berelson, "how young the institution of graduate study was by World War II —hardly more than two generations old. Many of the students of the first graduate professors were themselves still active in 1940 and were only then beginning to turn the system over to *their* students.") And when the best schools have expanded, they have usually drawn their younger instructors and professors from those recommended by the established professors in the elite schools. (The one major exception was the influx in the 1930s and 1940s of foreign scholars from European universities.) The chances for the "outsider" to break into the elite ranks depend, in large measure, on his ability to publish rapidly in the academic journals as a means of getting attention; one has here an additional dimension of the academic phrase "Publish or perish." But by and large the inbreeding remains.

It is not only for position within its own ranks that admission to an elite graduate school is important; it is important also for entree into contiguous elite groups as well. Because of the connections of the leading faculties with the executive agencies of government, and with the major foundations, the graduate student in an elite school is more likely to get a job in such agencies or a choice fellowship than someone from a school with lesser standing.

While the pattern of elite schools was laid down many years ago-going back, in fact to the first formation of graduate schools—the flow of government money in the past decade has tended to reinforce and extend this pattern of elite concentration. Given the fact that during the war and after, government needs (particularly in the physical sciences and military technology) were urgent, and that the leading researchers in each field were at the best universities, such a self-reinforcing circle was almost inevitable. As Harold Orlans has remarked about the creation of major new laboratories, "Each of these centers represents a unique national enterprise which can hardly be duplicated on every campus; its financing must be justified in terms of its individual purpose, rather than the criteria of programs catering to a number of institutions."

But even in the more general distribution of funds, small schools have suffered. According to a study by the Department of Health, Education, and Welfare in 1962, about 186 universities and technological schools, less than 10 percent of the 2,000 accredited institutions of higher learning, received 97 percent of all government research funds. In 1960, for example, the National Science Foundation spent over 90 percent of its money at 139 institutions which award one or more science doctorates. Actually, 60 percent of its total money went to the top twenty schools of the 139. Less than 10 percent of its money (about $4.2 million) went to 104 institutions that award lower science degrees. And not a penny went either to the remaining 801 institutions that award a master's or bachelor's degree in the sciences, or the 593 institutions below the four-year level, most of which presumably give instruction in mathematics and some other fields within the purview of the National Science Foundation.

While such disproportions are inevitable when one is seeking to get necessary research done, or to help talented persons in the various fields-after all, there is no democratic logic which insists that research money be distributed evenly—there is, however, a question about the concentration of disbursements in areas of pure science, or where the government is eager to encourage the spread of science education.[11] For some of its chief consequences have been to enlarge the distance between the elite universities and the other universities in the country and, of equal importance, to place a great strain on the liberal arts colleges which stand outside the university system.

All of this—the ascendancy of research over teaching and the paramount position of the graduate school within the university—points

---

[11] As Orlans remarks: "There are no Nobel laureates and probably no members of the National Academy of Sciences at the 1,785 institutions of higher education receiving no research funds from the National Science Foundation or the 1,600 receiving no research funds from any federal agency. Many who teach science at these institutions do not hold the doctorate and, at junior colleges, are trained to about the level of a good high-school teacher. Nevertheless, it strains credulity to imagine that not *one* member of the staff of these institutions has the capacity to conduct research of a quality comparable to that of the lowliest scholar now receiving federal research funds."

up the plight of the independent liberal arts college and of the under-graduate college within the universities. The new standard for judging the quality of an institution has become the number of distinctive contributions its members make to "research." Before World War II, when the humanities dominated the intellectual scene, the repute of a school was based on its contributions to scholarship, and since scholarship derives primarily from qualities of mind rather than from results which are dependent upon costly experimental apparatus or expensive research projects, colleges with a few brilliant scholars could hold their own in the competitive ranking of institutions. But with the rise of the sciences and social sciences, "research" rather than "scholarship" has come to predominate; and in the quest for research funds and the desire of individuals to give graduate courses based on their research, the colleges have suffered.

All of this, too, is related to the changing role of the professor in a national university system. The primary shift of emphasis is the now greater orientation of individuals to their disciplines as a source of recognition rather than to their universities. In many colleges and universities, there are still local stars whose names are luminous within the confines of the school. But increasingly, one's ability to be promoted quickly, to move to some more favored school, or to command research funds, depends on one's standing in the discipline rather than on service to the school.

A second facet of this change is the multiplication of tasks and the differentiation of functions of the professorial role. Forty years ago, a college professor taught his undergraduate classes, instructed a few graduate students, and wrote some books and articles. Today he will be a teacher, researcher, project director, administrator, and fundraiser. He will have dozens of dissertations to direct and serve on countless Ph.D. oral examinations. He will write or feel compelled to write articles and research reports, edit compendia and symposia, and, with the growing number of professional journals, join more editorial boards and referee more journal papers. He will be on departmental committees, university committees, professional association committees; attend conferences, local and international; and serve on government commissions, local, state, or federal.

Along with all this, the expansion of the national job market has greatly increased the mobility of the college professor. In previous years, a man would teach at a small college or, if talented, at his home university while working on his Ph.D., then move around two or three times, become an associate professor in his forties, and settle down for the remainder of his academic life. But this is no longer the case. It is still true that individuals over forty-five move infrequently, but in many fields a man may become an associate professor at age thirty or thirty-five and a full professor a few years later; and this age change is reflected in the increased mobility of those in such upper ranks. A recent study, for example, of 420 economists who had moved within a previous five-year period showed that 140, or one-third, held the rank of associate professor or higher.[12] And, interestingly enough as regards mobility in and out of the academic world, slightly more than a fourth of them had at some time or other worked in government, while about 40 percent had worked in business as well.

The expansion of the universities and the increased mobility have intensified the competition for professors of national reputation, producing at times an amusing game of musical chairs. A recent effort of two universities to attract "stars" (one because it was seeking to raise its repute, the other because it was seeking to repair a fading image) created such a fevered roundelay that though *in* the end few men had moved, the salary scale in several professions moved up with startling rapidity. Both schools sought men between the ages of thirty-five and forty-five—anyone younger was still unproven and perhaps a risk; someone older would be too strongly identified with the previous school. But in any field the number of first-class men in that age range is small, so the competing schools offered salaries between $20,000 and $25,000 a year plus generous research-leave time. In the instances where individuals were successfully enticed, the "raided" university in turn sought to snatch individuals from other schools or, where a competitive offer was matched, the salaries for other men in the department had to be adjusted accordingly. In consequence, offers to only three or four persons in a field created a ripple which affected several dozen more.

---

[12] Howard D. Marshall, *The Mobility of College Faculties* (New York, Pageant Press, 1961), p. 56.

We can at this point, perhaps, tie together these changes—the increasing force of research, the multifarious roles of the professor, the orientation to the discipline, and the increased mobility in a national job market—and sketch some of their consequences for the *instructional* role of the undergraduate college.

1. The emphasis on research has increased the power of the graduate school, since funds are more easily available to men teaching in the graduate school—if only because they have "command" over graduate students as research assistants. And with such funds goes the greater prestige as well. In the pecking order, thus, the individual who teaches undergraduates exclusively stands lower on the status hierarchy than one who teaches graduate courses; and within the college, the one who teaches only lower division courses stands below those who teach junior and senior courses.

2. The chief consequence of the multiplication of professorial roles has been the demand by the professor for a reduced teaching schedule and more time for research and public service. In many undergraduate schools, a four-course teaching load is still common, while in the larger colleges and universities a three-course load is the norm. Yet increasingly in the elite schools, professors will teach only two courses (one of which will be a research seminar), while asking for regular research leaves every two years or so. In a university divided into graduate and undergraduate schools, the reduction in teaching load is almost invariably at the expense of the college course. This requires a university either to consolidate courses or to increase the size of the faculty.

3. It is in the recruitment of new and younger faculty that the orientation to the discipline and the easy availability of research funds pinch the most. In the past a brilliant young scholar would have taught lower level or introductory college courses while working for his Ph.D., or in the first few years after he had earned his doctorate. But now the best graduate students are able to "buy off" teaching time with research money. Inasmuch as recognition and advancement are achieved primarily through publication rather than teaching, the impulse on the part of the younger man to substitute research time for the classroom is a strong one. Because the highest rewards and research money are to be found in the graduate school,

the desire to move out of the college and establish one's career on the graduate level becomes equally compelling.

The impact of all this on the students—at least for many who go to the elite schools—is obvious. For them the college is a "way station" on the road to graduate school. Given this emphasis, and the lengthening period of graduate education, some universities have sought to "squeeze" the college by allowing for "advanced placement" credits in the freshman year (for work taken in the high schools), and by permitting students to begin graduate work in their senior year. In many subjects, moreover, the content of the undergraduate courses is no longer shaped by the college faculty, but is determined by the graduate schools, which specify the kinds of preparation a student needs. In this way, the independence of the college tends to be reduced.

These changes, which I have sketched in generalized fashion, have affected the independent liberal arts college and the university-based college in different ways.

The independent colleges have suffered in two ways. One is in the quality of students. In those instances where bright students have decided at an early age to go beyond college into graduate school, such students often prefer university colleges, where they can take graduate work in their senior year or establish contact with a graduate professor, rather than the small independent college. For analogous reasons, because of the growing importance of the graduate school, the independent liberal arts college finds it increasingly difficult to recruit and maintain a topflight faculty that will stay at the undergraduate level for any long period of time. Some colleges, such as Amherst, Swarthmore, Williams, Oberlin, Reed, and the major New England women's colleges, can do so by offering high salaries, amenities like good housing, and a small student body. But even such schools face difficulties. The expansion of curriculum and the introduction of new courses—most colleges, for example, seek to offer work in Oriental civilization or Slavic studies as part of an expanded world outlook—make it hard for the independent college to recruit scholars in specialized fields.

Some colleges have tried to "upgrade" their status by offering graduate work in a few fields or by becoming universities. Other colleges within a common geographical locale have formed condominiums, or quasi-university clusters, in order to hire individuals in specialized fields whose courses would be open to students of all the colleges. But in such adaptations, the distinctive identity of the individual colleges may be jeopardized.

For the university-based college, there are other difficulties. While they can often call on the superior resources of the university for instruction in specialized fields, and at times command the services of distinguished figures in the university (in the sciences, for example, at Columbia and at several other major universities, these professors as a matter of pride will regularly teach undergraduate courses), the colleges by and large have become the "stepchildren" of the university. They lack the superior fund-raising power of the specialized schools such as engineering, or the specialized fields such as area studies. The increase in the number of graduate students and the reduction of teaching loads often mean that a professor will give up his college assignment when confronted with the pressures on his time. Younger men, eager for tenure at the university, are loath to spend extra time on teaching preparation, or (even if this is not the case) feel that teaching is unappreciated, compared to research and publications. And, within the close university setting, invidious distinctions between the graduate school and the college are often more visible, or are so felt by college instructors.

Yet all of this is merely prelude. It is estimated that by 1980 the college-age population (eighteen to twenty-one) will increase by almost 7.5 million to about twenty million, and by the year 2000 it will increase by another 7.5 to 10 million.

What proportion of these youths will attend college is not easy to predict. In 1959, for example, the Office of Education issued projections of college enrollments to 1970, assuming that the proportion attending college would rise from the 1959 figure of 35 percent to 38.7 percent in 1965, and to 42.2 percent in 1970. Within two years, the assumption was scrapped as too conservative, and the Office of Education increased its estimates for 1970 college enrollments by a million students. If these trends materialize, by 1970 the colleges and universities in the United States will have twice as many students as in 1960.

Little of this increase in enrollment is explained by population growth. For example, if college attendance rates had remained constant from 1950-1952 to 1958-1960, matching simply the increase in college-age population, the number enrolled would have increased by only 8 percent; but in that period, the number of students increased by about 40 percent. The simple fact is that more and more young people realize that a college education is a necessary prerequisite for any kind of well-paying job, and the federal government and the states, by various means, are making it possible for more of them to attend college.

The changes in magnitudes are quite awesome. In 1870, there were approximately 300 colleges and universities in the United States, comprising 5,530 professors and 52,000 students. Only 1.7 percent of the eighteen to twenty-one age group were in college. Just before World War II, the number of institutions of higher learning had increased to 1,690, the students to 1.35 million, and 14 percent of the eighteen to twenty-one age group were in college. In 1964 there were approximately 2,100 institutions, 400,000 faculty members, and 4.8 million students, who constituted 40 percent of their age group, in college.[13] By 1970, if median projections bold, there will be 7 million students in college, comprising 47 percent of their peers.[14]

[13] As George Keller reminds me, the government figures are somewhat deceptive. The 40 percent figure is derived by subtracting the 4.8 million from the total number of persons between ages eighteen and twenty-one. But actually only 68 percent of the undergraduates fall into the eighteen-to-twenty-one age category. Since there ate no figures for the actual ages of undergraduates in the earlier years, and since we do not know how many younger or older students will be in college in the next decade, these percentages are useful, then, only to illustrate trends.

[14] Government projections are made on three bases: *constant-rate* projections continue existing enrollments into the future, without change; *father's attainment* projections introduce, on an experimental basis, a variable which modifies the constant-rate principle by seeking to isolate a key causal factor of motivation; *trend* projections are based on age-specific college enrollment rates fined to an exponential curve. For an elaboration of this methodology, and for some of the basic statistics in this section, see Louis H. Conger, Jr., "College and University Enrollment: Projections," in Selma Mishkin, ed., *Economics of Higher Education* (Washington, D.C., Office of Education, 1962).

How can the educational facilities be expanded to meet this demand? Where will the teachers be found? How will the bill be paid, and by whom? Of the three questions, the last can be answered most readily: the bill will probably be paid in large and increasing measure by federal funds. But the other two are not answered as easily.

Can the university meet all these varied challenges and adapt to the new functions it is being called upon to perform? Even as rhetorical questions they allow us to sum up, even if only schematically, the salient features of the social and intellectual changes that confront the university today.

The university is a striking example of endurance among social institutions. Like cathedrals and parliaments, it was a medieval invention. "What has survived and is significant," as Sir Eric Ashby has remarked, "is the social purpose of the university, its independence from Church and State, and its peculiar method of internal government." In the next decades, all three of these characteristics will be tested.

The historic role of the university, more so in Europe perhaps than in the United States, has been the transmission of a traditional culture and common learning and the education of an elite. In the industrial societies, and particularly in the United States, the university took on a very different, triple-service function: as a ladder of social mobility for the middle class; as the place to train the emerging professional classes, particularly law,[15] medicine, and engineering; and as a community agency providing, in the state and municipal colleges, such varied services as agricultural extension, adult education, research for state and local legislatures, and aid for local business firms.

---

[15] Dean Keppel of Columbia observed; almost fifty years ago: "It must be remembered . . . that the beginnings of professional education in America are found not in the institutions of learning, but in the familiar personal association of the students wirh men in active practice. When in 1858 the trustees appointed Dwight as professor of law, it was not their intention to establish a professional school. They soon came to the conclusion, however, that success was more likely should the work be organized with a view of actual admission to the Bar. The prompt success of the Law School and its rapid growth were without parallel in the contemporary history of professional education." Frederick P. Keppel, *Columbia* (New York, Oxford University Press, 1914), p. 9.

In the advanced industrial societies, and in the emerging post-industrial society, the university is taking on a vastly different role. It is becoming one of the active shapers of the society, taking over, perhaps, the role which the business firm played in the past hundred years. One can see this by sketching the relationship of the university to the changing social structure of the United States.

1. The university is becoming one of the chief innovative forces in the society. Insofar as economic development is increasingly de pendent on research and new knowledge, the role of the university has been enlarged, and it is becoming one of the determinants, rather than a passive reflector, of social change.

2. The university is becoming the chief determinant of the strati-fication system of the society. Insofar as position in the society is increasingly determined by the kind and amount of education one obtains, the degree-granting power of the university (particularly the advanced degrees), the grading system, and the network of elite universities all become decisive to one's chances of moving up in the society.

3. The job of mass higher education will become the predominant task of the colleges in the last third of the twentieth century. By 1975, as many as half of all youths aged eighteen to twenty-one will be seeking some kind of college education and higher degree. The definition of "educated" will change radically, and the question what is "an education" will have new answers.

4. As society becomes more differentiated, both in knowledge and in tasks, the university takes over the function (once handled largely "on the job") of training persons for specialization.

5. Insofar as old skills will become obsolete and traditional sub-jects will erode, a new concept of "continuing education" will come to the fore. In the large business firms, as in the armed forces, attend ance at "advanced schools" has become a necessary step for promo-tion within these institutions. The older notion that the possession of a college degree is a plateau of life is vanishing. Educated individuals will require continual training and, in fact, may have as many as two or three different "careers" within a working lifetime. The for-malization of continuing education will be one of the next great tasks of the university. One sees this, in embryo, in the proliferation of

research institutes which provide advanced training courses, and in such postgraduate universities such as the Rockefeller Institute for Medical Research (which was recently chartered as the Rockefeller University) and the RAND Corporation, whose informal seminars and cooperative projects between different staff members become, in effect, postgraduate courses.

6. The university has become, at least in American life, the major focus of the intellectual and, to some extent, the established cultural life of the country. Most of the "highbrow" literary magazines, and even the established little magatines are now published on university campuses or edited by people whose source of livelihood is the university. The spread of the little theater movement, the multiplication of centers of music and art, the creation of small museums have become a distinguishing aspect of the universities in the last decade.

Whether the university is resourceful enough and sufficiently flexible to undertake all these new functions (and some of them are "new" simply because of an added quantitative dimension) is a question. One can already see the strains which have emerged.

The balance between research and teaching has already created considerable organizational tension in many universities. This is reflected not only in the depreciation of teaching (in California, as noted above, less than one-third of the yearly half-billion-dollar expenditure is related directly to teaching), but in the question of what status and tenure are to be given to the large number of research persons who have been brought into the university, particularly in the government-maintained projects and laboratories.

The growth of knowledge has lengthened considerably the time required to earn a Ph.D. The mean lag between B.A. and Ph.D. in the physical sciences has increased from 6.8 years in 1920-1939 to 7.4 in 1950-1959 and 7.8 in 1960-1961. In the biological sciences the mean increased from 8.0 years in 1920-1939 to 8.3 years in 1950-1959 and 8.9 years in 1960-1961. In other fields the current lag is even greater: 10.4 years in the social sciences, 12.0 in the humanities and professional fields, and 15.2 in education, (In some fields, notably education and the humanities, the delay is due to the fact that a man may have begun teaching long before completing the doctorate. The recipients of science degrees in 1957-1961 spent only 2.9 years in professional work between the B.A. and the Ph.D.) The principle of full financial support for a qualified candidate from his entrance into graduate work to the completion of the thesis would reduce the time materially. But the intellectual problem remains, and it is one of the significant pressures in the reorganization of secondary school and college curriculums, in order to accelerate the pace of the brighter students.

The multiplication of specializations raises the question whether every university should—or even can—teach "everything." Adam Smith's example of the "pin factory," almost two hundred years ago, is one of the earliest models of the advantages of the division of labor. It is debatable whether, particularly in graduate work, every university has to cover all the specialized fields. It may well be, as is already evident, that some universities will simply forgo some subjects and concentrate on particular strengths. Can the intellectual life be organized on such a division of intellectual labor?

The rapid changes in the conceptions of knowledge, the successive "paradigms," as Thomas Kuhn has called them, raise a basic question about the nature of curriculum. As Rene Dubos has cogently put it: "In a world where everything changes rapidly, the practical facts learned in school become obsolete. . . The only knowledge of permanent value is theoretical knowledge; and the broader it is, the greater the chances that it will prove useful in practice because it will be applicable to a wide range of conditions. The persons most likely to become creative and to act as leaders are not those who enter life with the largest amount of detailed specialized information, but rather those who have enough theoretical knowledge, critical judgment, and the discipline of learning to adapt rapidly to the new situations and problems which constantly arise in the modern world." One of the consequences of this argument is that the curriculum has to be reorganized not so much to teach "subject matter," as to make fundamental the nature of conceptual innovation and the processes of conceptual thought.

Yet such changes raise the problem of "a common learning." As Douglas Bush has pointed out, "the cardinal fact is that for centuries [from the Renaissance to the eighteenth century] Europe had a

cultural solidarity that transcended national and religious boundaries.
. . . All or almost all the great original thinkers and writers had more
or less the same kind of classical education and read, spoke, and wrote
the same language, literally or metaphorically or both—Copernicus,
Kepler and Galileo; Machiavelli, Ariosto, and Tasso; Calvin, Rabelais,
and Montaigne; Erasmus, Sir Thomas More, Spenser, Shakespeare,
Bacon, Milton; and a host of others. In fact, down through a good
part of the nineteenth century most of the great men of Europe and
America were brought up on the classics." To what extent, today, is
a common learning possible? And what are its constituents?

Finally, given the problem of educating seven million youths at a
rime in the colleges, is it possible to maintain standards? To what extent,
even in graduate schools today, can one maintain the personal relation,
the small seminar, the informal contact, the systematic exchange of
common work and experiment between teacher and student?

Most of these problems lie outside the purview of this book, though
they provide the context of the particular question—the nature of
general education in a college curriculum—with which this study is
concerned. Many of these problems confront not only the colleges
and the universities, but the entire system of education itself, and
that far afield we certainly cannot go. Yet some revisionary steps are
being taken in the secondary schools, and it is to these changes that
we turn in the following section.

In the Secondary Schools[16]

"Education has a national budget second only to that of national
defense. Yet only a small fraction of one percent of this budget has
been spent in research and development," the Life Sciences panel of
the President's Science Advisory Committee reported in April, 1962. In
recent years this situation has begun to change, particularly in the
efforts to reshape the secondary schools in the United States.

[16] I am indebted to two former students, Mr. Richard M. Andrews and Mr. Richard
A. Epstein, for help in the assessment of the Advanced Placement program.

There have been four significant changes in the high school in the past decade:

1. Curriculum reform. Largely through the intervention of col lege professors or the professional associations, revolutionary changes have been introduced in mathematics, physics, and biology, while other changes, less drastic and more open to challenge, have been made in English and social studies.

2. The Advancement Placement program. In a number of high schools, "college level" courses are offered to qualified students to prepare them for "advanced placement" tests given by the Educational Testing Service (E.T.S.) for the College Entrance Examinations Board. In some colleges, success in advanced placement allows a student to skip as much as a year (at Harvard, about 10 percent of the entering class is placed directly into the sophomore class); at other schools (Columbia, for example), advanced placement may excuse a student from a required course, but the student is encouraged to spend four years in the college, although taking graduate courses in his senior year. One outcome of the Advanced Placement program has been to break the lock-step approach and to encourage the nongraded high school, where students move through their high-school years at varying paces.

3. Improvement of teaching. Large sums have been spent by the Ford Foundation Fund for the Advancement of Education, and by the National Science Foundation, for workshops, conferences, summer study programs, and the like, which have upgraded the competence of thousands of teachers, especially in the sciences.

4. Interdisciplinary courses. "College-type" humanities courses, including English, history, music, and art, have been organized on an interdisciplinary basis. Similarly there have been interdisciplinary courses in the social studies. The movement has been more wide spread in the private secondary schools than in the public high schools, and in some instances they seem to have been designed more to upgrade the sense of status of the secondary school instructor than to reorganize curriculum. These are the most debatable of the many new innovations.

All of these changes, it should be pointed out, affect only a minority of students—as may inevitably be the case. Most of the subject matter reform is addressed to the top 20 percent of high-school students, though the biological sciences study materials were used by about 600,000 high-school students in 1964-65. Only about 25,000 students take the E.T.S. Advanced Placement tests—largely in mathematics, English, and American history—and it is sometimes unclear whether these students are preparing for advanced placement or preparing simply for the tests. But the first question about secondary education that one must raise is not curriculum but the educational "atmosphere" of the high schools, and the values of the students. This is a subject largely outside the scope of this inquiry, yet it must be mentioned, at least in passing.

The dismaying revelation of the numerous inquiries into the American adolescent in recent years—and we can take James Coleman's study, *The Adolescent Society,* as the most careful—is that academic achievement counts for little in the high schools. In most high schools bright students stand outside the highly ranked peer groups, which are concerned mainly with popularity.[17] Boys care mainly about cars and sports and athletic prowess; girls are concerned primarily with beauty and glamour and attractiveness. All of them regard daring and extracurricular activities as very important, and high-school elites confer the greatest weight to these aspects of student life. Brains and good grades bring few if any tangible rewards from adolescent peer groups.

Most of the sociological studies describe these attitudes as central to a distinct subculture, or "youth culture," as if they constituted a set of norms separate from those of the society at large. It is quite true that adolescents, like any group in the society, have a somewhat distinct set of social relations, but, as Bennett Berger points out, "almost all the values and interests of adolescents revealed by Coleman's data seem to be derivative from and shared by the great

[17] James Coleman, *The Adolescent Society* (New York, Free Press of Glencoe, 1961), The book is a report of research in ten Illinois high schools, selected to represent a wide range of communities from small rural towns to Chicago and ics suburbs. For an extensive commentary on the Coleman book that has some brilliant observations of its own, see the essay review by Bennett M. Berger, "Adolescence and Beyond," in *Social Problems* (Spring 1963).

majority of their parents; the kids even preferred Pat Boone to Elvis Presley better than two to one—as good an indicator as any of the tendencies to utter respectability."

The point Berger shrewdly makes is that the adolescent subculture performs important local community functions. The centrality of high-school athletics, for example, is sustained as much by parent and local booster organizations as by the students themselves. In many small towns, it is one of the important sources of spectator-leisure and an important focus of community spirit. Academic excellence, however, is a value apart. As Berger writes, "Relatively few can realistically expect to be brilliant students—few are bright. But many can aspire to be sociable, popular, and well liked through the kinds of activities in which anyone can participate and with which any adult can empathize." Their parents, too, care a great deal about prestige and popularity, and they engage in the search for these important illusions, using those criteria—a large car, a well-appointed house—which become the criteria for the adolescents themselves.

If predominant student values militate against intellectualism, the oppressive atmosphere—almost one of policing—in many of these schools tends to herd the students into tight routines. Edgar Friedenberg, who has studied numerous high schools in the country, describes, for example, a large high school about fifty miles from Los Angeles.[18] "It is a big, expensive building, on spacious but barren grounds. Every door is at the end of a corridor; there is no reception area, no public space in which one can adjust to the transition from the outside world. Between class periods the corridors are tumultuously crowded; during them they are empty. But at both times they are guarded by teachers and students on patrol duty. . . Its principal function is the checking of corridor passes. Between classes, no student may walk down the corridor without a form, signed by a teacher, telling where he is coming from, where he is going, and the rime, to the minute, during which the pass is valid. A student caught in the corridor without such a pass is sent or taken to the office; there a de-

---

[18] The following account is taken from "The Modern High School: A Profile," in *Commentary* (November 1963). A revised version of this essay appears in Friedenberg's *Coming of Age in America.*

tention slip is made out against him, and he is required to remain after school for two or three hours. He may do his homework during this time but he may not leave his seat or talk."

The school itself did seek to teach the high-school subjects conscientiously, and classroom content was handled at a creditable level. Students, in fact, felt they were receiving competent instruction. But as Friedenberg observes, "What is formally taught is just not that important, compared to the constraint and petty humiliations to which the youngster with few exceptions must submit." At the school Friedenberg has described there is no physical freedom whatever. Except during class breaks, the lavatories are kept locked, so that a student must not only obtain a pass but find the custodian and induce him to open the facility. "Indeed Milgrim High's most important arrangements are its corridor passes and its johns; they dominate social interaction. 'Good morning, Mr. Smith,' an attractive girl will say pleasantly to one of her teachers in the corridor. 'Linda, do you have a pass to be in your locker after the bell rings?' is his greeting in reply."

But such a regimental routine is more than simply an effort on the part of high-school authorities to minimize "disorder." It is part of a more pervasive, if unplanned, effort to harness the young into the organizational features of the adult world. Erik Erikson, whose thinking has guided Friedenberg's inquiry, has written of the adolescent's need for a "psycho-social moratorium": a period of years relatively free from adult pressures and responsibilities in which young people may seek to find out "who and what they are." In a double sense, this time-period is being eroded in American culture. On the one hand, there is the elaborate structure of pseudo- and quasi-adult activities in which student participation is often made obligatory. On the other, there is the pressure to plan careers early, the worry about which college one will be able to enter, and the concern about rising up the skill-and-status ladder after graduation. Without being overly simple, it is evident that the "opting out" of the system by the "beats" in the mid-1950s, and the more social-minded protest of an intellectual stratum in the 1960s, are reactions to the "harnesses" imposed by an organized society, just as in the early nineteenth century the nascent industrial working class reacted similarly, with spontaneous wildcat strikes and machine-breaking, to the disciplines imposed by an industrial society,

The problem of the reform of the secondary schools is clearly more than a matter of upgrading a curriculum to match the advances of new knowledge and new modes of thought. It is a matter, much more difficult to achieve, of raising to consciousness the underlying values of a middle-class society in a people who do not want such a confrontation with their lives. But this is, within the compass of this book, necessarily an aside.

The innovations in secondary school curriculum reform, especially in the sciences, have received so much notice that little more than a summary of the major changes need be given here, in order to provide a context for the later discussion of college programs.[19]

The oldest reform is in mathematics, and it is now in its second decade. Its earliest beginnings were in 1951 at the University of Illinois, when the Committee on School Mathematics, as a result of the demands of the undergraduate college, sought to improve the freshman courses. The interest subsequently shifted to high-school mathematics and over a ten-year period materials for grades 9 through 12 were produced and tested. The Illinois program emphasizes "learning by discovery" with the student doing (rather than being told about) mathematics. Verbalization, in fact, is discouraged for fear that premature or incorrect generalization may simply be a hindrance. The program, organized sequentially,[20] covers four

---

[19] A lucid if somewhat uncritical discussion can be found in *The Schools,* by Martin Mayer (New York, Doubleday Anchor, 1963). An evaluation with critical comments and suggestions fot further changes is contained in the report, "School Curriculum Reform," by John I. Goodlad, for the Fund for the Advancement of Education (March 1964). Some valuable discussion of the problems arising from reform is in "Innovation and Experiment in Education," A Progress Report of the Panel on Educational Research and Development, of the President's Science Advisory Committee (March 1964). And a comprehensive account of the range of programs in science education can be found in the document "Science Education in the Schools of the United States," Report of the National Science Foundation to the Subcommittee on Science, Research, and Development of the House Committee on Science ami Astronautics, 89th Cong., 1st sess., 1965. I have profited, too, from conversations with Charles Silberman of *Fortune* magazine, who has prepared a comprehensive study on "Education and the New Role of Knowledge" for Time Inc.

[20] The program, organized in eleven units, is as follows: 1) the arithmetic of real numbers; 2) prenumerals, generalizations, and algebraic manipulations;

years, but though the materials are designed for all students, it is assumed that many students will drop mathematics after a year or two, so that the last two years are actually designed for those who are somewhat more interested in mathematics than is the ordinary student.

The best known and most widely used of all the "new" mathematics programs is that of the School Mathematics Study Group (SMSG), an effort which grew out of a two-day conference in February, 1958, sponsored by the American Mathematical Society, and which has been underwritten by the National Science Foundation at a cost of approximately $6 million for the first five years. Texts are now available for grades 4 through 12, while texts for kindergarten and the primary grades are in preparation. The SMSG approach is not experimental, and conventional topics form the bases for its courses. What is central, and represents a departure from the traditional "math" is the effort to concentrate on concepts and their relationships—the structure of mathematics—rather than rote learning or progressive school "problem" approaches.

The most radical experiment in the teaching of mathematics is the work of Patrick Suppes of Stanford University, a logician who is developing a mathematics program for kindergarten and the first three grades based on "set theory," and a program in mathematical logic for able fifth- and sixth-grade children. According to Suppes, "all mathematics can be developed from the concept of set and operations upon sets." He views sets—or simply the idea of groupings and relationships within groups—as appropriate for young children because sets are more concrete and facilitate mathematically precise definitions.

The effectiveness of these programs, as Professor Goodlad (whose descriptions I have followed) has noted, has not been fully tested. "This is due partly to the difficulty entailed in evaluating such goals, for example, as 'an intuitive grasp of fundamental principles,' partly

---

3) equations and inequations, applications; 4) ordered pairs and graphs; 5) relations and functions; 6) geometry; 7) mathematical induction; 8) sequences; 9) exponential and logarithmic functions; 10) circular functions and trigonometry; and 11) polynomial functions and complex numbers. Units 1 to 4 are intended for the first high-school year; units 5 and 6 for the second, units 7 and 8 for the third, and units 9 to 11 for the fourth year.

to the absence of criteria for competing programs." Yet whatever the doubts about particular approaches, there is little question that a vast and positive upheaval is under way. Whatever the differences among mathematicians about *what* to emphasize, they support the "new math" for its idea of teaching concepts (rather than rote drill), the creation of skills for arithmetic calculation and algebraic manipulation, the emphasis on the nature of the real number system and the nature of probability, and the sense students acquire of mathematics as a language—i.e., as a means of ordering relationships through symbols rather than simply a set of techniques.

In the summer of 1963, the Cambridge Conference on School Mathematics, convoked by Educational Services Incorporated (which has borne the brunt of organizing the new physics curriculum), laid down some guidelines for the ideal mathematics curriculum of the future. The conference proposed a curriculum in which, by the end of high school, students would have reached "a level of training comparable to three years of top-level college training today," i.e., they would have completed two years of calculus and one semester each of modern algebra and probability theory. The carrying out of such proposals admittedly lies far in the future since there are little more than a few hundred elementary and high-school teachers in the country who would be capable of teaching these subjects in the secondary schools today. Yet the group felt that the achievement might be reached within twenty years.[21]

---

[21] One significant fact pointed out by the conference is that, since the beginning of the century, there has been a three-year "speed-up" in the teaching of mathematics, i.e., in the range of materials covered in the secondary school curriculum, without any large-scale organized effort it change.

While the basic tone of these reports is optimistic, some voices have been raised in warning about the contents of the change, and about the pace of introduction. Alvin Weinberg, director of the Oak Ridge National Laboratory, writing in *Science* (August 6, 1965) has dubbed the new math a "puristic monster" representing the "spirit of the fragmented research-oriented university," useful only to a small minority of students. Howard Fehr of Columbia University's Teachers College has stated that "About 75 percent of all high-school students are studying the new mathematics, but only 25 to 35 percent of their teachers have been trained in the new mathematics." And Max Beberman of Illinois, who initiated the first experiments, has warned that the hasty introduction of the new programs was harming the teaching of mathematics to children. For a comprehensive survey of these criticisms, see the report, by Harry Schwartz, in the New York *Times*, January 25, 1965.

The most publicized curriculum reform, and the one with the greatest impact on the sciences, is in high-school physics, which began in 1957 under the leadership of Jerrold Zacharias of M.I.T. Interestingly enough, the Physical Science Study Committee, which worked out the new curriculum, began initially in revolt against the separation of chemistry and physics at the high-school level, and sought to work out a unified course for both subjects. But as the President's panel on Educational Research and Development wryly observed, "This revolt was short-lived; it proved impossible in 1956 to bring physicists and chemists under the same roof, and the PSSC proceeded to devote its efforts exclusively to physics."

The approach to the teaching of physics, as in mathematics, is primarily "heuristic," a term now associated with the work of the Hungarian mathematician George Polya of Stanford.[22] The emphasis is on reasoning and approaches to solutions, rather than on rules or on modes of computation. Much of the work is done in the laboratory, where the students are introduced to problems of discovery and verification of physical phenomena. The course was developed in part as a reaction against what the committee felt to be an excessive emphasis in high-school physics courses on the technological applications of the ideas of physics. Hence the emphasis was shifted "away from technology toward a deeper exploration of the basic ideas of physics and the nature of inquiries that can lead to these ideas." The course, in four parts, opens with fundamental concepts of time, space, and matter, leads to a detailed examination of light, proceeds to the discussion of motion, and ends with the exploration of electricity and the physics of the atom. Since the first year of operation in 1957-58, when eight teachers and 300 students used the course, approximately 4,000 teachers and 170,000 students, or between 40 to 45 percent of all secondary school students enrolled in physics classes in the United States, participated during 1963-1964.

The reorganization of the chemistry curriculum has come about later than that of physics, and though it lacks the unified impact of the Zacharias revisions, it has begun to reach more students. The

---

[22] The art of "Heuristics," or more simply the art of discovery, is exemplified in Professor Polya's delightful little book, *How to Solve It,* a Doubleday Anchor paperback.

Chemical Bond Approach Project, with headquarters at Earlham College in Indiana, grew out of an effort of a group of chemists in 1957 to write an introductory chemistry course, initially on the freshman college level, "based on conceptual schemes. . . since conceptual schemes play a major role in the organization of chemistry today," rather than presenting chemistry as "an encyclopedia collection of chemical reactions and laboratory techniques."

Using the theme of "chemical bonds," or the ties between atoms, as the central concept, the attempt is made to work out the structure of chemicals and to present these in geometrical terms. The idea of "models" is introduced by confronting the student with the idea—used also in electrical engineering theory and to some extent in general systems analysis—of the "black box." One can know what goes into the box and what comes out; but one does not know exactly what happens within the box. Thus, one can only infer a set of actions and logically construct a set of models to account for changes.

A broader if less radical effort has been initiated by the Chemical Education Materials Study, which was appointed by the American Chemical Society in 1960 to revise the chemistry course at the high-school level. Less ambitious than the Chemical Bond project (there is less emphasis on speculation and theorizing, and more attention in the laboratory to observation of experiments), the behavior of substances is explained principally according to the theory of atoms and energy exchanges, and the course then moves into problems of the structural relations in the various states of matter. By 1964, a final textbook and laboratory manual was being used by more than 100,000 students.

Perhaps the most massive effort to reorganize a high-school science has been made in biology, where, since 1959, more than 2,600 persons have contributed to the work of the Biological Sciences Curriculum Study (BSCS), headed by Bentley Glass—a twenty-seven-member steering committee selected from the American Institute of Biological Sciences and several teacher organizations. In its review of high-school biology the committee found that the biology being taught in the high schools in 1960 was from twenty to a hundred years behind the advances in the field, the reason being that such topics as

organic evolution, individual and racial differences, sex and reproduction in the human species, birth control, and similar topics had
often been taboo.

Unlike some of the other science programs, the BSCS assumed that
most of the students would have but a single course in biology,
and since the field itself is quite diverse, with significant differences
as to what might be considered important, the BSCS did not attempt
one comprehensive program but presented instead three different,
overlapping courses—the so-called Yellow, Green, and Blue versions,
plus a Teacher's Handbook edited by Joseph J. Schwab of the University of Chicago in which the differences among the three versions
are explored and the teachers themselves are introduced to the problems
of conceptual renovation.[23]

[23]The three texts axe published by different houses: *Biological Sciences: An
Inquiry into Life* (Yellow version; Harcourt Brace and World); *High School
Biology* (Green version; Rand McNally); *Biological Sciences: Molecules to
Man* (Blue version; Houghton, Mifflin). The *Teachers' Handbook* is published by
Wiley. Two laboratory books are *Animal Growth and Development* and *The
Complimentarity of Structure and Function,* both published by Heath.
The emphasis in the Blue version is on the molecule, in the Green version
on community and population from an ecological and biotic framework, and in the
Yellow version on a comprehensive course in the whole of biology.
As Professor Goodlad summarizes the contents: "Nine unifying concepts run
through each of the three versions of BSCS biology: changes of living things
through time (evolution); diversity of type and unity of pattern of living
things; genetic continuity of life; biological roots of behavior; complementarity of
organisms and environment; complementarity of structure and function; regulation
and homeostasis—the maintenance of life in the face of change; science as
inquiry; intellectual history of biological concepts. Approximately two-thirds of
the content is the same for all three programs...."
The Green version emphasizes the biological community, beginning with the
complexity and diversity of life and coming to cellular structure relatively late
in the course. Major topics are the following: the biosphere dissected; patterns in
the biosphere; the individual dissected; evolution, behavior, and man. The Yellow
version, emphasizing cellular biology at the outset, divides the subject matter into
seven sections: cells, microorganisms, plants, animals, genetics, evolution, and
ecology. The Blue version stresses physiological and biochemical evolutionary
processes with emphasis on the contributions that molecular biology has made
to the general understanding of the universe. Topics are: biology—the interaction
of facts and ideas; evolution of the cell; the evolving organism; multicellular
organisms—energy utilization; multicellular organism—the integrative systems;
higher levels of organization.
BSCS courses differ from traditional courses in that they place greater
emphasis on molecular and cellular biology, on the community and world biome,
and on the study of population. They stress investigation and principles, the
universal rather than the applied aspects of biology.

Table 4
Number of Students Using Curriculum Reform Materials

Group	1959-60	1960-61	1961-62	1964-65
School Mathematics Study Group	23,000	173,000	626,000	1,350,000
Physical Science Study Committee	22,500	44,000	75,000	200,000
Chemical Bond Approach Project	800	4,000	10,000	50,000
Chemical Education Material Study		1,200	11,500	210,000
Biological Sciences Curriculum Study		14,000	52,000	580,000

Source: National Science Foundation report, "Science Education in the Schools of the United States."

In the last five years, the innovations in the mathematics and science curricula have spread with amazing rapidity (See Table 4). Yet there have been criticisms principally because the innovations have helped only a minority of students. The Physical Science Study Committee course, for example, was aimed consciously at the college-bound student, and at the brighter half of that group. Martin Mayer reports Jerrold Zacharias as saying that the course is aimed only at the top third of the intelligence distribution, but Mayer concludes that "many teachers feel that only the top 10 percent have much chance of handling it successfully." A similar criticism has been voiced by a British biologist and inspector of English schools, J. K. Brierly, in an appreciative review of the biological materials (*Science,* February 14, 1964), who argued that the level of the texts are probably pitched too high for the fifteen- and sixteen-year-olds for whom the course is intended. ("Matters are made worse by the fact that the physics and chemistry courses usually follow the biology course. The *Teachers' Handbook* gives some excellent summaries on the physics and chemistry underlying biology, but it would require a very able teacher indeed to build these into the biology course which is full enough in itself.")

The validity of such criticism is questionable. Whether one could —or should—ever design a common course for all students in the high schools, given the varying capabilities and different intentions, is moot. A multi-track system, as has already developed in the colleges (see chapter 5), is probably more desirable. In fact, a new project has been established at Harvard, under the auspices of the National Science Foundation, to develop a physics course for less able students, including those who are not college bound. The emphasis here will be less on the verification (and mathematical reasoning) of physical theories than on the relationship of physics to other intellectual currents.

A more serious criticism, as Professor Goodlad has written, is that "the curricular reform movement so far has been focused on single subjects—planned, generally, from the top down," and it lacks an integrative focus. The President's panel on Educational Research and Development has been cognizant of this weakness and, in its "progress report" of Anarch, 1964, has signaled an intention of taking a unifying step. "The division of science, at the secondary school level, into biology, chemistry, and physics is both unreasonable and uneconomical," it declared. "Ideally, a 3-year course that covered all three disciplines would be far more suitable than a sequence of courses which pretends to treat them as distinct. Today, such a 3-year course would be difficult to fit into the educational system. . . . It is understandable that the groups which developed the existing programs, each of which faced great problems of its own as it worked towards its goals, were reluctant to embark on the larger task of giving coherence to the sum of their efforts. With the programs now complete or approaching completion, it may be that the time has arrived for this necessary next step."

Yet such an effort would require more than the reform of the curriculum; it would require the reorganization of the entire secondary school system itself. At present there are about 21,000 senior high schools in the United States, but only about 4,000, in James B. Conant's estimate, are large enough to provide adequately for a typical student body. One-third of all the high-school seniors, argues Conant, are attending high schools that are too small to provide, except at excessive cost, the range of offerings that should be available. It may well be, given the criticisms of Friedenberg and others, that secondary schools should not be made too large; but an adequate reorganization of the schools, providing for more buildings and more teachers, may require a cost far beyond what the United States, so far at least, has been willing to spend or even think about.

But even within the more limited purview of the present-day reforms, the existing structure of the schools, as Professor Goodlad points out in his Ford survey, tends to vitiate some of the curriculum changes. "There is an absence," he writes, "of experimental effort to fit together the various subjects or combinations of subjects into a reasonably unified curriculum. The schools are left largely alone to choose between the 'old' and the 'new,' to select from among several varieties of the new in some fields (mathematics, for example), to determine time allocations, to establish patterns of continuity from elementary to secondary schools, and so on. These problems are compounded for local schools by [a high rate] of student transiency and the fact that in many parts of the country, elementary and secondary school districts are separately organized and administered. Such problems are not likely to be resolved within existing patterns of the current curriculum reform movement."

This quick overview has dealt, so far, largely with mathematics and the sciences. There have also been reform movements in English, social studies (economics, anthropology, and sociology), and foreign languages, but with the exception of the last, either the reform movements are still in embryo or no real thought has been given to the problem.

The most deplorable situation is in English, both as to curriculum and to teacher preparation. A survey in 1963, by the National Council of Teachers of English, indicates that roughly *half* the high-school English teachers in the country felt that they were badly prepared to teach literature, while 67 percent felt ill-prepared to teach composition. In fact, about half of all high-school students in the country are being taught by teachers who did not major in English while in college; in many small high schools, where teachers are pressed to do many different subjects, the attitude seems to be that if a teacher can read she can teach English.[24]

The reading lists are equally ridiculous. "A tenth-grade student in a conservative system such as that in Louisville," reports Martin

---

[24] The situation is even worse among elementary school teachers. At least one-third of the 900,000 public school teachers of English have taken no formal course of any sort in the last decade; of those who have, they have taken four times as many courses in education as in English. In the colleges ten years ago, 29 percent of the English teachers had Ph.D. degrees; only 12.6 percent held the degree in 1963. The survey is included in the report *The National Interest and the Continuing Education of Teachers of English.*

Mayer in *The Schools,* "will he asked to handle *Silas Marner, A Tale of Two Cities, Julius Caesar,* and *Idylls of the King.* In Kansas City, the minimum will be *House of Seven Gables, Cimarron* by Edna Ferber, and *Spring Came on Forever* by Bess Streeter Aldrich, whose sweet romances, otherwise unknown to literature, have become a national high-school staple." In the reading program in English literature, "Everything before the nineteenth century has almost disappeared except Shakespeare and the excerpts in the anthologies; and most serious British twentieth-century literature is considered too subversive of 'values' to be tolerated." The American literature course, continues Mayer, "has had to rely more on twentieth-century novels, and the instincts of the school systems. . . are to concentrate on Aldrich, Edna Ferber, and Pearl Buck."[25]

That these are no isolated examples can be seen from the recent book by Lynch and Evans which examines the high-school English textbooks.[26] As Diana Trilling remarked in a review of the book, "Following Mr. Lynch and Mr. Evans in their patient tour through the anthologies and grammar or composition books on which virtually all high-school work in English is based, where is the reviewer to stop for *the* dramatic demonstration of our debasement?" For example, among the poets most frequently anthologized in ninth-grade readers, Ogden Nash makes twenty-two appearances against Walt Whitman's ten. In twelfth-grade readers (for high-school seniors), the most frequently anthologized author of short stories is O. Henry, followed fairly closely by Stephen Vincent Benet and Jesse Stuart.

[25] As an example of the kind of knowledge a high-school student is supposed to have and is tested for, Mayer cites the third-year state-wide Regents examination in New York, which is required of all pupils in the state. "[It] offers a literature section of forty short-answer questions, of which twenty are to be answered. Sampling down the list, there is a question about *Macbeth* ('In her sleep-walking scene, Lady Macbeth reveals her (1) distrust of Banquo, (2) suspicions of Macduff, (3) pride in her husband, (4) suffering for her crimes'), questions of similar difficulty about A. J. Cronin's *The Keys of the Kingdom,* about *A Man Called Peter, Captains Courageous, The Rivals,* 'The Outcasts of Poker Flat,' Sherlock Holmes, the second stanza of 'The Star-Spangled Banner,' a recent book by Kenneth Roberts, Poe's 'Fall of the House of Usher,' Browning's 'Last Duchess,' *Cress Delehanty,* an O. Henry story called *Reach for the Sky,* Paul Galileo's *The Small Miracle, Winnie-the-Pooh, Kon-Tiki, Treasure Island,* etc."

[26] James J. Lynch and Demand Evans, *High School English Textbooks: A Critical Examination* (Boston, Atlantic-Little Brown, 1964).

The two chief sources of the short stories used by anthologists are the *Saturday Evening Post* and the late *Collier's,* with such supplementary sources as *This Week, Woman's Day,* and *Catting All Girls.*

Admittedly this situation does not hold for the "best" high schools in the country; but these are a tiny minority comprising a few hundred in all of the more than 20,000 secondary schools in the nation. Some effort is now being made under the leadership of Harold C. Martin, formerly of Harvard, as head of the Commission on English, an independent agency of the College Entrance Examination Board. But as Francis Keppel warned, while he was the U.S. Commissioner of Education, the teaching of English is so poor as to threaten the nation's entire educational system.

The situation is not much better in the social studies. The fundamental shape of the present social studies curriculum was laid down in 1916, in a report issued by the National Educational Administration's Committee on Social Studies, in which it was urged that the curriculum should teach Good Citizenship. Most sequences still follow the line laid down at that time.

In most schools, the students in the academic program will take something called "world history" in the tenth grade, a year of American history in the eleventh grade, and the twelfth grade, often still labeled simply "Civics," is devoted to problems of democracy, though many schools allow alternative electives in economics, a potpourri of social studies, or even, in some cases, comparative studies (e.g., Oriental civilization). So far, only tentative and largely uncoordinated efforts have been made to tackle the problem.

A highly successful high-school geography project has been under way since 1961 in which some new courses and materials have been tested quite extensively. An anthropology curriculum study project, sponsored by the American Anthropological Association and supported financially by the National Science Foundation, has produced a book, *The Emergence of Civilization,* which was used experimentally in 1963-64 and was well received. Various groups are tinkering with an economics unit; one, supported by the Carnegie Corporation, is headed by Lawrence Senesch at Purdue. And Educational Services Inc., which grew out of Jerrold Zacharias' reform efforts in physics, has begun a wholesale effort, under the direction of Elting Morison, the historian from M.I.T., to develop a single curriculum which will comprehensively organize the social studies into a coherent unit. But all these are only beginnings.

In addition to curriculum reform, the two major innovations in the 1950s were the recruitment of more highly qualified teachers for secondary schools, and an "advanced placement program" for qualified students, both initiated by the Ford Fund for the Advancement of Education.

Of the $50 million spent by the Ford Fund in its first decade (1951-1961) about half went into programs for the recruitment and training of teachers. A substantial portion of the latter money went to so-called fifth-year programs, whereby college graduates would return to universities for concentrated work in a single discipline, in preparation for high-school teaching. These fifth-year programs were a reaction against the traditional emphases in teacher training upon "methods courses" and, in the language of the Fund, sought to substitute substantive study for professional courses in teacher training. The major project sponsored by the Fund during this period was the Harvard Master of Arts in Teaching program, established in 1952 by the Harvard School of Education in cooperation with twenty-nine northeastern colleges. The Harvard program combines specialized study, methods courses, and an internship program whereby students teach in local schools under the supervision of the master's program faculty. Since 1952, about three-quarters of the graduates of the Harvard School of Education have been in this master's program for high-school teachers. How much "upgrading" there has been in secondary school teaching across the country is difficult to evaluate. Certainly the large number of summer institute programs, especially in the sciences, and the various workshops have improved the competence of many teachers. Perhaps the most important consequence, however, of the Ford and other programs has been to increase the status of the secondary school teacher and to make him more aware of the crucial role he plays in the educational process.

It is the effort to accelerate the bright student, however, that has received the greatest attention in the past decade and a half; and here the results, one can only say, are mixed. In 1951, the Ford Fund sought to break the lock-step process whereby students moved *en bloc* from grade to grade into college. There was, said a Fund report, "the lack of sufficient flexibility to accommodate the vast differences in ability, interests, and maturity that prevail among young people of secondary school age." Consequently, the Fund sought to encourage two diverse schemes: an early admissions program, whereby qualified students would be admitted to colleges after their second or third year of high school, and an advanced placement program, whereby high-school students, in their senior years, would take special "college-level" courses, and, upon the successful completion of advanced placement examinations, would receive exemption from college courses and advanced standing in their college credits.

The early admissions program at first received the greated attention and publicity. In 1951 and 1952, for example, about 410 students who had completed only two years of secondary school were admitted to Columbia, Chicago, Wisconsin, and Yale on Fund scholarships for early admission. While an evaluation program conducted in 1957 concluded that these students did slightly better scholastically than a group of regular students, and showed no more psychological strain than the older students, the early admissions program has not caught on in the colleges. Whether it is the intangible fact that the fifteen- to seventeen-year-olds, who made up the early admissions group on the whole, felt out of place among their older classmates, or simply that such a program was too difficult to administer, the fact remains that the initial enthusiasm for this type of acceleration has largely diminished.

The Advanced Placement scheme, on the other hand, has shown a steady growth, but here, too, the fact is that the program has taken hold only in a small group of select secondary schools, largely in the New England and Middle Atlantic states, whose students have gone mainly to the Ivy League colleges. In 1962-63, for example, a total of 21,769 students took Advanced Placement examinations, or less than 2 percent of all the students then entering college. In that year, only fifteen high schools that had more than a hundred students taking Advanced Placement, while one-third of all the students in the nation taking Advanced Placement went to thirty-seven universities. The secondary schools having the largest number of Advanced Placement candidates in May, 1963, were:

Phillips Academy (Andover, Mass.)	246
Bronx High School of Science	233
Phillips Exeter (N.H.)	172
Regis High School (N.Y.C.)	165
Evanston Township (Illinois)	156
New Trier (Winnetka, Ill.)	155
Irondequoit (Rochester, N.Y.)	135
Mount Lebanon (Pittsburgh)	129
Hunter College High School (N.Y.C.)	126
Stuyvesant High School (N.Y.C.)	122
Lawrenceville School (NJ.)	120
Midwood High (Brooklyn)	117
John R. Buchtel (Akron)	116
Ann Arbor High (Michigan)	113
Taylor Allderdice (Pittsburgh)	107

The colleges with the largest number of Advanced Placement candidates were:

Harvard	635
Yale	496
Cornell	472
University of Michigan	397
Princeton	386
M.I.T.	327
Columbia	326
Stanford	306
University of Pennsylvania	290
City College of New York	284
Northwestern	248
Brooklyn College	228
Dartmouth	222
Wellesley	183
Smith	182

University of California (Berkeley)	180
Rochester	168
Brown	158
Rensselaer Polytechnic	158
Radcliffe	155
University of Illinois (Urbana)	154
Oberlin	152
Brandeis	138
Queens College (N.Y.)	136
Williams	125
New York University	125
Michigan State	125
Vassar	124
University of Utah	123
Pembroke	117
Syracuse	117
Duke	114
Fordham	110
University of Colorado	107
University of Chicago	106
Barnard	102

Although the Ford Fund began the Advanced Placement program in 1952, it was taken over in 1955 by the College Entrance Examination Board as an official activity of that organization. Standardized tests are now administered nationally, a procedure which allows for comparability in the performance of candidates. Tests are administered in thirteen subjects, but almost 60 percent of the examinations are taken in English, mathematics and American history. The following is a summary of the number of subjects and candidates taking examinations in the spring of 1963:

American history	4,952
Biology	1,634
Chemistry	2,500
English	8,579
European history	1,672

French	1,191
German (intermediate)	250
German (advanced)	78
Latin 4	438
Latin 5	240
Mathematics	5,853
Physics	713
Spanish	549

Except in physics, mathematics, and chemistry the ratio of boys to girls taking the examinations is about even.

The Advanced Placement program is costly. It requires special preparation by the teachers, a high teacher-student ratio in the classroom, extra books and materials, and the like. One of the reasons why the Advanced Placement program has taken hold more quickly in the northeast and Middle Atlantic region is that this area is one of the wealthiest in the country, and has both the largest number of specialized schools (such as Bronx Science, Stuyvesant, and Hunter College High) and the greatest number of serious college preparatory schools (Phillips, Philips Exeter, Lawrenceville) than any other section of the country; and these schools have taken greater advantage of the program than others. In the South and the Midwest, the strong tradition of localism and states' rights has worked against the introduction of the program, even when needed funds are available. The Mountain States schools have accepted the program in principle, but have neither the funds nor the trained teachers to introduce the program in any extensive way. The California system presents a special case, in that while it has the funds and the talents to introduce an advanced program, it resents the intrusion of national groups, and only one of its schools (University High School of Los Angeles) appears on the list of fifty schools having the largest number of candidates.

Most colleges accept performance on the standard Advanced Placement examination (a mark of 4 on a scale of 5 is usually required) as the basis for giving credit, though some colleges prefer to administer their own tests. Thus Chicago, for example, conducts its own placement examinations since, except for languages, few of its courses match the typical "AP" subjects, and it places students on the basis of these tests. Columbia will accept performance in Advanced Placement foreign language examinations as a sign of proficiency, but sets its own placement examinations for students seeking to take the "high speed" track in physics, chemistry, and mathematics.

In what ways can one evaluate the Advanced Placement program? Harvard, which has endorsed the program wholeheartedly, encourages entrants to seek advanced standing and has a full-time director to administer the program. In 1963, of 1,300 freshmen, about 50 percent (635) had taken one or more Advanced Placement examinations and 155 had sufficient Advanced Placement work to be offered sophomore standing directly from secondary school. Most of these, interestingly enough, were students who concentrated in mathematics, physics, and the natural sciences rather than other fields. The results, as an evaluation of a seven-year period disclosed, were impressive. Of those who had entered with some college-level work in high school, about half had earned degrees with high honors at graduation, and of those who went directly into sophomore standing, more than 80 percent graduated with honors.

Yet the Harvard program has its risks and costs. For one, those students admitted directly as sophomores are forced, usually, to choose a major immediately, yet experience with the class as a whole indicates that 50 percent of the freshmen change their majors after entering college. This means that students entering the college have to be quite certain of their major interest, or they risk losing a period of time if they change—a cost that might induce some of these students to continue with a major even though they might otherwise have wanted to change programs. More important for the curriculum of Harvard College, those students entering with sophomore standing, or with considerable advanced placement, usually are "forgiven" two of the three required general education courses, and only have to take one outside their concentration. Thus the general education program becomes one of the victims of the advanced standing program, for the students often plunge almost immediately into their specializations and miss out on the broad humanities and social science programs.

Performance on examinations can only give a "gross" sense of the Advanced Placement program. Impressionistic evidence suffers from subjectivity, yet it can, perhaps, give a person a better appreciation of the experience itself. In the spring of 1964 I asked student interviewers[27] to report on the Advanced Placement program in five schools in the New York metropolitan area. These were the Bronx High School of Science, Stuyvesant High School, the Great Neck (L.I.) North Senior High School, Regis, and Horace Mann. The first three are public schools, two of them in New York City, the other in a wealthy upper middle-class suburb; Regis is a parochial school, run by the Jesuit Fathers, whose six hundred students, drawn from all classes, are all on scholarship; Horace Mann is a well-established, expensive private school with an excellent faculty and extensive plant. Three of the schools—Bronx Science, Stuyvesant, and Regis—pick students entirely on the basis of competitive examination. Regis, for example, selects 150 freshmen from all parts of the New York metropolitan area from over 5,000 applicants. Bronx Science admits less than 900 students a year from an equal number taking the entrance examination. (While no public data is available, it is understood that the average I.Q. of the Bronx Science student is above 135.) Great Neck North and Horace Mann have no similar selective entrance requirement. But Great Neck North serves a community that is largely upper middle class and predominantly Jewish, a group highly concerned with academic preparation, and about 90 percent of its graduating seniors go on to college. Horace Mann is exclusively college preparatory, highly receptive to innovation, and one of the leaders in private school education in the country.

Clearly, it would be difficult to find a less representative sample of the typical American high school than the five chosen here. But it is these schools, with the interests, resources, and selected student bodies, that lead the way in experimental programs and techniques in the secondary schools. And it is such schools which provide the

---

[27] Student interviewers, I felt, would make the high-school student less conscious of being under observation, and, equally important, these observers could compare the advanced placement work more directly with their own high-school work, and with their experiences in Columbia College, particularly with the Humanities and the Contemporary Civilization courses, the special concern of this study.

"talented tenth" of the nation's student body, and which are the main resource for the Ivy League colleges. Thus the selection has relevance for our problem.

At Bronx Science, of the 885 seniors, 226—or little more than one-fourth of the graduating class—were enrolled in advanced placement courses. (Of these, 132 were taking one course, 78 were taking two, and 16 were taking three, a total of 226 students taking 336 courses.) The administration had no plan to expand the program, believing that all those who could possibly benefit were already included, and that further expansion would distort the school program entirely. The organization of the program and the selection of students are entirely in the hands of the administration. Students cannot choose advanced placement courses as electives, but must apply; and selections are made on the basis of past records, recommendations by teachers in the department, and the score in the PSAT examination (junior year aptitude examination).

A Columbia student observer, Richard A. Epstein, reported on an English class at Bronx Science. "There is only one English class at Bronx Science, a fact which may reflect the predominant scientific orientation of the student body. Yet there had been ninety applicants, of whom twenty-five had been chosen. The class discussion, which I listened to over two periods, was devoted to Flaubert's *Madame Bovary.* There were a number of oral reports on various chapters by several students, each of which was followed by a discussion led by the teacher, who was excellent in stimulating the students to think about the questions that had been raised. Despite the high-school method of instruction, the level of classroom discussion compared favorably with discussions that I have heard at Columbia. Students spoke of the difference between the subjective world of the characters and the objective world of the author; they were concerned to differentiate between 'illusion' and 'reality'; they traced themes throughout the book, page by page; and they analyzed selected passages aloud in order to demonstrate Flaubert's style and method. And they did it all with a good deal of sympathy and understanding.

"The mathematics, chemistry, and physics classes comprised the bulk of advanced placement courses at Bronx Science. Again the teaching methods are those typically found in high school. There is little use of formal lectures. The class analyzes together homework problems which students recite on, or put on the blackboard. But the pace is rapid and the class is energetic. The mathematics classes use a standard introductory text, and they cover it at least as thoroughly as most freshmen calculus courses." The physics and chemistry courses, according to student evaluators, were first-rate, and one estimated that "these students knew as much physics and chemistry at the end of one year as I did after three terms of standard college physics and two terms of accelerated college chemistry. Only self-esteem prevents me from saying that they know more as high-school seniors than I did as a college sophomore."

While both Bronx Science and Stuyvesant (where the same generalizations would apply) are oriented towards the sciences, Regis places heavy emphasis on the humanities. It does not offer advanced science courses of the caliber of the two specialized New York public high schools. About forty seniors take a second year of chemistry, but less than half of these seemed to have sufficient confidence to take the Advanced Placement chemistry examination. So far as the school is concerned, the student decides for himself whether to take the examination, a policy different from that of the public schools, which require alt students who register for the advanced placement courses to take the examinations. In mathematics, there is no regular calculus course, though some students were meeting with a mathematics instructor after hours to prepare for the calculus examination.

It is in English and history that Regis prepares its students so impressively. In 1964, about a hundred of the 150 sophomores in the school took the Advanced Placement examination in American history after only one year of study (as against three and even four semesters for the average high school), and this group had a better than average performance. Perhaps the most interesting course, from the standpoint of this study, is the world history course. The standard high school advanced placement syllabus is similar to a competent college course in world history, such as the "World History from

1450" at Barnard. But the emphasis at Regis is on readings, from Aristotle, Bodin, Hobbes, Locke, Rousseau, Montesquieu, and similar authors, and the course, both in scope and intent, followed closely the first-year Contemporary Civilization course at Columbia. What is striking—and it is a point we shall return to shortly—is that of all the "college-level" courses at these five schools, only one, at Regis, anticipated the readings contained in the Columbia Contemporary Civilization and Humanities courses.

At Horace Mann, the advanced placement classes in mathematics, world history, and English were all on a high level. The world history course did not have the philosophical and critical orientation of the one at Regis, but was a high-grade, straight history course relying on texts and such supplementary readings as Isaiah Berlin's *Karl Marx* and Crane Brinton's *The Anatomy of Revolution.* The most interesting experimental feature at Horace Mann was a Colloquium in English, open only to selected students, which discussed *Portrait of a Lady, Portrait of the Artist as a Young Man, Ghosts, Oedipus Rex, Pride and Prejudice,* etc. This featured seminar discussions, individual tutorials, and a separate library for the Colloquium students.

Advanced placement courses at Great Neck North in English, chemistry, mathematics, and French were on a level comparable to that of Bronx Science and Stuyvesant. But the numbers who participate tell a revealing story, especially for those concerned with the extent and impact of the advanced instruction in high schools on college curricula. Great Neck North is not a specialized school such as Bronx Science or Stuyvesant, or a self-conscious school for training an intellectual elite such as Regis, or an intensive college preparatory school such as Horace Mann, but a suburban school in a wealthy upper middle-class community, and thus typical in many ways of similar suburban schools in Chicago, Los Angeles, and other great metropolitan centers whose graduates go on to the "good" colleges. Yet of a total of 440 seniors only 15 were enrolled in the Advanced Placement program in English, about 15 were taking mathematics (half of these were also in the English program), and about the same number in chemistry. In all, it would be fair to assume that somewhat less than 10 percent of the seniors in one of the best public high schools in the country participated in the Advanced Placement program.[28]

In the light of all this, let us revert to one of the questions which prompted this inquiry: Do the general education courses at Columbia College have to be reorganized because of the advances in curriculum and preparation in the secondary schools? The answer would seem to be, at this point and for the near future, no. Whatever the progress that has been made in the revision of mathematics and the sciences, and the general improvement in foreign language instruction, there seems to be little evidence that any substantial changes have been made in the social studies and humanities areas to force a reconsideration on these grounds in the Humanities and Contemporary Civilization courses. (That these courses should be modified for other reasons is a different question, discussed in chapters 4 and 5.)

A review of the experiences of Columbia College with the Advanced Placement program, as well as several studies conducted by the College of the experiences of Columbia students in the Humanities and Contemporary Civilization courses, tends to substantiate this judgment.

In recent years, the number of entering freshmen in Columbia College taking one or more Advanced Placement exams has risen from 30 percent in 1961 to 43 percent in 1964. (The experience of the secondary schools, as well as the history of the program in other colleges, indicates that the percentage will probably level off, in the near future, at about 50 percent.) Not all students score sufficiently high, of course, to gain credit (one must score a 4 or a 5) and about one-fourth of the entering freshmen receive some amount of credit for advanced standing.

But a breakdown of the examinations taken indicates a somewhat

[28] Great Neck North, like many of the high schools of its class, offers "enriched courses" which are not run under the auspices of the Advanced Placement program. The senior year social studies course, for example, is devoted to the "great issues." This special course is open to any student, and, in consequence, the quality of work is variable. The instructor is left to his own devices with regard to curriculum, presumably because the "great issues" change from year to year. As one Columbia observer reported: "As a former student at Great Neck, I know this program has yielded fruit that varies from teacher to teacher and from year to year. Some of the results are fine; others are best passed over in silence. It is of little significance so far as the reevaluation of general education is concerned."

more skewed picture. The largest single bloc of students, 149 in 1963, took the English placement examination, but only 18 of these (most highly qualified secondary school students) scored 4 or better.[29] By contrast, 46 of the 145 students taking the mathematics examination scored 4 or better, as did 13 of the 34 taking physics, and, the best single performance, 44 of 83 students in American history.

In only a very few cases does performance on the Advanced Placement examination exempt a student from the Contemporary Civilization or Humanities courses; what happens is that such a student is exempted from a sophomore course in his specialty (e.g., History 9-10 in the case of American history) or is put into the "advanced introductory," or "high-speed" track in mathematics and the sciences. Nor does much of the work in the advanced placement courses directly prepare a student for the Columbia general education courses. The English advanced placement syllabus is primarily on recent literature (I make the distinction, necessarily so, between "recent" and "modern"), while the Humanities readings are predominantly the classic writings of Western civilization. While the emphasis in the advanced placement English is on literary analysis and methods of literary criticism (largely textual and thematic, rather than discussions of genre), there is little effort to deal with philosophical or moral contexts. The advanced placement courses in world history give a student some better preparation for the background readings in Contemporary Civilization, but they do not equip him to deal with primary sources and documents.

All of this is reinforced by two studies of the experiences of Columbia College students in the Humanities and Contemporary Civilization courses in 1963 and 1964.[30] Thus, all the students in the Hu-

[29] At Columbia College, a student does not automatically win credit on the basis of the advanced placement score. In each instance, a student's paper is given to the appropriate department for review, and the department is not necessarily guided by the score on the test. In some instances, a student has been given credit for English who may have received only a 2 on the examination, and credit has been refused to some who have scored 4 or better. But for gross comparisons, the performances indicated above will serve.

[30] In April, 1963, and April, 1964, questionnaires were distributed to all students in the Humanities and Contemporary Civilization classes asking the students about their preparation for the courses, A total of 664 students answered the questionnaires in 1963 and 642 in 1964, The differences in responses in the two questionnaires were almost nil. (Thus 11.8 percent in 1963 and 11.7

manities course were asked: "Of the works assigned, approximately how many had you read before entering Columbia?" Less than 1 percent had read "all of them," 4 percent had read "most of them," 11.7 percent had read "about half," 68.5 percent had read "a few," and 14.3 percent had read "none of them." To the check question, "To what extent do the readings and class work in Humanities A duplicate work done in high school," half the students reported less than a 5 percent overlap with high-school work. Only twenty-three students (of the 642) had covered more than half the work in secondary school.

The background of the student—i.e., whether he came from a private prepatory or a public school—did account for some significant differences in the character of prior reading. Thus of the 160 prep-school graduates, 45 reported they had read half or more of the Humanities readings, as against only 53 of the 429 high-school graduates. Yet this difference was not reflected significantly in the grades of the students, nor in their enthusiasm for the course. Of those who had read the books prior to college, about half thought the rereading very valuable, and more than an additional fourth felt it was fairly valuable.

A similar distribution was found in the responses to the Contemporary Civilization questionnaire. Less than 17 percent of the students had taken courses in secondary school similar in content to the Contemporary Civilization course, although when the figures are broken down by type of school, the percentages do change somewhat: i.e., 28 percent of those from private prep schools, 13.6 from public high schools, and 5 percent from parochial high schools had taken courses with material similar to Contemporary Civilization.

To the question: "How well do you feel your secondary school prepared you for the kind of class discussion that takes place in Contemporary Civilization," a total of 22.5 percent answered, "very

percent in 1964, for example, said they had read about half the books in the Humanities course before coming to Columbia.) In all citations, therefore, the results reported are of 1964, and the N, against which percentages were computed, was 642. Thanks are due to Professor Terence K. Hopkins of the sociology department for the preparation and tabulation of the questionnaire. The Humanities questionnaire was done under the supervision of Professor Robert J. Belknap; that of the Contemporary Civilization by Professor Robert K. Webb.

well," and 26.2 percent answered, "fairly well." Again the type of school revealed significant differences: 45.9 percent of those from private prep schools (of a total of 135) answered, "very well," as against 16.9 percent of the public high-school students (of a total of 462) and 12.5 percent of the parochial students (of a total of 40) about the kind of preparation in their secondary schools. Slightly more than 25 percent of the public high-school students, 22.5 percent of the parochial high-school students, and almost 30 percent of the private prep students felt that their secondary schools had prepared them "fairly well" for the work in the course.

Students were asked which of the major books read in the Contemporary Civilization course had been read in whole or in part or not at all before coming to Columbia.[31] Between 20 and 25 percent had read Machiavelli's *The Prince,* Marx and Engels' *The Communist Manifesto,* and a work of Voltaire. But except for Plato's *Republic* (read by about 9 percent), none of the other authors' works cited had been read entirely by more than 5 percent of the students. Five books each had been read "in part" by about a fourth of the students, another three books by slightly more than 10 percent. On a "reading index," about 22 percent of the students had read none of the sixteen books, 40 percent more had read between one and four books, while at the other end of the scale, only 2 percent had read all sixteen, and 5 percent between twelve and fifteen books. (Again the breakdown of the reading index by type of school revealed significant differences; only 7.4 percent from the private prep schools had read none of the books, as against 26.6 percent from the public high schools and 20 percent from the parochial schools; at the other end of the scale, more than 16 percent from the private prep schools had read twelve or more books, as against little more than 5 percent from the public high schools, and none from the parochial schools.)

While there is some evidence, thus, that students from private prep schools are better prepared and have read more of the works used in the Humanities and Contemporary Civilization courses than those

---

[31] Sixteen books were listed, beginning with Plato's *Republic* and ending with the *Communist Manifesto.* The other authors included Aristotle, Augustine, Aquinas, Luther, Machiavelli, Calvin, Descartes, Hobbes, Locke, Rousseau, Voltaire, Adam Smith, Edmund Burke, and John Stuart Mill.

from public schools—and the proportion of Columbia students from private prep (not including private parochial) schools, though rising in recent years, is about 30 percent of the entering classes—the amount of work taken in secondary schools does not preempt to any significant degree the work offered by Columbia College in the freshman year. These experiences, to repeat, offer few grounds for changing the Humanities and Contemporary Civilization courses.

A Critique of the Secondary School Reforms

The reform in curriculum and the Advanced Placement program clearly are transforming the secondary school. The biggest change has been to substitute a principle of "ability grouping" for the lock-step process in which the entering class went through a common program *en bloc.* This move has also accentuated the tendency to break up the "comprehensive" school and to sharpen the differences between the specialized and elite schools, public and private (probably no more than 500 in the country), from the large number of ordinary schools. But even this development provides little reason to assume, so far at least, tbat such changes signify an erosion of the liberal arts college and a swing to the kind of educational system of France, Germany, and the Soviet Union, where students move directly from advanced secondary schools to specialized university work. Apart from the sociological fact that established institutions, no matter how desiccated, take a long, long time to change, there are two (if not more) significant intellectual reasons why the liberal arts college will continue to play a crucial role within the American educational system.

One is the fact that there is a significant "limit" to the kind of curriculum change possible in the secondary schools: what is possible in math or the sciences does not necessarily carry over into the humanities and the social sciences. To put it more formally, the structure of knowledge, or at least the structure of the acquisition of knowledge, in the physical sciences is vastly different from those in the humanities and the social sciences. It is not, as some observers have claimed, that physics is a "hard" science and sociology a "soft" science. There have been many instances where "received truths" in the natural

sciences have been surprisingly overturned and a field left in an intellectually chaotic state. Nor is it necessarily, as one writer put it, that
mathematics and the scientists follow an inductive or heuristic approach,
and the social sciences do not. Many sciences are almost entirely
hypothetically deductive, and work from axiomatic principles, while
some social sciences operate with a raw empiricism that might startle even
Francis Bacon. For pedagogical purposes, at least, the difference between
mathematics and the sciences, on the one hand, and the social sciences
and humanities, on the other, is that mathematics and the sciences pose
intellectual puzzles, the "solutions" of which are objective and do not
depend upon personal experience, while the understanding of human
predicaments is, in large measure, a function of experience.

There is, it seems to me, a different kind of imagination at work
in the intuiting of problems in physics and mathematics, than in the
understanding of the *Oresteia* or in reading Plato's *Symposium.* This is
not to suggest that a high-school student may not be able to understand
something about these latter works; but the *kind* of understanding is one
that necessarily will go through successive changes as the individual
gains a firsthand sense of different kinds of experience in life.[32] This may
be one of the reasons a person may be a great mathematician by the age
of twenty, but it takes an additional twenty years for an individual
to become a great literary critic.

The mistake which seems to be in the making in the renovation of
the secondary school curriculum, one which repeats in its way the
error that the proponents of general education made in the 1940s
and 1950s, is to assume that the same kind of changes, and the same
educational theory, work "across the board" in all subjects. What

---

[32] Perhaps one *of* the traditional folk-tales about Talmudic education may sharpen
this point. Usually, a youth will begin the study of Talmud at age ten or eleven,
poring over these books to learn the methods of exegesis and hermeneutics. The
Talmud itself is simply a set of "law books," the codification of the first Five
Books of Moses (the Pentateuch) by logical categories (ritual practices, commercial
practices, and the like) plus the rabbinical commentaries over the texts and decisions
arising out of the conflicts in interpretation. In Talmudic analysis there is always
kadarka, the rightful way, and *lo-kadarka,* the unnatural way. The familiar story
is told of a group of Talmudic *chochem* (wise-guys) of age ten or so who, on
reading the section on sexual practices, ask the teacher, "Rabbi, and what is *lo-
kadarka* here?" And the rabbi, answering with a smack, asks, "And *Kadarka* you
know already?"

I shall argue—and the point is elaborated considerably in the next two chapters—is that because there are different principles which govern the acquisition of knowledge in the sciences, social sciences, and humanities, the building of curriculum necessarily must take into account these differences.

To state the matter most baldly: the acquisition of knowledge in mathematics and the sciences is largely *sequential,* in which one can build subject matter on subject matter in linear fashion, so that students can take *measurable* steps at their own pace in these fields. Knowledge—or rather "understanding"—in the humanities is, to continue my visual metaphors, largely *concentric,* in which a few major themes—the nature of tragedy, the different kinds of love, the discovery of self—are returned to again and again, in and through many different doors, as one's comprehension enlarges through experience.[33] In the social sciences, the pattern of knowledge is one primarily of *linkages,* in which the understanding of one kind of phenomenon cannot be self-contained but is possible only by an understanding of linked contexts: thus, an understanding of the operations of a "command economy" is dependent on an understanding of the nature of a mobilized or directed political order, just as knowing the operations of a "market" economy is dependent on the knowledge of a particular kind of legal order and the nature of the institution of contract.

If these arguments are correct, then it seems to me that one can quite successfully "accelerate" and extend back into the secondary schools the teaching of the more factual, exact, and "abstract" subjects such as foreign languages, the physical sciences, and mathematics, taking over, as has been true in the past, many "college-level" subjects into the high-school years. But the same approach is not so possible for the discursive and inexact subjects. The effort which

[33]To tell another talmudic story: a disciple asks a famous rabbi; "How does one become wise?" The rabbi, surprised, says simply, "One studies and works hard." "But," remonstrates the disciple, "many people study and work hard and are not wise." "Then," says the rabbi, "I suppose one studies, works hard, and has experience." But the dismayed disciple again points out that many persons have studied, worked hard, and have experience, and still are not wise. "But then one needs good judgment," replies the rabbi. "But how does one get good judgment?" asks the disciple in despair. "By having *bad* experience," retorts the rabbi.

is now under way in some of the more fashionable preparatory schools, for example, to teach college-type "humanities" programs can only end in a modishness that will quickly wear out, and that, during its tenure, might succeed only in "taking the edge off," diminishing the shock of recognition for works which should be confronted primarily in later years.

There is, I believe, an "orderly" division of labor between secondary schools and colleges in which different concentrations and different kinds of preparations are allocated. And if this argument is accepted, then it also follows that the reorganization of a college curriculum should be attempted with these divisions in mind; and the specification of courses and the identification of necessary "tools and techniques" must derive from the underlying principle in each field.

The second reason why the liberal arts college still retains a vital function has less to do with curriculum than with the nature of the adolescent "beast." The "hidden and instinctive wisdom" of the American college, as the late, wise William De Vane, former dean of Yale College, put it, has been the "unforced intellectual maturing" that was allowed the American student.[34] The college years have been for the student the time to try himself and his mind, to test his many ambitions and to confront the many competing intellectual ideas. The current "erosion" of the American college, in fact, does not derive from any meaningful development of curriculum or changed institutional structure, but from the pressure on the student to choose a career early, to define a vocational intention, to specify a major, to narrow his interests, and to accelerate through school.

---

[34] De Vane writes: "After the close of World War II, France obviously underwent an 'agonizing reappraisal' of many of its social institutions, among them its educational system. I was visited by it least two delegations from France enquiring into the nature and procedure of the American college. It was evident that these delegations felt that the American college provided something that the French system lacked, and badly needed. I agree, and suggested that the unforced intellectual maturing that was allowed the American student had its practical advantages in matters of initiative and decision, that our team sports and our cooperative activities (which in their imbalance we so decry) might possess a hidden and instinctive wisdom. It should be added that the French system of education has not changed." William C. De Vane, "The College of Liberal Arts," *Daedalus* (Fall 1964).

Clearly not all acceleration is bad. The new emphasis on "ability grouping," the freedom of students to set their own pace in schools, the creation (as will be discussed later) of "multiple tracks" in subjects, in which the content of introductory courses in physics, chemistry, mathematics, et al., is adapted to the different needs and interests of different kinds of students are all necessary ways of expanding the period of "unforced intellectual maturing." But the hue and cry to foreshorten the college years, to speed a boy into sophomore standing and spin him into graduate school in the senior year—these are not only destructive of the college; they are, more sadly, destructive of the student himself.

This quick sketch of the social canvas and the intellectual land-scape was intended to illustrate the context of change within which the American college is seeking to redefine itself. The problem of *the* American college—if such animal there be—lies far outside the scope of this inquiry. But these changes do pose direct problems for the colleges which have pioneered in the idea of general education—Columbia, Chicago, and Harvard—and all three have, in varying degrees, been calling their programs into question, I have sought to describe these responses in chapter 5. But my task—and my interest—are more than description. If the intellectual arguments I have sketched in the preceding pages are valid, then they call for the reorganization of general education itself. What I have tried to do, therefore, in the next chapter, is to state my presuppositions (or prejudices), and in chapter 5 to make some proposals for some new sequences at Columbia College itself.

Chapter Four

THE NEED FOR REFORM:
SOME PHILOSOPHICAL
PRESUPPOSITIONS

Among the paradoxes with which St, Paul describes the character, the vicissitudes and the faith of the Christian ministry, the phrase "as deceivers yet true" is particularly intriguing. Following immediately after the phrase "by evil report and good report" it probably defines the evil reports which were circulated about him as charges of deception and dishonesty. This charge is refuted with his "yet true." But the question arises why the charge is admitted before it is refuted. Perhaps this is done merely for the sake of preserving an unbroken line of paradoxical statements. If this be the case, a mere cation of rhetorical style has prompted a very profound statement. For what is true in the Christian religion can be expressed only in symbols which contain a certain degree of provisional and superficial deception. Every apologist of the Christian faith might well, therefore, make the Pauline phrase his own. We do teach the truth by deception. We are deceivers, yet true.

Reinhold Niebuhr, BEYOND TRAGEDY

A statement of presuppositions is the declaration of a point of view. Since this book is neither wholly descriptive nor wholly prescriptive, it is only fair that I make explicit the compound of prejudices, opinions, and values that have guided this inquiry. In sketching these presuppositions, I do not seek to present an ordered philosophy or to explore the "ultimate grounds" of belief about the nature of man and society; this is not an exercise in dogmatics—theological or pedagogical. At best, these presuppositions may serve two purposes: since I seek, in the following pages, to describe the design of social change, present and future, which affects educational practice and philosophy, these presuppositions may serve to indicate the "value relevance" that leads me to select one, rather than another, set of changes as the most significant for the reconstruction of liberal education; and since, in the following chapter, I will make prescriptions for the curriculum, these presuppositions might be regarded as the working principles that underlie my recommendations. To that extent, this section is more than a warning about prejudices and pieties; it is meant to be a guide to the perplexed, to make intelligible the heart of the inquiry itself.

There is not, I believe, in education—and perhaps not in life—a quota of eternal verities, a set of invariant truths, a single quadrivium and trivium that must be taught to a young man lest he be charged with the failure to be civilized or humane. There are tasks—tasks appropriate to the elucidation of tradition, the identification of societal values (which can be rejected as well as accepted), and the testing of knowledge—which have to be met by a college. One hundred years ago, the curriculum of Columbia College was within the genteel tradition, to educate a small elite. Sixty years later, general education was introduced at Columbia in response to the altered social character of the student body, and to a need for answers to questions about the goals of society that had been provoked by the war. In a similar fashion, the influential Harvard Redbook twenty years ago confronted the problem of maintaining high standards of excellence in the face of egalitarian demands for mass education, and bridging the two by a common language. Some of these recent tasks remain; newer ones have emerged.

But one has to locate the arenas of change if one seeks to determine what is in need of change. Society, the system of social arrangements to meet needs and solve tasks, is today changing rapidly, especially as technology, the instrument of change, becomes more amenable to definition and direction. Culture—the deposit of experience, the realm of judgment, and the arbiter of standards—changes more slowly, for in the domain of mind many truths and values coexist and there are

no simple tests, such as functional rationality in economics, to determine the better mode. Human nature, that stubborn compound of
passion and intelligence, unlimited appetite, and parochial upbringing, changes more slowly still. The educational process has to take
all these dimensions into account in shaping the balance of experience
and imagination that becomes for the individual a working principle
in ordering his life.

Each generation—such is the nature of modernity—seeks to discover
its own entelechy and, in so doing, to renew history as the present and
to reshape the past, to assimilate the received ideas and to choose those
relevant to its concerns. In this regard, the university with respect to its
traditional function is in an anomalous position: it is called upon not
only to conserve the past and reinterpret the present, but also to test the
new. In fact, the confrontation of the "new"—the new not of sociology
or the sciences, for these are part of a continuing tradition, but the new
of sensibility and of that which calls itself post-modern—is the most
perplexing challenge to the university today. It is first and foremost the
problem of the humanities, since these are the bearers of tradition.

Whatever else may be said in criticism of American colleges (at
lease of the best of them), they cannot, as Lionel Trilling has pointed
out, be called "indifferent to the modern." In fact, the tide—the literature
of Yeats, Eliot, Lawrence, Joyce, Proust, and Kafka, and of such
forebears as Rimbaud, Baudelaire, and Dostoevski—runs so strong
as to swamp us all. This is a literature whose force, as Trilling puts it,
"may be said to derive from its preoccupation with spiritual salvation.
It is a literature which has taken to itself the dark power which certain
aspects of religion once exercised over the human mind."[1]

This facet of modernity, emphasizing will and passion, subverts
established order not because it reshapes experience (as any positive
inquiry must), but because it taps an energy, demonic at its source,
that overflows the containing vessels of art and because it insists on

---

[1] Lionel Trilling, "Commitment to the Modern," a commencement address at
Harvard University, July, 1962, reprinted in the *Harvard Alumni Bulletin* (July 7,
1962), pp. 739-42.

its own subjective experience and desire as the standard not only of esthetic but of moral truth as well.

Its successors, calling themselves "post-modern" or "post-Christian," have lost even the concern with salvation itself. In the first novel of Camus and the "anti-novels" of Butor and Robbe-Grillet, we perceive an anaesthesia of feeling; and in the writings of Burroughs and Genet we have crossed the borders of hallucination and degradation. There is a rejection of the moral order because it is not rational and just but cruel and insensate. The result is either nihilism or gnosticism—forms of private knowledge and belief which in their moral radicalism are subversive of society itself.

Latter-day nihilism, the post-modern, remains moral and post-Christian, however, in that it is a search for an ultimate, even a theological ultimate, although it has no hope of a savior or any possibility of redemption or salvation. There is the sense of despair without the possibility of any grace. One lives then, at the extreme, in the continuing search for sensation and experience and novelty, since there is no seeming meaning beyond these. The radical "I"—an "I" far beyond the "ego and its own" (in Max Stirner's phrase) envisaged by nineteenth-century romanticists—lives with a sense of unlimited desire but is constantly trapped by the recalcitrances of society, and thus seeks to destroy it.

This new phase of modern culture may at first seem remote, a nerve of experience that touches only a few. Yet art has an imaginative power that transforms private chimeras into public realities. For art, as Ortega y Gasset has pointed out, is the freest activity of the human imagination, of human actions the least dependent on social constraints and conditions, and for this reason, the first signs of changes in collective sensibility become noticeable in art. It is, one can say (in the phrase of De Quincey) the realm of proleptic wisdom. Just as the agonized fantasies of a Rimbaud a hundred years ago prefigured the cruder cult of adolescence today, so the writhings of a Burroughs, or the anti-art of some modernist cults, may foreshadow the vulgate language and destructive impulses of thousands more tomorrow.[2]

---

[2] A number of these themes are expanded in my essay "The Disjunction of Culture and Social Structure: Some Notes on the Meaning of Social Reality," *Daedalus* (Winter 1965).

The anamoly of all this is that the thrust of modernity—what Professor Trilling has called the "adversary culture"—has itself become an established force, nowhere more than in the university, while retaining its adversary stance.[3] The intention of modernity, in opposing middle-class culture, was to permit a radical detachment (the cant word today is "alienation") of the individual from the conventions of the time and from the very idea of convention itself. It was to establish the autonomy, if not the authority, of "the ego and its own." But the "I," as Professor Trilling remarks, has become an "us." And the new class which maintains this "adversary stance" has developed the power to overturn old canons and to establish new categories of its own. In such a state of affairs, the creative tension between modernity and tradition goes slack, autonomy becomes a collective, and modernity itself becomes a convention. The most radical and new meets with little opposition, even when it is most destructive of tradition, for novelty and the new have become the tradition itself. And for those emerging out of this tradition, who rail against this situation because of their need to go "beyond" the modern and the new, the artistic effort is concentrated no longer in subverting the moral and social order but, beginning in underground fashion, becomes an assault against the final taboos of cultural and psychic life itself.

Can we, as Professor Trilling suggests, "complicate, not retract" this commitment to the modern? Or is it all too late? In Trilling's view, if radical subjectivity is to be maintained in all its potentiality of creativeness, it must be met with a countervailing force. "It must be confronted with the mind that insists that the world is intractable as well as malleable. And such a countervailing force must, I believe, be specifically offered to the radical subjectivity of our students, else they will never develop their powers of intellectual mastery; they will fall into inertness and the weariest of all conventionalities, the conventionality of an outworn radical mode," It is the rational intellect today, says Trilling, not sensibility, which works in the interests of experience.

The realm of sensibility has enormous power because it engages

[3] See Lionel Trilling, *Beyond Culture* (New York, Viking, 1965), pp. ix-xviii.

the taproots of emotions; the discipline of mind has its appeal in the order it imposes on feeling. But the issue is not fully joined by counterposing mind to sensibility in the hope that in the ensuing dialectic the process of *aufheben* (in the Hegelian sense of interpenetration) will raise the moral consciousness to a higher level. For both modern mind and modern sensibility unfold not only in contradiction to each other but in complicated response to a social structure which encompasses both. The interplay of consciousness and society is, after all, one of the major themes of the great masters of modern social science—of Marx, Weber, Durkheim, and Freud—and any understanding of modernity (and the post-modern responses) is intelligible only in the context of their discussion. Truistic as this may be, it is still startling to realize that rarely in the university are the literary and the sociological imagination joined in a common enterprise in the effort to illumine both.

Is it the task of the university to be a clerisy, self-consciously guarding the past and seeking assertively to challenge the new? Or is it just a bazaar, offering Coleridge and Blake, Burckhardt and Nietzsche, Weber and Marx as antiphonal prophets, each with his own call? No consensual answer is possible, perhaps, because the university is no longer the citadel of the traditional mode—only the simple-minded can believe it is—but an arena in which the critics once outside the Academy have, like the tiger (or Tyger) once outside the gates of society, found a place—deservedly—within. And the tension between past and future, mind and sensibility, tradition and experience, for all its strains and discomfitures, is the only source for maintaining the independence of inquiry itself.

If the confrontation of modernity with tradition and of rational intellect with modernity is one of the tasks of a college in responding to the sentient few, the humanizing of the educable many is, perhaps, the great task of liberal education today. The question is not "who is this new man, the American?" but "who is the generic man that stalks the world today?"

All of ancient wisdom recognized the double nature of man; as *chia* (wild animal) or *halachic* (law-abiding); Apollonian and Dionysian; Caligulaic and Stoic; sinner and redeemed; instinct and reason; impulse and intelligence. But each age has also seen man through a special prism fashioned to its controlling view of man's centrality. For the Greeks, virtue and reason constituted man's essential nature, and man realized his potential through the rule of measure and the life of the mind. The Christians saw man as struggling against powerful sinful impulses, hopefully transfigured by the healing power of love. The bourgeois world-view, concentrating on things—property and money—introduced a test of functional rationality for the efficient allocation of labor power and the maximal use of resources. The "reactive" philosophies of the late nineteenth century—Nietzschean, Sorelian, Paretian, and Freudian—showed us the irrational forces that are dammed up and spill over when the "self," divided by functions and curbed by social repression, breaks loose.

Modern social science, reflecting on man in a complex, interrelated, differentiated world, has given us a still different picture—that of behavioral man. Behavioral man is a learner, capable of great feats. Far removed from his animal origins on this evolutionary scale, he has created many tools for shaping and even transforming his environment. But in his relations with other men, behavioral man is a seeker not of truth but of deceptions, about himself as well as others. As Bernard Berelson and Gary Steiner have observed, after itemizing an inventory of "scientific findings" about human behavior:

> He adjusts his social perceptions to fit not only the objective reality but also what suits his wishes and needs; he tends to remember what fits his needs and expectations, or what he thinks others will want to hear;... his need for psychological protection is so great that he has become an expert in the "defense mechanisms"; in the mass media he tends to hear and see not simply what is there but what he prefers to be told, and he will misinterpret rather than face up to an opposing set of facts or point of view; he avoids the conflicts of issues and ideals whenever he can by changing the people around him rather than his mind, and when he cannot, private fantasies can lighten the load and carry him through....
>
> For the truth is, apparently, that no matter how successful man becomes in dealing with his problems, he still finds it hard to live in the real world undiluted: to see what one really is, to hear what others really think of one, to face the conflicts and threats really present, or for that matter, the bare human feelings. Animals adjust to their

environment more or less on its own terms; man maneuvers his world to suit himself within far broader limits.[4]

So, as the authors conclude, behavioral man is social man—social product, social producer, and social seeker—to a greater degree than he is philosophical man, or religious man, or political man, or the great man held up as avatar by common folk. The traditional images of man have stressed motives like reason or faith, impulse or self-interest; the behavioral science image stresses the "social-adjusting" definition of all these.

Is this then the whole truth or even just an added truth? Berelson and Steiner chose for their epigraph a phrase from T. S. Eliot's *Burnt Norton:*

> Go, go, go said the bird: human kind
> Cannot bear very much reality.

But what, then, is reality? It was Zeuxis, the Ionic iconographer, who painted grapes so naturally that, as Pliny tells us, the birds flew up to peck at them. But who was the deceiver, and who the deceived?

What are we to say of a world where man has become a searcher of deceptions, about himself as well as others, without seeking for truth? Can one accept behavioral man on his own terms? Or does the university have a responsibility to change this man—for the portrait of modern man in *Human Behavior* is an indictment of contemporary society, an indictment that brings the university before the bar of humanitas? If nothing else, the nature of behavioral man is a justification for strengthening the humanities in liberal education.

In elliptical fashion, I have begun with two realms, that of sensibility (and the demonic) and that of social man (and his self-deceptions), and posed perhaps extreme formulations about each. Yet this was not done for rhetorical or paradoxical purposes, but to define two aspects of the culture as these present themselves in the form of tasks for the university. For the lure of sensibility attracts those sentient and talented individuals (as well as their modish camp followers) who, in exploring the limits of esthetic and moral radicalism, fall at times into a

[4] Bernard Berelson and Gary A. Steiner, *Human Behavior: An Inventory* of *Scientific Findings* (New York, Harcourt, Brace, and World, 1964), p. 664.

dandyism, a beat or nihilistic mood which subverts not only the existing order but tradition itself. While the self-deceptions—and often
the single-minded careerism—of behavioral man (the mass-man fore-
shadowed by Ortega y Gasset) muffle a social conscience and a spirit
of critical inquiry which are the necessary attributes of a civilized
man. In what way, then, can or should the university confront both
challenges?

The university cannot remake a world (though in upholding
standards it plays some part in such attempts). It cannot even remake
men. But it can liberate young people by making them aware of the forces
that impel them from within and constrict them from without. It is in
this sense, the creation of self-consciousness in relation to tradition, that
the task of education is metaphysics, metasociology, metapsychology,
and, in exploring the nature of its own communications, metaphilosophy
and metalanguage. This, in itself, is the enduring rationale of a liberal
education and the function of the college years.

In the more limited and specific ways that such purposes can be
embodied in a curriculum, the content of liberal education, in dealing
with the above tasks, can be defined through six purposes:
   1)   To overcome intellectual provincialism;
   2)   To appreciate the centrality of method (i.e., the role of con-
        ceptual innovation);
   3)   To gain an awareness of history;
   4)   To show how ideas relate to social structures;
   5)   To understand the way values infuse all inquiry;
   6)   To demonstrate the civilizing role of the humanities.
In this chapter I shall discuss the first three, since the presuppositions
should be made explicit, and conclude with an argument about the general
pattern of the organization of knowledge. The remaining three points
are discussed in the chapter on curriculum, since they can only be
elaborated by concrete examples,

Provincialism is a source of arrogance, and knowledge a source of
humility. It takes a high degree of sophistication, Freud once wrote,
to believe in *chance.* For a primitive, as for the provincial, the world

is completely determined and highly ordered. Everything has its particular causes—the will of God, the sequence of the ritual, the conspiracy of the powerful—and the "book" or the custom tells us so. For the provincial, as for the primitive, knowledge is unsettling because it leads not to truth but to uncertainty and tentariveness. And few people can live comfortably in a shifting universe. The strength of Shakespeare, Keats said, was that he had "the power of remaining in uncertainty without any irritable reaching after fact or reason." Yet without such exploration there can be no possibility of freedom, the freedom defined by Kant as self-imposed and self-determining choice.

Intellectual provincialism takes two forms. One of them consists of the hold that myths, ideologies, or biases can have upon the minds of men; and from the beginning of philosophy, social thinkers have sought for ways to transcend these limitations. For Plato knowledge of the Ideal was the means of overcoming the contingency of the immediate; for Tracy Destutt ideology, or the trust in sense impressions, would "purify" ideas; for Herbert Spencer sociology would eliminate prejudice or nationalistic blinders. The most enchanting, if not most comprehensive, tableau was that of Francis Bacon. In his *Novum Organum,* Bacon enumerated four types of distortions of thought, which he called the "idols of the tribe," the "idols of the cave," the "idols of the market place," and the "idols of the theater."[5]

The idols of the tribe are the prejudices common to all: the tendency to see and believe only what is agreeable, to suffer from illusion, and to interpret everything anthropomorphic ally. The idols of the cave are prejudices peculiar to the individual, so that everything is seen from a particular angle of vision. (Bacon cites the case of his contemporary, Dr. Gilbert, who, "after he had employed himself most laboriously in the study and observation of the loadstone, proceeded at once to construct an entire system of philosophy in accordance with his favorite subject.") The idols of the market place, Bacon decided, were those distortions of thought that arise out of the confusions of language, confusions which he felt abounded particularly among the medieval Schoolmen: the assumption that things corre-

[5] Francis Bacon, *Novum Organum* (ch. 1), in E. A. Burtt, ed., *From Bacon to Mill* (New York, Modern Library, 1944), pp. 34-35.

spond to names (e.g., witches), or the tendency to overlook the difference between the literal and the metaphorical meaning of a term (e.g., *finite* and *infinite* when applied to physical and nonphysical objects). In consequence, said Bacon, "great and solemn disputes of learned men often terminate in controversies about words and names." Finally, the idols of the theater: "In my judgement," Bacon wrote, "all the received systems (of philosophy) are but so many stage-plays, representing worlds of their own creation after an unreal and scenic fashion."[6]

A sophistication gained from idol-breaking is easy to achieve. But there is today a different, second kind of provincialism which is more recalcitrant to change—that which arises out of expertise. For the most provincial, often enough, is the specialist who has mastery of one technique or function and is ignorant of the worlds beyond.

More than a hundred and fifty years ago, Friedrich Schiller, in his *Letters on Aesthetic Education,* had placed the responsibility for the decline of the individual on the differentiation of functions:

> When the commonwealth makes the office or function the measure of the man, when of its citizens it does homage only to memory in one, to a tabulating intelligence in another, to a mechanical capacity in a third; when here, regardless of character, it urges only towards knowledge, while there it encourages a spirit of order and law-abiding behavior with the profoundest intellectual obscurantism—when, at the same time, it wishes these single accomplishments of the subject to be carried to just as great an intensity as it absolves him of extensity—is it to be wondered at that the remaining faculties of the mind are neglected, in order to bestow every care upon the special one which it honours and rewards?

The consequence, for Schiller, was that in art and scholarship the intuitive and speculative minds had become estranged, and each had zealously excluded the other from its respective field of application. A hundred years later, the process of specialization had become the very engine of intellectual progress. Whitehead, perhaps more eloquently than anyone else, has called attention to its dangers.

---

[6] In destroying these idols, Bacon sought to pull down the towers of scholasticism and establishes empiricism as the foundation of inductive inquiry. But science itself is no longer so provincial as to rule out hypothetical-deductive systems, or the foundations of rationalism, as means of gaining knowledge.

Another great fact confronting the modern world is the discovery of the method of training professionals who specialize in particular regions of thought and thereby progressively add to the sum of knowledge within their respective limitations of subject. . . . This situation has its dangers. It produces minds in a groove. Each profession makes progress, but it is progress in its own groove. Now to be mentally in a groove is to live in contemplating a given set of abstractions. The groove prevents straying across country, and the abstraction abstracts from something to which no further attention is paid. But there is no groove of abstractions which is adequate for the comprehension of human life. Thus, in the modern world, the celibacy of the medieval learned class has been replaced by a celibacy of the intellect which is divorced from the concrete contemplation of complete facts.

The dangers arising from this aspect of professionalism are great, particularly in our democratic society. The directive force of reason is weakened. The leading intellects lack balance. They see this set of circumstances, or that set; but not both sets together. The task of coordination is left to those who lack either the force or the character to succeed in some definite career. In short, the specialized functions of the community are performed better and more progressively, but the generalized direction lacks vision. The progressiveness in detail only adds to the danger produced by the feebleness of coordination.[7]

The conventional approach to this problem, within the field of education, is to argue that one needs to give the prospective specialist a "broad" background in the humanities, a "solid" grounding in general education, and more work in philosophy or the classics. But all of these answers, commendable as they are, beg the question—*for the problem is not just the lack of cultivation of the person but the increased narrowness of the intellectual tasks themselves.* And this is not redeemed by making a man an amateur, a connoisseur, a gentleman in realms outside his subspecialized field.

Much of this is analogous to a debate that took place a number of years ago on the problem of what to do about repetitive work, or the extreme division of labor—the dehumanization of work—in factories. One school of thought, the liberal-minded "prophets of play," argued that technology is irreversible, and the only solution was to abandon the worker to this Moloch during the day, but permit him

[7] Alfred North Whitehead, *Science in the Modern World* (New York, Macmillan, 1960), pp. 282-83.

to find his satisfaction in the creative use of leisure. (Could a worker engage in "creative play" if his hours at the bench were spent in soul-deadening work?)

Actually, there were some answers in the realm of work—"enlargement of tasks," the rotation of jobs, worker control over pace, an increased degree of responsibility, and similar notions, but these were rarely applied because American industry, wedded to the idea of efficiency, would not at that time assume the added costs and possible loss of productivity which such changes would entail.[8]

But the character of intellectual work, surely, is a different matter, and the university, unlike industry, cannot be indifferent to the provincialism which is inherent in the specialization of fields and the consequent creation "of semiskilled intellectuals" to staff them.

Are there any answers, other than the pursuit of cultivation outside the hours of one's work? I think there are, for while specialized tasks may always exist, no educated man need hold to a particular specialization for long.[9] This means, in effect, a more liberal conception of specialization itself, one that emphasizes not the specific subject, or the training for a concrete task, but the grasp of a discipline and the grounding in method. Only in this fashion can a man relate the particular task to the general intellectual field and thus acquire sufficient agility of mind and mobility of skills to move from problem to problem in the unfolding development of knowledge itself.

To this intellectual rationale must be added the practical consideration that in the coming post-industrial society, training for a specific task, or concentration in a specific skill, risks the quick obsolescence of that training as well. For in a society of rapidly expanding knowledge, in which it may be expected that a man, in the sciences and social sciences at least, may have to "re-train" himself twice and three times during a lifetime, specialization easily becomes a form of fossilization. Only a broad grasp of method, and of the nature of

---

[8] For an account of the debate, see my essay *Work and Its Discontents* (Boston, Beacon Press, 1956). Since them, a number of corporations such as I.B.M. and Polaroid have taken substantial steps to make work exciting and meaningful for its workers.

[9] An economist friend told me recently that he had once been the "zinc-and-lead man" in the construction of the input-output *tableau economique* that Wassily Leontieff was constructing for the American economy. Since he was a good economist he didn't stay long at the task.

conceptual innovation and renovation, can prepare a person for work in the decades ahead. It is in this sense that an emphasis on the "centrality of method" joins an intellectual to a practical need.

I have remarked a number of times in this book on the centrality of method, on conceptual innovation; the phrases now need to be made concrete.

In contrasting general education with specialism, the Harvard report of 1945 defined the first as "that education which looks first of all to [the student's] life as a responsible human being and citizen" and the second as occupational training through the acquisition of an art or a technique. On reflection, both definitions seem wide of the mark. One cannot civilize a man "in general," for it is only by confronting him with problems that are meaningful to him, most directly by the moral choices that may occur in the pursuit of his own profession, that one can tell whether or not he has learned to apply the humane arts. As for the second: to acquire a technique without at the same time becoming aware of the intellectual context of the art, is to quickly outmode that training itself.

In fact, I do not think that the distinction between general education and specialism really holds. One must embody and exemplify general education through disciplines; and one must extend the context of specialism so that the ground of knowledge is explicit. The common bond of the two is the emphasis on conceptual inquiry. To this extent, in the reconciliation of liberal education and specialism, training cannot deal with techniques in the narrow sense, but with the foundations of knowledge itself: i.e., how a particular discipline establishes its concepts; how these concepts, seen as fluid inquiry, need to be revised to meet new problems; how one establishes the criteria of choice for one, rather than another, alternative patterns of inquiry. In effect, general education is education in the conduct and strategy of inquiry itself.[10]

[10] For an illustrative "paradigm" of this organization of inquiry, see Joseph J. Schwab, "What Do Scientists Do?" *Behavioral Science,* V., No. 1 (January, 1960).

What Schwab has sought to do is to formulate the types of conceptual structures, and the alternative patterns of inquiry, accessible to the man of science. These are organized around six "decision points" which occur in the course of inquiry, and by the positing of adequate criteria for the formulation of the next steps in creating further propositions. These decision points and choices,

There are three rationales for establishing the centrality of method, or of conceptual inquiry, as the foundation for college education-cutting across general background as well as the specialized courses, One is the point already alluded to—that in the present phase of the organization of knowledge, one can no longer train people for specific intellectual tasks or provide a purely vocational training. In effect, obsolescence of specializations indicates that one cannot any longer educate a person for a "job." One has to provide the means for intellectual mobility, for continuing education, for mid-career refreshment; and this can be done only by a grounding in the modes of conceptual inquiry.

Beyond this sociological fact is the second of the rationales—the overturn in the structure of scientific thought that was initiated by the conceptual revolution in physics in the mid-1920s.[11] For a short time during the late nineteenth century, a number of leading sci-

says Schwab, "summarize what I have seen in some 1,000 scientific papers written by European and American scientists over the past five centuries in the biological sciences and the three 'behavioral' sciences. Most of the papers are from the last two centuries, from the biological sciences (including clinical medicine and psychiatry) and psychology."

These alternative patterns of inquiry, it should be pointed out, are not fixed sequences that can be applied to all fields. The order in which different modes appear is not constant across different fields or different problems. Nor is the choice of one pattern or another intrinsic to a specific discipline; in fact, as Schwab points out, "a relatively stable personal preference contributes mightily to the view of a scientist about what ought to constitute his science; these personal preferences represent a configuration of personality types among scientists which is relatively stable; this personal factor and ephemerals of circumstance rather than the inexorables of logic or of history often determine what is better or best for a given science or scientist at a given time."

The alternative patterns of inquiry, then, are a logical ordering of the different ways open to particular sciences or investigations, apart from the specific point at which any individual scientist begins his own inquiry.

[11] I follow here the line of reasoning used by Thomas Kuhn in his *Structure of Scientific Revolution* (Chicago, University of Chicago Press, 1963), and I borrow some specific examples from Joseph Schwab's *The Teaching of Science as Enquiry* (Cambridge, Harvard University Press, 1964), pp. 9-14.

Kuhn's general argument is that changes in the structure of scientific thought do not come about simply through the cumulative growth of knowledge or the disproof of previous theories, but by the replacement of one basic paradigm (or an organized framework of questions and inquiry) by another. For a comprehensive explanation of the nature of paradigms and their application in the social sciences, see Robert K. Merton, *Social Theory and Social Structure* (Glencoe, Ill., Free Press, 1957), rev. ed., pp. 13-16, 50-55.

entists—Karl Pearson, W. K. Clifford, and Lord Kelvin, among others—held the view that science was a matter of uncovering the "facts of nature" and reporting on what was immediately observable and measurable.

The discovery of radioactivity, the exploration of the world of the atom, the principle of relativity, the new conceptions of space and time created an upheaval in science so vast that some of the oldest and least questioned of our notions about the physical world could no longer be treated as literally true, or literally false. It was not that the revolution in physics consisted only of denying those ideas that had previously been accepted. The revolutionary assertions, as Schwab points out, "did not come about because direct observations of space, place, time, and magnitude disclosed that our past views about them were mistaken. Rather, our old assertions about these matters were changed because physicists [were forced] to treat them in a new way—neither as self-evident truths nor as matters for merely empirical verification. They were to be treated instead as principles of enquiry—conceptual structures—which could be revised when necessary in the direction dictated by large complexes of theory, and diverse bodies of data, and numerous criteria of progress in science."

All of this implies, for the nature of scientific inquiry, the disappearance of the "self-evident givenness" of fixed dimensions, or the idea that facts can be treated as self-existing givens. In one sense it is a return to the original Kantian proposition that knowledge is contingent on the knower and on the questions he asks to organize and guide his operations. But contrary to Kant, the new scientific conceptions do not arise out of some fixed *a priori*, for the selection of facts depends in each case upon conceptual principles of the inquiry, and these are not fixed but subject to change.

This conceptual revolution is not restricted to physics alone. As a mode of inquiry it has changed the character of all the sciences,[12]

[12] There are, of course, investigators who remain committed to a "naive empiricism" as the most pragmatic mode of achieving new knowledge in a field. Perhaps its outstanding practitioner is B. F. Skinner of Harvard, who is probably one of the most influential behavioral scientists of the mid-twentieth century. Skinner advocates a "nose-first" style of research. He argues that unformalized principles operate in his, and in most, research. Conjecturing, conceptualizing, theorizing are in his view expendable if not harmful preoccupations. Nature, for him, is "out there," to be discovered and explored by the

In biology, the primitive guiding concepts of a "living machine" or of "structure and function" are no longer taken as "facts" but as conceptual schemes, to be reordered in the light of new conceptions of organism. The change is apparent, though only imperfectly charted, in the social sciences as well.

In the social sciences, the two dominant modes of inquiry, before the last twenty-five years, were a crude positivism or a simple, descriptive history. The positivism, initiated principally by Comte, sought to discover "regularities" in social phenomena on the model of the regularities in Newtonian physics. Elements of volition, human consciousness, goals and purposes were treated either as epiphenomena, or as sociopsychological "givens" to be derived from an uncomplicated Benthamite principle of pleasure-pain, the economic calculus of maximization, or the Hobbesian conception of human nature. In the case of certain aggregate phenomena (demography, migration, the differentiation of cities), some "laws" of varying validity were established. But by and large this crude positivism, or "social physics," has failed.

Descriptive history, the dominant mode of social scientific thought, has been the effort to provide causal explanations of single events, or consequences of events, by an exact determination of "facts." But when pressed by the simple methodological demand to account for

scientist. The model of science Skinner has in mind is Baconian, not post-Einsteinian, physics, and if upheavals shake the conception of the material universe held by physicists this is of little moment to him.

As a sympathetic critic, V. Edwin Bixenstine, puts it: There is a Skinner paradox. "His preachment is: do not theorize; rather observe, explore, follow your nose [but] Skinner's own temperament is much more inventive than it is curious. He is startlingly creative in applying the conceptual elements of his—let's be frank—*theory* to a wide variety of issues, ranging from training pigeons in the guidance of missiles, to developing teaching machines, to constructing a model society! . . . That Skinner has operated so effectively under this handicap is a tribute to his talent. I wish we were all as capable. We are not."

As for the admonition to follow one's nose, as Professor Bixenstine delightfully puts it: "Our biologist friends tell us that, in the course of evolution, the olfactory sense was undoubtedly the first significant *distance* receptor. But man seems constitutionally averse to depending on his nose. Recent evidence suggests that most of his 'smell brain' is not employed in analyzing smells at all; rather, it seems to be involved in complex emotional and dispositional states. Man will never be content with following his nose; he is wholly oriented toward the farthest possible extension of his perception. To theorize is the logical fulfillment of his nature. It is his true 'sixth sense,'" V. E, Bixenstine, "Empiricism in Latter-Day Behavioral Science," *Science*, CXLV (July 31, 1964), 464-67.

the selection of "relevant" facts, the historian has either lapsed into an extreme empiricism of "multicausal" explanation or has resorted to some sweeping philosophy of history, be it a great-man theory, a Marxian explanation of material causes, or some Spengler-Toynbee version of cyclical development. The difficulty with the historicist approach is that because events are seen as discrete or as evolutionary "stages" of development, there has been little possibility—owing to the lack of a general conceptual scheme—of asking comparative questions (such as why economic rationality developed first in the West) or accounting for variations in social systems (e.g., the different social developments of England, the United States, Canada, and Australia out of a common "political culture").

The "revolution" in sociology in the last few decades, beginning first with the work of Max Weber, and extended largely by Talcott Parsons, Edward A. Shils, and Robert Merton, consists largely in the creation of *analytical concepts* that can be applied to *any* social system within a society, from simple pair groups, such as the family, to large complex organizations, or can be applied to the comparison of total societies, instead of using descriptive or discrete concepts whose utility is limited to the immediate phenomena observed. Thus social groups can be analyzed systematically on the basis of "norms," "role differentiation," "institutionalization," or on the basis of the specific properties of groups, such as size, kinds of cohesion, formal and informal organization, patterns of communication, patterns of influence, etc. Societies or large-scale political organizations can be looked at in terms of the "functional requisites" necessary to keep the social unit operating. Social systems can be compared by determining whether the criterion of reward is universalistic or particularistic, whether social position is based on a criterion of achievement or ascription, whether emotional orientations toward others are neutral or affective.[13]

The extent to which these particular methods—or other conceptual schemes—will continue to be useful remains to be seen. What is clear is that some kind of analytical scheme is now felt to be necessary.

[13] The most relevant works for this approach are Talcott Parsons' *Structure of Action* (New York, McGraw-Hill, 1937), especially ch. 13 and 14, with their discussion of analytical concepts; his *Social System* (Glencoe, Ill., Free Press, 1951), ch. 2; and Robert K. Merton, *Social Theory and Social Structure* (Glencoe, Ill., Free Press, 1957), ch. 2 and 3.

This is particularly so with the rise of the new states and the emergence of so many different kinds of political societies in Asia and Africa, for without some analytical scheme, no systematic comparison of societies, to account for variation and change, is possible.

In the last fifteen years, this conceptual revolution in sociology has moved over into political science as well, and one finds Weberian typologies of authority and legitimacy (traditional, rational, and charismatic) replacing the older formalistic concepts of sovereignty, while in the work of Gabriel Almond and his students one finds an effort to extend the sociological dimensions of political analysis with such concepts as "political culture" (to define the social arena of politics) or "political socialization" or "national identity."[14]

One can also note this form of inquiry being used in the humanities as well.[15] Professor E. H. Gombrich, in his masterly work on perception in art, has argued that our sense of esthetic experience is a "convention," and that styles of painting, for example, are a function simply of agreed-upon modes (or conceptual frameworks) of recognizing objects. Thus the "flat" style of Egyptian painting is due not to a lack of naturalistic knowledge on the part of the Egyptian artists but to a convention; and our recognition of this and other styles is one of our own conventions. In a perhaps less direct way, the literacy criticism of Northrop Frye, with its use of the idea of "convention," indicates a similar orientation.[16]

All of this may be merely modish, or it may portend a genuine large-scale shift in intellectual orientation. Yet there is enough evi-

---

[14] Almond's chief efforts are to be found in *The Politics of Developing Areas,* edited with James S. Coleman (Princeton, N.J., Princeton University Press, 1960), and *The Civic Culture,* with Sidney Verba (Princeton, N.J., Princeton University Press, 1963).

Other political scientists, economists, historians, and sociologists who are working with these analytical schemes, particularly on comparative questions applied to the problems of economic and social development, are S. M. Lipset, David Apter, S. N. Eisenstadt, Karl Deutsch, David Easton, Lucian Pye, Harry Eckstein, David Landes, Bert Hoselitz, and Everett Hagen.

[15] In one sense, neo-Kantianism has always been strong in the field of the history of culture—e.g., the idea of conceptual inquiry, as we find it expressed, say, in the work of Dilthey.

[16] For representative works, see E. H. Gombrich, *Art and Illusion* (New York, Pantheon Books, 1960), and Northrop Frye, *Fables of Identity* (New York, Harcourt, Brace, and World, 1963).

dence, in the sciences and social sciences, to indicate that the pedagogy of thought must take seriously, if only controversially, this great change in methods of thought and analysis.

The consequence of these revolutions in conceptual inquiry—the third rationale for establishing the centrality of method as a keystone of general education—is that the duration of a revisionary cycle in scientific knowledge has been drastically shortened. "In many sciences," Professor Schwab claims, "the rate of revision [of theoretical knowledge] is twenty to a hundred times what it was much less than a century ago." Almost every field today is in a state of fluid, rather than stable, inquiry; one can no longer assume a fixed body of received knowledge as the guide to further problems. The result is that the biology or chemistry or physics or sociology or economics that one learned thirty years ago is wholly inadequate to the newer conceptual structures that guide inquiry at the frontiers of these fields today.

All of this calls into question the prevailing way that science is taught and even how research is organized. The idea of science as a bounded map of knowledge to be filled in by successive advances of research and experiment assumed the existence of a fixed body of principles that guided the pattern of experiments. But the principles were not treated as problems in themselves. The revision of knowledge, whether one calls it a new paradigm or a state of "fluid inquiry," is not the adding of material to the subject matter *per se* but the development of new principles that will redefine that subject matter and guide a new course of stable inquiries.

Yet, as Professor Schwab points out, "it is precisely here that our system of rewards and of education has been remiss. We have maximized the social, financial, and psychological rewards for technical and stable contributions—new fuels, new missile designs, new vaccines, new antibiotics, first syntheses of organic compounds. Where we have at all designed our school and our science programs to attract young people to the sciences, the designs have been shaped to attract the potentially competent technician and the avid, able, but docile learner. Our teaching laboratories invite students to discover the satisfaction of techniques mastered. They emphasize the desirability of patience, accuracy, and precision. They testify to the soundness of existing knowledge. But rarely indeed do they invite students to discover the limitations of present knowledge or to identify unsolved problems and areas of present ignorance. Much less do they invite students to invent, to devise and explore possibilities alternative to current formulations. Our classroom work is imbued with the same dye of established law and accepted knowledge. This is obvious in the premium put on 'learning the lesson.'"[17]

The responsibility of educators is a heavy one. It requires a consistent self-consciousness in science and social science education. To cite Schwab again; "No mere updating of course content will suffice. Mesons, phosphate bonds, DNA, and population genetics can be taught just as dogmatically and rigidly, and as little to the present purpose, as the nineteenth-century cell theory or the impervious atoms and elements of Mendeleef's periodic table."

What is required is a radically new approach to science teaching as conceptual innovation, conceptions that involve scrutiny of the organizing principles of each discipline as an integral part of the imparting of the discipline itself.[18] It is in this sense, perhaps, that one joins hands with the old notion of the quadrivium (arithmetic and music as the exemplars of proportion and harmony; geometry and astronomy representing the structure of things) and the trivium (grammar, rhetoric, logic representing the structure in words). In that ancient formulation an "art" was a technique, and the seven liberal arts that constituted the core of education were not so much areas of knowledge as tools for getting and dispensing knowledge. But the purpose of such techniques was also, at least for the creative few, to lead them to *scientia,* or the structure of ideas itself. It is in this sense that the centrality of method has a focus, and a goal—the idea of the creative formulation of change, of *scientia.*[19]

In this emphasis on the centrality of method, there is, as I have argued before, a positive new role for the college as an institution standing between the secondary school and graduate research work.

[17] Schwab, *The Teaching of Science as Enquiry,* p. 39.

[18] As my colleague Leon Lederman, the physicist, scrawled in the margin of an earlier draft: "But, but . . . This *is* the way we teach it!! ? How else?" This is how *he* teaches; but regrettably, not all do.

[19] See James S. Ackerman, "On Scientia," *Daedalus* (Winter 1965).

One of its fundamental purposes must be to deal with the modes of conceptualization, the principles of explanation, and the nature of verification. The world is always double-storied: the factual order, and the logical order imposed upon it. The emphasis in the college must be less on what one knows and more on the self-conscious ground of knowledge; how one knows what one knows, and the principle of the relevant selection of facts.[20]

In this emphasis on method, one risks that sterile debate—whether you can teach method apart from subject matter. The answer, of course, is that one cannot. But the shoe is really on the other foot: can one teach a subject without an awareness of method? In this respect, the distinctions, for pedagogical purposes, between conceptualization, discipline, and subject matter should be clear. A *concept,* in this specific usage, is a term that allows us to group together different phenomena, or selected aspects of phenomena, under a common rubric. (One can ask a child what a whale and an elephant have in common, and he might correctly answer *size;* a boy in secondary school might say: despite the fact that one lives in the water and the other on land, they are both mammals, because they have similar physiological processes.) The grouping we make is a function of whatever different purpose of analysis we may have in mind. A *discipline,* then, consists of a coherent group of interrelated concepts that can be applied to kindred phenomena and that allow one to make theoretical or explanatory statements about the relationships of these phenomena. A *subject matter* is a related class of phenomena that can be analyzed by a particular discipline. (Thus sociology is a discipline and ethnic-group relations a subject matter; economics is a discipline and international trade a subject matter.)[21]

---

[20] Stefan Dedjier has cited an old Chinese proverb: Give a man a fish and you have fed him for a day; teach him how to fish, and you have fed him for a long time. To this one must now add the coda: Teach him how to recognize the best places to fish, and you have immeasurably increased his yield.

[21] What, then, are history and political science? One would have to say that they are subject matters investigated, in the case of history, by specific tech niques (e.g., the validation of documents) and defined rules of evidence, and, in the case of political science—when sociology and economic concepts are not brought into play—by *ad hoc* empirical case methods rather than disci- plines.

In a marginal note Dean Truman has entered a demurrer; "This assumes a

All of this leads to the preliminary proposition—a point I shall emphatically come back to in the discussion of curriculum—that the nature of college education can now be envisaged as a series of logical steps in which first comes the acquisition of a general background, second the training in a discipline, third the application of this discipline to a number of relevant subjects, and fourth the effort to link disciplines in dealing with common problems. It is this progression, involving at each step of the way an awareness of conceptual innovation and method, that is the heart of the ordering of a curriculum.

What is the role of history in this conception of liberal education? In his *Phenomenology,* Hegel made the remarkable observation:

> The manner of study in ancient times is distinct from that of the modern world, in that the former consisted in the cultivation and perfecting of the natural mind. Testing life carefully at all points, philosophizing about everything it came across, the former created an experience permeated through and through by universals. In modern times, however, an individual finds the abstract form ready made. In straining to grasp it and make it his own, he rather strives to bring forward the inner meaning alone, without any process of mediation; the production of the universal is abridged, instead of the universal

sharper line between a subject matter and a discipline than would seem warranted. Political science, even before 'political behavior,' had elements of discipline—in your sense—though insufficiently explicit and thus lacking in coherence. But is this difference from sociology or anthropology one of degree or of kind, as you assert? I would argue that political science is a discipline—weakly developed—and international politics *is* a subject matter. Even if one accepted your view as presently valid—and I don't—how long must it remain so? Is it inherent? I doubt it."

Dean Truman convinces me, but only in part. As I indicated (see footnote 15), a number of political scientists are seeking to construct analytical schemes, and some, like Morton Kaplan or David Easton, have presented fully coherent conceptual systems. But political science, even more than sociology, is riven by the dilemma whether it is to be historical or analytical, and the practitioners in the field are more resistant—perhaps the problems as they have defined them make it so—to the use of analytical models.

There are a number of social scientists who argue that since politics always involves choice, political science can be "reduced" to economics, and that different models taken from decision theory (such as utility-preference models) can be applied to politics. For some interesting work in this direction, see Anthony Downs, *An Economic Theory of Democracy* (New York, Harper, 1957); Duncan Black, *The Theory of Committees and Elections* (Cambridge, Cambridge University Press, 1958), and Mancur Olson, Jr., *The Logic of Collective Action: Public Goods and the Theory of Groups* (Cambridge, Harvard University Press, 1965).

arising out of the manifold detail of concrete existence. Hence nowadays the task before us consists not so much in getting the individual clear of the stage of sensuous immediacy, and making him a substance that thinks and is grasped in terms of thought, but rather the very opposite: it consists in actualizing the universal, and giving it spiritual vitality, by the process of breaking down and superseding fixed and determinate thoughts.[22]

The passion for the abstract is a great danger, especially for students, because they lose a sense of the concrete and of the actuality of events, which give not only dramatic meaning but a kind of sensible-ness to the nature of human dilemmas. In his essay "The Commitment to the Modern," Lionel Trilling cites a relevant experience he and I had in conducting, with Steven Marcus, a joint English-sociology seminar on Victorian England. Our interest was in the way novelists and social inquirers look at a society, and we took a period, fairly unified in temper, in which the problems so characteristic of today were first encountered: the impact on a traditional social structure of the rise of industrialism, urbanization, social mobility; the expansion of profession; the entry of masses into political society and the claim for participation in democracy—in short, the upheavals of class structure and the ways in which Victorian England tried to deal with them. We read Dickens, George Eliot, Thackeray, Henry James, and other novelists who had created fictional worlds that reflected these social conditions; and we also read the social documents (the Parliamentary Blue Books, the Northcote-Trevelyan report, the Chadwick report) and the social investigators (Mayhew, Charles Booth) that sought to provide a factual picture of these changes. As Professor Trilling reported our experience:

The subject we were dealing with was not a contemporary one although the concepts we used were peculiarly of our time; we were investigating the assumptions of the society of Victorian England, and the first thing that struck us was the *uneasiness* of our students in dealing with a *historical* subject. Despite the vivacity of their minds, they found it almost impossible to imagine the actuality of personal and social situations in the fairly recent past. The distant past might perhaps have given them less trouble, as being nearly in the realm of

[22] G. W. F. Hegel, *The Phenomenology of Mind,* ed. by J. B. Baillie (London, Allen & Unwin; New York, Macmillan, 1961) p. 94.

fantasy and comprehensible as such. Many of them, as it happened, had concerned themselves with the study of religion, and they were surely most: gifted in their understanding of the more arcane aspects of theology; but if we raised questions about the Thirty-Nine Articles, or the disabilities of Dissenters, or the functions of a bishop, they were not merely impatient of such Philistine considerations; we had the distinct impression that, whatever religion *was* for them, it clearly had nothing to do with an (actual) religious community, a church, or prayer.

In the classic conceptions of liberal education (the quadrivium and the trivium), history played little, if any, role in the curriculum. When Plato sketched in his *Republic* a plan of studies, he mentioned arithmetic, geometry, astronomy, and the like; he did not even allude to history. History was praised most highly not by philosophers but by the rhetoricians. The fundamental change became marked only in the sixteenth century (Machiavelli can be taken as a convenient symbol) with the repudiation of classic political philosophy and a novel emphasis on history.[23] It became customary, by the end of the seventeenth century, to speak of the "spirit of a time," and by the middle of the eighteenth century Voltaire and others were discussing the "philosophy of history" in the sense that the changes in societal forms themselves were now seen as posing philosophical problems about basic ontological categories.

History as the "queen" subject flourished in the nineteenth century. Hegel forged a synthesis of philosophy and history through his "cunning of reason." Marx placed his towering emphasis on the temporalness of institutions. Ranke sought to write history as it "actually was." A "historical school," particularly in Germany, brought about a historical jurisprudence and a historical political science for studies that were considered, falsely, to be "unhistorical."

The domination of the historical method in the social sciences, particularly in the nineteenth and early twentieth century, was due largely to two influences: the belief (held by the German historical school) that one could explain the meaning of a social phenome-

[23]For contrasting discussions of this change in intellectual climate, see Leo Strauss, *Natural Right and History* (Chicago, University of Chicago Press, 1953), especially ch. 1; and Karl Lowith, *Meaning in History* (Chicago, University of Chicago Press, 1949).

non by its origin—i.e., the principle of genetic explanation; and the theory of social evolution (held by such diverse thinkers as Comte, Marx, and Spencer), in which the past was seen as a unilinear succession of stages, and the future as unfolding in inevitable fashion from the present. These two modes of historicism fell into intellectual disrepute following the "pragmatic critique of the historico-genetic fallacy"[24] (the argument that the consequences of an act are not wholly explainable or predictable from its antecedents) and the intellectual failure of Marxism, at least of its vulgar side, with its overly determinist view of history. Further denigrations of historicism (e.g., Karl Popper's), the transformation of sociology into an analytical discipline, the rise of the "new criticism" in literature, with its emphasis on the text alone (rather than on historical context) as the only relevant universe of discourse, all contributed even further to the decline of history as a social science or a humanistic study. Where history has flourished as a subject (such as the American Studies program after World War II), it has more often been an instrument of national identity and national consciousness rather than an intellectual enterprise in its own terms.

Yet there are, it seems to me, valid intellectual reasons for the restoration of history as a central subject. This is not history as a "philosophy of history," or as a guide to salvation, either religious or secular.[25] It is history for the purpose of liberal education itself. For the sense of the past and the knottiness of fact are the necessary means of transcending contemporaneity and "actualizing the universal."

[24] For an early but still cogent argument, see the essay by Sidney Hook in *Essays in Honor of John Dewey* (New York, Holt, 1929).

[25] To Nietzsche, for example, history was the handmaiden of life's purpose. Life, he said, was an unhistorical power, which can be maimed by an excess of history or by a history that, out of covert malice toward the present, denies its claims and achievements. But, he went on, "the fact that life does need the service of history muse be as clearly grasped as that an excess of history hurts it. ... History is necessary to the living man in three ways: in relation to his action and struggle; in relation to his conservatism and reverence; in relation to his suffering and desire for deliverance." The need for history, he insisted, "is not that of mere thinkers who only look at life, or of the few who desire knowledge and can only be satisfied with knowledge; but it always has a reference to the purpose of life, and is under its absolute rule and direction." Cited in Lionel Trilling's "The Scholar's Caution and the Scholar's Courage," an address published by Cornell University, October, 1962.

I put forth five mundane reasons for the study of history:

1. To redress the passion for the abstract by emphasizing the con crete, thus demonstrating a social situation in its manifold complexity and actuality and showing "that the world is intractable as well as malleable." Literature and art also emphasize the concrete, and these have their obvious place in the scheme of liberal education. But his tory, in this sense, has been neglected, and shabbily so. And history, as I shall try to show in chapter 5, is the logical first step in the or dering of a curriculum.

2. To provide a "vocabulary of reference" for the historical imagination, both to stretch the imagination and to forestall the limited (and sometimes false) analogies that can be invoked to justify or explain events. It is striking, for example, to see the paucity of historical analogies used by statesmen and strategists to satisfy or explain events. (Thus Khrushchev repeatedly invoked the Treaty of Brest-Litovsk, and that alone, in arguing with the Chinese about why he signed the nuclear-test ban; or one hears from American military strategists the obsessive references to Pearl Harbor to justify the need for an overwhelming counterforce.) Such analogies risk be coming deceptions: at best they are poor rhetoric; at worst an in stance of the historico-genetic fallacy.

3. To emphasize the role of contexts in establishing the meaning of ideas. One need not argue that the development of ideas (or of literary and artistic forms) is solely the product of the logical de velopment or the immanent unfolding of these ideas and forms them selves. The history of ideas (and institutions) necessarily involves the idea of historical context.

4. To identify the relevant antecedent events that have shaped the present. Can one understand the problems of the *tiers monde* without knowing the history of imperialism? Or the nature of modernity without knowing the history of romanticism and the social position of the intelligentsia? Or the contending forces for world leadership without knowing the history of nationalism, fas cism, and communism, and their respective ideological impulses? This is not to say that the "immediate present" must serve as the criterion of historical examination, but a liberal education has to

present to the student a sense of the fundamental social forces of the time.

5. To be a source for comparative analysis. This is not a degradation of history but the expert use of it as a laboratory for the kinds of explanation and generalization that other social sciences seek to make. At the present moment, for example, more than fifty new countries in Asia and Africa are trying to achieve nationhood and a viable existence as societies. Over the past hundred years another fifty or so countries, in Latin America and Asia, have been struggling to create a stable political system and an effective state. Only with the help of the historian, and his skill at unraveling the actual stories of the development of these countries, can some valid generalizations about national identity, legitimacy, the sociological conditions of democracy—the crucial problems of political science in the broadest sense—become possible. But in this effort the historian himself has to become aware of the conceptual prisms of the sociologist and other social scientists.[26] Here the problem is not the creation of an interdisciplinary movement, but a sophistication of each craft in each other's skills.

The teaching of history necessarily involves a sense of fact and chronology; but beyond them is the problem of meaning and explanation, and here the pedagogy, if not the practice, of history must combine with the methods of conceptual inquiry. For while the exact determination of a sequence of events is the craft problem of the historian, the significance of events, the choice of what is to be scrutinized as relevant, a sense of what alternative courses were open, and even the choice of a generic term to identify the events are functions of the conceptual framework one chooses.

Take, for example, the French Revolution. Was the Revolution an

[26] A personal experience: A few years ago, in preparing an essay on late-nineteenth-century European history for the background reading book in Contemporary Civilization ("Capitalism and Its Critics, 1879-1914"), I was struck by the fact that none of the standard texts in European history (such as H. A. L. Fischer's *History of Europe*) discussed or even mentioned what, from a sociologist's point of view, was one of the crucial problems of the time—the rates of social mobility. While exact statistical data on this question would clearly be hard to come by, the general idea itself, and its import for the changes in the society and its politics, were not even raised.

event of 1789, with the creation of the Constituent Assembly; or was the Revolution the coming to power of Robespierre in 1793? Was the significance of the French Revolution the fact that it brought a new bourgeois class to power, or that it introduced a new principle of legitimacy? To explain the French Revolution, does one invoke a Marxian theory of the contradiction between an outmoded feudal order and the rise of new material conditions of generating wealth? Or does one accept a Paretian view, that the cause was "blocked" social mobility and therefore an inadequate "circulation of elites"? Does one take a Tocquevillian view that the Revolution occurred because the political authorities were unable to cope with the rising resentments and rising expectations of classes that were better off just before the Revolution than at any rime before? Or does one show, in a view like Crane Brinton's, that revolutions have an inherent momentum that is bound to produce excesses? Does one, within a more delimited historical canvas, take the view that the Revolution was precipitated by the tension between Paris and the countryside, or that it was a sequence of events produced by the inability of the French economy to sustain the hunger of the Paris crowds? And if one accepts any of these general interpretations, how does one explain, from the standpoint of theory, why a violent revolution occurred in France and not in England?

In a different sense, the history of the Roman Republic from Marius and Sulla to Augustus can be read as an exciting narrative of human ambition, but also as comparative sociology: of the consequence to a society of the recourse to military force, even when it is done to maintain tradition (the intention of Sulla); of the role of a mass army drawn from the "mob" in becoming an arbiter of politics (as under Marius); and of the nature of Caesarism and its consequences for the principle of legitimacy.

The simple point is that any discussion of history has to be more than the recital of "facts"—though knowledge of the facts many pedagogues now call for, in their horror at students' ignorance of simple basic chronology, is certainly necessary. The discussion has to be put in a context wherein the student understands the nature of evidence, the reason why a scholar chose some facts rather than others, and the guiding conceptual frameworks that lie behind the selection of evidence. It is only by contrasting such schemes that a student can grasp what is problematical about interpretations and controversial about meanings.

This is not history as historiography, or what successive historians have written (though this is relevant for the sociology of a historical problem). Nor is it an effort to read "lessons from the past" for the purposes of the present. It is an effort, as one objective, to see history as the efforts of peoples and societies to deal with some recurrent problems of social order and, as a second objective, the presentation to the student of the principles of historical explanation and the nature of evidence, as ways of understanding basic social processes.

This is not to argue that historical problems (and periods) are all equivalent, or that new and different dimensions are not introduced by such factors as the cultural traditions of a society, the changing roles of production and consumption because of technology, or that even such elements as the size and speed of communications do not introduce new variables. But one can still argue that the logical criteria for all generalizations can be applied to historical explanation.[27] And one can say that certain crucial variables of the political order—such as the nature of authority and legitimacy (the relation of ruler to ruled and the kinds of moral justifications invoked for rule), the relations between economic and political power and the recruitment or restriction of elites (the relation of the stratification system to the authority system)—are basic structural forms that all societies must define, albeit in different but limited ways.

In concentrating on the principle of conceptual inquiry as a basic element in liberal education, I do not mean to argue that this mode of inquiry is the royal road to all knowledge, or that knowledge is even of one piece. As J. Robert Oppenheimer wrote recently:

The unity of knowledge, long thought of as corresponding to a structure in which the foundation stones imply the whole, has today a very different topology; very much more than a temple, it is a network, as William James foresaw, with no central chamber, no basic truths from

---

[27] For a discussion of such criteria, see Ernest Nagel, *The Structure of Science* (New York, Harcourt, Brace, and World, 1961), ch. 15.

which all else will follow, but with a wonderful mutual relevance between its many branches, and with beauty illuminating the growing tips of knowledge, even in the most recondite and unfamiliar branches.[28]

In fact, as I outlined the argument in chapter 3, and would extend it here, the pattern of knowledge is fundamentally triadic, and different principles govern the acquisition of knowledge in the sciences, the social sciences, and the humanities, with important consequences for the theory and practice of pedagogy. In the sciences (and in mathematics), the learning is *sequential:* within any science, stipulated levels of prerequisites define the kinds of knowledge necessary before one can proceed to the next level. In the social sciences, the pattern is one of *linkages* between fields. Elements of economic policy, for example, are understandable only in a political context, and this in turn is dependent upon some conception of the social community. In the humanities, knowledge is *concentric;* one moves within many different circles of meaning in the effort to attain, if ever, an understanding of a text and an experience.

In the sciences, as one can quickly see from an examination of different college catalogues, courses are standardized and sequential. In mathematics one moves from algebra, geometry, trigonometry, and calculus to the more advanced work in differential equations, linear and multilinear algebra, geometric topology, and so on. In Physics, one begins with mechanics and heat, goes on to electricity and magnetism, and then to light and atomic physics. These courses are not taught as "historical disciplines" (though the history of science is important for cultural and intellectual history), for science is a self-corrective system for disposing of useless facts. There is a memory of all false starts and blind alleys (and perhaps more important, a criterion for the identification of such trails). But one begins with the models that explain, as clearly as possible, the phenomena and problems of the field, in accordance with the best techniques of measuring and validating the theories that one has derived, using a given conceptual mode.

The social sciences are multilinear and necessarily linked to each

[28] J. Robert Oppenheimer, "The Added Cubit," *Encounter, XXI,* No. 2 (August, 1963), 44-47.

other. The concept of a "command economy," for example, is not just an examination of the administrative techniques of planning; it involves an understanding of the political controls and bureaucratic structure such an economy entails, as well as the kind of social system (the nature of incentives, patterns of occupational recruitment, and social sanctions) such a polity requires. In a similar way, the idea of a "market economy" requires a knowledge of the legal framework (e.g., the law of contracts) and the political structure in which such a society operates. Anyone working in the field of economic development, for example, soon realizes that he may need not only some knowledge of politics and sociology but a personality theory and family structure as well.[29]

The function of the social sciences is to indicate the differentiations and variations in human actions; hence the emphasis on linkages. The humanities have a different intent: to heighten sensibility (that fusion of intellect and feeling) and to impart a sense of coherence about human experience—heroism, pride, love, loneliness, tragedy, confrontation with death. The purpose of the classroom, the function of the teacher and critic, is to make the creative accessible. A great novel has no "nature," as if it were a natural object and therefore subject to some fixed discussion of its qualities and properties (though there are logical orderings of genre), but it can be read in different ways; and each of these ways is a different and valid facet of human emotions. Knowledge—and understanding—in the humanities is gained not by the solution of abstract puzzles which may be logically independent of personal experience, but precisely through experience. Hence the "concentric" sense of uncovering new meaning, as one confronts, over a period of time, a genuinely imaginative work.

In emphasizing the centrality of the humanities, there is no need to argue that poetic statement and metaphysical image are a truth larger than the empirical validations of science. The justification of the humanities is that they combine, as Jacques Barzun has put it, "fixed rea-

---

[29] Cf. the recent books of David McClelland *(The Achieving Society)* and Everett Hagen *(Theories of Social Change),* which argue that economic development and entrepreneurial innovation are inhibited in overly rigid, authoritarian family-structured societies.

son with wayward spirit," and this unique combination of order and freedom, rule and spontaneity, limitation and potential is a necessary realm of experience for renewing the animal spirits and the guiding intelligence of man.

If this triadic division has any validity, then a number of pedagogical consequences may follow, particularly for the relation of specialized work in college to graduate school, on the one hand, and of the colleges to the secondary schools, on the other. In the social sciences, for example, it suggests that a crosshatching arrangement may be necessary, wherein a student who wanted to study sociology in graduate school would as an undergraduate major not in sociology but in history and economics, or psychology and anthropology. This is not to argue for interdisciplinary courses in the early college years, but quite the contrary. Where interdisciplinary courses have failed, it has been because they have taken up "cross-hatch" topics before a student had any knowledge of the disciplines required. In those courses, a student was introduced to the social sciences through the topic of "culture and personality" before knowing any anthropology or psychology; or to the topic of "planning and the market" before knowing any economics or political science. This is not meant to derogate such topics. But if they are to be valid as social science subjects, students should have some knowledge of the disciplines first, rather than pick them up, *ad hoc,* along the way, in the general social science course. The argument here is that a grounding in a discipline, in its conceptual frameworks and analytical techniques, should be the prerequisite for interdisciplinary work. Students who seek to pursue one or another social science field in graduate school would do well not to specialize in that subject in college but to concentrate on disciplines that would provide the contextual basis and the linkages for a better understanding of his own subsequent graduate specialization.

This also suggests that the current and even growing vogue for "social studies" or "social science" in the secondary schools is essentially wrong, for most of these courses compound the error of the interdisciplinary social science courses that flourished in the colleges after World War II, and that are now on the decline. Such high-school courses introduce large problems of public policy as the "interesting" way of arousing student interest, before the student has any competence, in an abecedarian sense, in dealing with these questions. My feeling is that the secondary schools would be more strongly advised to concentrate on history and anthropology, where large amounts of useful factual information in simple interpretative schemes would serve as the foundation for later college studies, rather than on the social science courses that now predominate.

In an equal sense, a conception of the humanities that sees its mean-. ing as gained not just through logical explication, but as a function of enriching experience and maturity, suggests that the vogue for the "humanities" in the secondary schools, wherein students can claim "I've read Plato and Nietzsche" or one term is spent on the Greek plays, is a false conception of what students can gain from the humanities. This is not to suggest that the secondary schools stick to "easy" readings and the "hard" readings be left to the colleges, that Shakespeare's historical plays belong in the high schools and *Lear* and *The Tempest* in the colleges (though the idea is not without merit), but that in approaching the humanities it be made as clear as possible that the unraveling of complex meanings in a dramatic tragedy, say, is a continuous one, in which deeper understanding arises through an individual's enlarged experience of the world. It is fair to say that the teaching of the humanities has become modish in the better secondary schools, because it is an easy way to become "like" a college, and their approach is misdirected. The secondary schools would do better to concentrate on the original intentions of the trivium, to assume the discipline of the written and spoken word by dealing with the skills of composition (which, as all college teachers will attest, are sadly neglected), with knowledge of genres and the more formal classificatory and instrumental elements that can prepare a student for the "fixed reason" of the humanities rather than its "wayward spirit" only.

To know how to read—to understand the structure of a work, its principal terms, and "primitive" assumptions—and to know how to write are continuing tasks in any education, but they must begin in the secondary schools. In addition, some of the work given in music humanities and art humanities, about the history of these subjects and the classification, of types, can be concentrated more easily in the secondary schools, releasing more time in the colleges for work in philosophy, poetry, and literature, where more complex problems of meaning are involved. Equally, the present-day intensive instruction in foreign languages in the secondary schools suggests that concentration at that level on the acquisition of language skills is a fruitful approach, leaving more time for college work in the literature of these languages.

The more coherent organization of the natural sciences and mathematics, with the defined sequential levels of work in these subjects-its lesser dependence on "experience"—and the recent work in the teaching of the "new math," the "new biology," and to a lesser extent the "new physics" in the secondary schools, suggests that intensive work in these disciplines can begin quite early and that, consequently, specialization in *these* subjects can be started much earlier in the college years.

This threefold division points, therefore, to a division of "pace" in the college years. It is easier for some students than for others to learn mathematics and sciences, and the more exactly defined levels in these fields make it easier for some students to advance faster along these sequences than others. This suggests that the idea of a "common core" of early college years, in which all students take a common curriculum of two years in the sciences, two in the humanities, and two in the social sciences may be too rigid. The division of pace indicates that a "vertical" organization of subjects, in which different "tracks" are laid out for the advancement of students in different fields, may be the more suitable form of college organization. But this brings us to the heart of curriculum planning—the task taken up in chapter 5.

Chapter Five

THE CONTEMPORARY CURRICULUM

> Let the tutor make his charge pass everything through a sieve and lodge nothing in his head on mere authority and trust: let not Aristotle's principles be principles to him any more than those of the Stoics or Epicureans. Let this variety of ideas be set before him; he will choose if he can; if not, he will remain in doubt. Only the fools are certain and assured. . . .
>
> If [the student] embraces Xenophon's and Plato's opinions by his own reasoning, they will no longer be theirs, they will be his. . . . He must imbibe their ways of thinking, not learn their precepts. And let him boldly forget, if he wants, where he got them, but lee him know how to make them his own.
>
> —*Montaigne,* OF THE EDUCATION OF CHILDREN
> *(translated by Donald M. Frame)*

In his visionary *New Atlantis,* Francis Bacon described a temple of knowledge, Salomon's House, or the College of Six Days Work, "instituted for the production of great and marvelous works for the benefit of man." In this house, says the Master speaking to his visitors, "we imitate the flight of birds. . . we have ships and boats for going under water." There is a perspective house to demonstrate light, a sound house for music, and "houses of deceits of the senses, where we represent all manner of false apparitions, impostures, illusions, and their failures." This delightful disarray is, perhaps, one recipe for a curriculum.

From a different view, one can see a curriculum, paraphrasing Reuben Brewer's definition of a poem, as an ordered experience built up through various kinds of meaning, controlled in turn by various uses of (conceptual) language.

My own prescriptions may end up somewhere between these two.[1]

Let me begin this chapter by restating my commitment to general education within the framework of a liberal arts program in a college. By a liberal arts program, I mean an emphasis on the imagination of the humanities and history and the treatment of the conceptual grounds of knowledge in the sciences and social sciences, as the central core of the college's concern. By general education, I mean the focusing of this concern on courses which cut across disciplinary lines (as in the case of contemporary civilization and humanities programs) to deal with the history, tradition, and great works of Western civilization, and on courses which deal with the integrative problems or common subject matters of several disciplines. By a college, I mean a four-year school, standing between the secondary school and the graduate institution, which performs a function that differs from the other two. To restate the rationale:

1. The alternative to this view of the college's role would mean the adoption of a quasi-variant of the European system, combining the secondary schools with a professional university education—the proposal Burgess and Butler made more than sixty years ago. In this scheme, the secondary school (on the pattern of the English sixth form, the French *lycee* and the propaedeutic year, and the German Gymnasium), would provide the broad humanistic background in history and philosophy, and the student would then proceed directly to the university, there to specialize in a scholarly field or be trained for a profession.

One difficulty with this scheme is that even today the American secondary schools do not provide an adequate background: at best they have tended to ape the first year of college education at the expense of training in fundamental skills; at worst they have dissipated student time by indulging in fads. Second, the triadic distinction of knowledge, which I presented in the preceding chapter, indicates that while sequential work in the sciences can begin fruitfully

---

[1] The happy middle is not always the best measure of truth. The story is told of a dispute among theologians: one group argued that there were perfect logical proofs for the existence of God; another argued that there were no logical proofs for the existence of God; and the third argued that the truth lay in between.

in the secondary schools, it is unlikely, intellectually speaking, that an equal concentration in the social sciences and the humanities is possible during these years. And third, even though secondary schools can be strengthened, they cannot supersede the distinctive role of a college.

2. The college, standing between the secondary school (concentrating on facts and skills) and the graduate school (with its necessary emphasis in specialization and research), can exercise a singular function—the training in conceptual analysis in the grounds of knowledge, the criteria of theory, and the standards of judgment.

3. The college is the place now where a student legitimately begins his training in a discipline. But it is also the place where, unlike the graduate school with its concentrations on narrow problems, it is possible to deal with the interrelations of disciplines, and to apply these disciplines to general problems. It may have been an intellectual mistake, as I think was evident in the past history of the Contemporary Civilization B course (the second year), to attempt such generality before training in a specific discipline was acquired. Yet if it was a mistake, it lay in the timing not the intention. The creation of what I have called, in the Columbia context, "third-tier" courses (see below, page 256) may be a different way to achieve this necessarily general interrelation of knowledge and synoptic vision.

4. For the young student himself, it is important that the college experience be unhampered and distinctive. It should be the testing years—the testing of one's self-and one's values; the exploration of different fields before settling in to a single one; and the experience of belonging to a common intellectual community in which diverse fields of knowledge are commingled. In short, the college can still be one of the few places of broad intellectual adventure, the place where one can resist, momentarily, the harness that society now seeks to impose at an earlier and earlier stage on its youth.

To restate a rationale is to set forth the grounds of judgment and the statement of values. But the liberal arts college today is now confronted by a number of problems. General education, we are told, is in a state of "crisis." (In the American temper, a problem is often seen as a crisis.) The demands of society, the changes in the secondary school, intellectual and institutional difficulties combine to undermine the college as we have known it. It may be useful, therefore, to summarize at this point the challenges which have called the liberal arts program (and, indeed, the very idea of a college itself) into question, and to enter some demurrers to these formulations. These challenges are:

1. The pressure to speed up college work and commence specialization early, as a greater proportion of college students enter graduate schools and the professions, because the time necessary for com pleting these advanced studies has lengthened—to four years or more in acquiring a Ph.D., and to as much as ten years beyond college in the instance of medicine. In consequence, students are unable to begin earning a living and supporting families until they are in their late twenties and early thirties.

The answer to this problem should perhaps be found not in the unwise compression of college time, but in greater financial support of young men and women during their graduate study. There is little reason to assume that in a complex, post-industrial society a man is qualified, in the professional sense, to earn his own living at the age of twenty-two. And since the skills that are acquired have a social utility, there is no reason why society should not bear the costs and carry the student through the training period. (In part this is already being done through varying combinations of government and university fellowships. But what is now given on a hit-and-miss and often unfair basis—science students can get support easily, those in the humanities cannot—should be done comprehensively.)

2. The pretensions of the secondary schools about "upgrading" and "enriching" their courses, and thus claiming to preempt the first year or two of college. While some very useful work has been done in mathematics, sciences, languages and, to a lesser extent, American history—fields where specific skills can be strengthened or a factual body of materials can be absorbed—some real damage is being done in the social sciences and humanities by giving students the illusion that they already "know" the basic ideas in these fields.

3. The intellectual difficulties encountered in organizing the gen eral education courses. But these difficulties, though genuine, do not constitute any reason for eliminating these courses, but for revising

them. And this is a process every good college, Columbia among them, has engaged in since the initial formulation of these courses. This revision is, in fact, the subject of this chapter.

4. The institutional difficulties of staffing that arise out of the changed balance in the university between college and graduate school, and the more general upheaval in the "market" for college professors. This is a problem, quite serious in its implications, that I can touch on only briefly in the concluding chapter.

In the light of all these changes and challenges, the colleges do have the responsibility of self-scrutiny and reappraisal. The questions of social policy in the financial support of graduate students, the character of secondary school instruction, and the institutional difficulties of the colleges lie outside the realm of my immediate responsibility; questions of curriculum do not.

One can begin the examinations of the intellectual and institutional difficulties of general education by returning at this point to the recent experiences of the three colleges, Harvard, Chicago, and Columbia, which have been the foci of this investigation.

Changes at Harvard College

The general education program at Harvard, in the words of a recent review committee, has been eroded. "What was being eroded was sometimes a technical detail; at other times it was a basic principle or what would have been considered a basic principle by the authors of the Redbook. The result, as it seemed to the committee, was that a program that originated with a strong sense of urgency and direction was becoming increasingly difficult to defend or even to understand."

The erosion of principle came about in the blunting, or in some instances the surrender, of the original program's emphasis on the "classic" themes—the achievements and monuments of Western civilization—combined with an historical orientation in subject matter and approach. Shortly after its beginnings, as I indicated earlier, a Harvard committee, headed by Jerome Bruner, recommended that the courses in the natural sciences concentrate on the current knowledge of a science, its principles and methods, rather than the case-history approach which had been the innovation of President James B. Conant, or the older history of science method derived from George Sarton. In other fields, analytical approaches have also been introduced.

But other elements, institutional and sociological, contributed to the erosion. Since the general education courses at Harvard were primarily courses given by "great men," the repetition of these courses over the years inevitably involved a loss of enthusiasm or interest on the part of these men; or, to use the formal language of sociology, there was a "routinization of charisma." When individual professors took leave of a general course for a year or two to concentrate on their own specialties, other "great men" had to be found. The result was a disruption in a course's continuity, or a sense of uneven equivalences as new courses were offered in place of the old.

Competition among departments interested in broadening their own introductory offerings often led to a blurring of the lines that defined a course as general education or departmental. Thus the social relations department—sociology, anthropology, and social psychology are grouped at Harvard into a common department—offered a broad introductory course in social science that was indistinguishable from a general education course. Such departmental courses tended to draw students away from the second-level elective general education courses in the college, and reduced the scope of the "gen ed" offerings,

Student interest in general education—what at Harvard was called the "Exeter syndrome"—slackened considerably, Exeter graduates (nearly a hundred of whom enter Harvard every year) tended to feel they had "had it" so far as general education was concerned, and sought to move directly into sophomore standing, advanced placement, or early specialization. This attitude spread at a great rate through much of the freshman class.

Finally, the structure of the large courses and the impersonality of the freshman year induced a feeling, particularly among the growing percentage of Harvard students coming from public high schools (currently about 60 percent), that the general education program was simply an extension of the kind of classes they had had in high school, and did not represent what a college ought to be. (Harvard has twelve hundred male and three hundred women undergraduates in the first year.) What was needed they felt was more "small group" instruction.

These last two factors led to the introduction in 1959 of what has been the most radical modification of the general education program, the freshman seminars. The seminars—the cost of which was met initially by a grant from Edwin Land, the head of the Polaroid Corporation, who felt, on the basis of his own college experiences, the need for such an innovation—typically comprise eight to ten students, who meet once a week, for two to four hours in the afternoon or evening, through one semester. There is no set pattern to the courses. As a Harvard report summarized the offerings: "Some seminars aimed to provide 'committed' freshmen early experience of adult and advanced work within a specialized field. Such, for example, was Donald Menzel's seminar on the growth and behavior of sunspots. A second kind of seminar examined the nature of a broad area of inquiry by treating in depth a sharply focussed but representative subject. Clyde Kluckholm's seminar on the Navajo Indian was an enterprise of this kind. And there have been some seminars, finally, that set out to demonstrate the nature of a wide area by considering, from the start, broad questions. Such were the seminars directed by David Riesman, which ranged through literature, philosophy, anthropology, and psychology to study the relation of the individual to society."[2]

In the four years ending in June, 1963, the program offered 130 seminars, and included 1,132 students. About half the seminars were in the social sciences, and a fourth each in the sciences and the humanities.[3] One hundred seven members of the faculty led seminars,

[2] The quotation is taken from the document, "The Freshmen Seminar Program: A Report to the Faculty of Aits and Sciences," Harvard University (February, 1963).

[3] One way of indicating the range of the courses is to "sample" every tenth seminar in the alphabetical listing of the program to show the variety offered: William Alfred on dramatic literature; Mary Bunting on microbial genetics; Joachim Gaehde on the history of art; Oscar Handlin on American history; William Klemperer on selected papers in chemistry; Kenneth Lynn on American literature; Anthony Oettinger on the theory of automatic computing machines; Krister Stendhal on biblical thought; Wallace Woodworth on readings in music.

some for one year only, others for several years. In each year since 1959, there has been a turnover of faculty, and thus of seminars, of approximately 66 percent. "That turnover," states the report of the program to the faculty, "reflects in part our determination to preserve the vitality of the seminars and of the program."

If one takes 1963 as a representative year, 322 Harvard and Radcliffe freshmen, or about 20 percent of the class, enrolled in the seminars, but of these, interestingly, 104 were women, representing about 30 percent of the Radcliffe class, and 218 were men, or little more than 15 percent of the Harvard class. The reasons for enrollment are varied: for some it is "something different," for others it is a chance to try a field and some intensive work in it to see if they would like to continue in that subject; for many, it is an opportunity to work at close range with an important intellectual figure, and to learn in a small group.

Clearly the innovation has been a useful, if costly, one. The question whether the seminar program can continue in its present form is moot. The turnover in faculty may be part of a determination to maintain vitality, but it also indicates that the "great names" at Harvard will teach such a freshman seminar once or twice, and then return to their own pursuits. Unless the program is able to attract these individuals on some rotating basis, it will be forced, as in the use of section men in the large general education courses, to fall back on young instructors, vagrant personnel, or others who, while individually stimulating, may be less attractive to students than the opportunity to work with important people. The routinization of charisma is no less of a problem here.

The task for Harvard has been twofold: to integrate this new institutional development, which has been almost a rival to the older program, into the general education structure; and to "rationalize" the offerings in the general education program. The Doty Committee, for example, noted various gaps and neglects in the intellectual coverage of the general education sequences: music is not represented; the visual arts are dealt with only in two courses at the second-group (nonrequired) level; the behavioral sciences have no home in the program (there is no economics or sociology at the required level, psychology is represented in one course at the elementary level, anthropology is available as a natural science alternative to physics or chemistry); non-Western societies are studied only in a handful of courses at the second-year, elective level; and half the students at Harvard and Radcliffe take only one science course during their college years.

To strengthen the requirements in the sciences, the Doty Committee in its report to the faculty in May, 1964, proposed a structural reorganization of the program, eliminating the traditional threefold division of the sciences, the social sciences, and the humanities, and replacing it by a twofold division of humanities and science. Of the social sciences, history was "allocated" to the humanities, while the behavioral sciences were grouped with the sciences.[4]

"This division," stated the committee, "is not advanced as the basis of a theory of knowledge: it is simply a device for effecting a program of nondepartmental education within the constraints of the problem as we understand it." In addition, the committee proposed a division of *electives* "to preserve a place in the program for courses by distinguished members of the faculty without the requirement that they fit into either of the other two main divisions," and a domain where experimental courses perhaps in non-Western cultures and the creative arts, could be offered.[5]

---

[4] Said the committee: "As a consequence of these considerations we propose that for the purposes of general education the areas of relevant learning be simply divided between the *humanities,* which in our usage will include history and the full range of subjects traditionally grouped under the humanities, and the *sciences,* which will embrace natural science, mathematics, and the behavioral sciences."

[5] Under the proposed general education reform, students would have been required to take two full-year courses (or four single-term courses) in each of the three divisions, science, humanities, and electives, plus a one-term course in English composition. Of the courses in the sciences, at least one would have been in the natural science category, the other in the natural sciences (including mathematics) or in the behavioral sciences. However, in both the humanities and the sciences, two full departmental courses were allowed as a *substitute* for one general education course. Of the two-term requirement in the electives, there was also a permissible substitution of other general education courses in the humanities and sciences, or courses in departments outside the concentration sequence. Students also would have been required to demonstrate proficiency in a foreign language.

If the proposals had been adopted the net result would be the *reduction,* actually, of required general education courses. Under the Doty proposals, a

After a year of intensive debate, the Harvard faculty, in March, 1965, voted more than two to one to reject the Doty Committee recommendations, even though its views had represented the consensus of a powerful committee and its policies had previously been approved, nine to one, by the Committee on Educational Policy. Two elements emerged during the debate which accounted for the defeat of the proposals. One was the opposition to the idea of replacing the three-way division among general education courses (social sciences, natural sciences, and humanities) with a twofold division wherein history would be allotted to the humanities and behavioral sciences (including "appropriate portions" of government put into a science category). The second, contrary in motive, was an opposition to any formalized general education and a desire simply to institute a distribution requirement, preferably departmental courses, in place of any specific set of general education courses.

Following the defeat of the Doty Committee report, the Harvard faculty debated a number of alternative schemes. In November, 1965, the Committee on Educational Policy, headed by Franklin Ford, dean of the Faculty of Arts and Sciences, proposed a plan which sought to maintain a commitment to general education, but went far toward meeting the wishes of those who wanted to introduce departmental work at an earlier time than hitherto before. It was a proposal which was frankly a compromise. (Said the Harvard *Crimson* in an editorial: "It may not stand a philosophical test, but it is not a philosophical document. It was not derived from first principles, but from faculty votes, and its only philosophical base is the small part of the Redbook program left unchanged by voted statute or administrative convenience.")

Under the Educational Policy Committee proposal, which was adopted by the Harvard faculty, each student is required to take at least four year-long courses outside the area of his field or concentration. Three must be in general education, and a student has to

---

student would have been required to take but one general education course in the humanities and the natural sciences, and could fulfill all other requirements from departmental courses. At the same time, a student specializing in the natural sciences could fulfill his "gen ed" science requirement without having to take any courses in the behavioral sciences.

take at least one course in each of the three areas offered by the Committee on General Education (i.e., social science, humanities, and natural science). But he need not, as previously required, take the lower-level (i.e., broad introductory) courses; he can, instead, take an upper-level course if he has taken, before hand, certain departmental courses, or their equivalents, as prerequisites. Students majoring in the natural sciences can forgo any general education courses in that field.

The most striking innovation in the new proposal is that it allows students to skip the lower-level general education courses by making these voluntary. At the same time, as Dean Ford noted, "it would be possible for a departmental course to count at par value in the total general educational program without imposing upon the new committee the painful, if not impossible, task of assigning exact substantive parity (e.g., equating Economics 1 with Social Sciences 2)." Thus, it has created open competition between the departmental courses and the general education courses at the lower level. Students who want to take upper-level general education courses can do so only by taking some departmental course first, and then taking some upper-level general education course in a subsequent year. In effect, new sequences would now be introduced in which general education courses build upon a disciplinary introductions, rather than the obverse, as before. (To this extent, the program moves in the direction of the kind of "third-tier" program as proposed in these pages.)

The critical point, of course, is that the broad historical courses in the first-year general education program become further whittled down from the original Redbook emphasis. For John Finley, the Master of Eliot House and the strongest proponent of the original general education program, the plan represents a "departmental take-over" of the general education program. To some extent, this is true. But what the proposal also does is to recognize the complaint of a large number of entrants (the "Exeter syndrome") who feel that they are already well prepared, and resent their "confinement" in the lower-level courses by permitting them to skip the lower-level general education courses. Thus, by allowing students to take upper-level courses in fulfillment of the requirement, considerable flexibility is introduced into the system. The cost, however, as Dean Ford has noted, is the loss of a "shared experience," which itself had been one of the rationales of the introductory general education courses.

The new Harvard scheme is, quite clearly, a "halfway house." It can move, in one direction, towards a complete distribution requirement in which students would be free to take any electives outside a field of concentration, or it can move in the other, of building more dearly specified sequences in which general education would become an application of, or a testing of, disciplinary knowledge in broader contexts.

Changes at the College of the University of Chicago

The College of the University of Chicago is in the throes of readjustment that may lead to the almost complete reversal of general education as practiced there for twenty years.

Originally (as will be recalled from the discussion in chapter 2) the college offered *only* courses in general education, in which a minimum of fourteen year-long courses over the four-year period were required for the B.A. degree. But the inability of the college to sustain that program, and the pressures for specialization, led to a reorganization of the college in 1957-58 in which an effort "was made to introduce a major system and to initiate a regular four-year baccalaureate program. The formal structure of four divisions, corresponding to those of the graduate school—in the social sciences, humanities, biological sciences, and physical sciences— was redefined, and students were required to concentrate in one of the four divisions, as a requirement for the degree. In addition, a "lower college," consisting of two years of required common-core courses, and an "upper college," consisting of one year of specialization in any of the four divisions, plus a year of electives, were established.

There were, however, a number of institutional difficulties in implementing the program. All students were required to demonstrate competence in *ten* courses to fulfill the common-core program.[6] But since no student was required to take more than *eight* of the core

---

[6] The ten courses were: a year of biological science, a year of physical science, two years of humanities, two years of social science, and a year each of English composition, a foreign language, mathematics, and the history of Western civilization.

courses in the first two years, two courses were "mitigated" for the student even if he failed to "place out" of these courses by examination. Thus all students automatically, in one way or another, were excused from at least two required courses. This, understandably, led to some confusion.

In reducing the number of courses, other difficulties emerged. There was a concurrent intellectual problem in that because of the compression of topics, some of the courses, particularly in the social sciences and the humanities, were awkwardly joined. Originally, each division offered three year-long courses in a required sequence. In the social sciences, for example, the first year emphasized political theory and American constitutionalism, the second year concentrated on personality, social structure, and culture, the third year on the problems of freedom and planning. Because of an unwillingness of the staff to forgo any of the topics, the compression of the courses into two years meant that economics was distributed in the first-year course, and the problems of freedom and bureaucracy in the second. In the humanities courses, music, painting, poetry, and literature were commingled in the first-year course, and history, drama, lyric poetry, fiction, and philosophy in the second; but because of compression, the block of time allotted to each field was quite short, and students shuttled from topic to topic and from subject to subject.[7]

The upper half of the college program had difficulties of another sort. Originally, the faculties of the college and the divisions were

---

[7] The word *commingle* is an effort to describe the intercalation of the different arts in the same course. As the course chairman observed in a memorandum to the staff: "I would like to observe for the benefit of new staff members that the presence of art, music, and literature in the course and the relation between the arts has long been a source of perplexity to students and to some of out university colleagues. . . . This is not a course in synesthesia, and the presence of the three arts does not imply any particular theory about the similarities or the differences between art, music, and literature. The main reason for the way in which we handle the arts in two- or three-week blocks, rather than following the conventional method of devoting a quarter of each, is simply our belief that students will learn more if they have time for assimilating their learning in each of the arts over a year-long period. In addition, since they usually have but one instructor for all three arts, students tend to develop a closer and more profitable pedagogical relationship with their teacher. Thus instructors should not feel at all compelled to say anything about the relationship of art, music, and literature, though such discussion is not necessarily to be avoided if it seems sensible and relevant."

distinct, and the members of the college were recruited largely because of their interest and competence in general education rather than for their specialized training. This made it difficult to introduce a major or concentration program because in a number of fields there were not enough specialized persons to give the courses. An effort to have the graduate division take over responsibility for the undergraduate courses was made, but this was possible only if the two faculties could be joined, and in a number of instances the graduate department refused to accept some of the college faculty, despite their tenure.

But all this—the effort, first, to build a general education program based on fourteen year-long comprehensive courses, and then the slow and unwieldy modifications which produced a unified, if compressed, lower college with a field specialization in the upper years—is now gone. In October, 1964, Edward Levi, the provost of the university, proposed a radical new scheme that, following its adoption some months later by the university and the board of trustees, goes into effect in the autumn of 1966.

Under the Levi plan, the college will be "divided" into five collegiate divisions, each under a Master, which will function with a high degree of autonomy as "area colleges," and offer a comprehensive program in each field. The five area colleges will be physical science, biology, social science, humanities, and a collegiate division which would concentrate on "civilizational" studies. Unlike the small, decentralized colleges that have been created at the University of California at Santa Cruz, which are on the "Oxbridge" model, the Chicago divisions not be separate residential colleges. Students at the College of the University of Chicago will live in common dormitories, but the colleges will be "intellectual unities" (paralleling to some extent the "schools" at the University of Sussex in England) which will offer inter-disciplinary and specialized sequences within each field.

Students in the new college will take four general courses in common, though the exact pattern remains to be worked out by the faculty. It is intended that two courses will be taken in the first year, one in the second, and some kind of integrating seminar in the final year. These common courses would be the core of general education. Within each college the exact relationship between specialized major sequences and more general courses remains to be worked out by each faculty. In the social science division, for example, a student might take a degree with a detailed specialization in economics, or he might take a broad program in public affairs as preparation for work in government, business and law.

While the new Chicago proposal is a large step away from the conception of a common general education program, or of broad synthetic courses as a comprehensive curriculum for all students, there is a new kind of rationale discernible in its emphasis on intellectual method. It is this: although students in each of the separate colleges might be deficient in areas other than their own concentration, by gaining a detailed knowledge of how to read the materials in a specific field, they would be able to search out its structure of "meta-meanings," so that they would understand the principles of description, exposition, and argument in other subjects as well. Thus while there would be specialization, the emphasis in each field would be on the structure of inquiry, as it is manifest in the subject matter.

In moving, first, toward some effort to instill specialization, and now, toward an area concentration as the basis of undergraduate preparation, the University of Chicago has finally reversed the original intention of a common four-year education. Curiously enough, despite all the early radical talk about the innovative nature of the comprehensive general education courses, there was, in the last decade at least, little genuine experiment in these sequences (although considerable re-juggling of course content). The considerable intellectual excitement at the college during that period was in the sequence in non-Western culture, and in senior seminars, where teachers felt more free, in teaching a course in their own fashion, than in having to contend with the drag of large staff courses.

This may, in itself, point to a general institutional lesson—that all revolutions fade, and after a while look tedious to their successors. Even revolutions have their pieties, and none more so than those which have loudly trumpeted new truths. It may be that Chicago, having gone so far in one revolution, now has to go much further in reversing itself, and that other schools, such as Columbia, which have evolved in less spectacular fashion are in a stronger, if less intellectually exciting, institutional position. But excitement, without object, is often a fruitless emotion. It is alleged that Robert Maynard Hutchins once remarked, "The trouble with my successors is that they do not have the courage of my convictions." That may be so. But what one can say about the College of the University of Chicago today, if not of ten years ago, is that some new convictions are being forged.

A Side Glance at England

Paradoxically, at a time when the scope of general education in the United States is being- reduced in favor of narrow specialism, the idea of general education is growing more popular in England, particularly at the seven new English universities formed in the early 1960s.[8]

All of the new universities are, in varying ways, experimenting with curriculum. One of the innovations is for each new university to build in strength in a few areas only. The idea that to be respectable each university has to offer, as far as possible, every academic subject has been abandoned. York is recruiting a high proportion of students, initially, in the social sciences and later in the natural sciences. East Anglia, in addition to other innovations, is seeking to relate biological studies to agricultural environment. But in almost all these schools, the older idea, characteristic of "Oxbridge," that a student read for three years only in a single area (e.g., classics or modern history), has been abandoned. At Colchester, the University of Essex teaches all arts students some science in the first year, as well as a compulsory course in statistics. At Warwick, there is a first-year course in logic and language "as a means of creating a common mode of discourse between all sides of the university." The idea of general degrees and linked subjects is common to all the new universities, with the possible exception of York.

[8] For a background discussion of the British educational scene, see Sir Eric Ashby, *Technology and the Academics* (London and New York, Macmillan, 1958).

It is the new University of Sussex, at Brighton, with its radical structural and intellectual innovations,[9] that has attracted the greatest attention. Sussex, the "oldest" of the seven new universities (it was chartered in August, 1961), groups its faculties not in departments but in "schools." By 1964 there were five such schools—the School of English and American Studies, the School of European Studies, the School of Physical Science, the School of Social Studies, and the School of Educational Studies. (Additional schools are being planned —African and Asian Studies, Applied Sciences and Engineering, and Biological Sciences.)[10]

The schools are in no sense super-departments, for the same subject may be studied as a major in more than one school. The purpose of the school structure is to link students and faculty in a common field, rather than in single disciplines, although courses in each discipline are offered. Some of the schools follow the pattern of the American "area program" studies, so that a student in the School of English and American Studies does work in both literature and social studies. But, in the effort to provide linkages between fields, there are "papers" (the British term for course) common to the School of Social Studies and the School of Biological and Applied Sciences, and to Social Studies and Technology.

A student takes a degree (i.e., a concentration) in science, arts, or social studies. Certain common, first-year requirements are required of all students. Thus before a student is admitted to either arts or social studies, he has to take two general courses required of all students seeking these degrees. One is in "Language and Values." To quote the prospectus: "To be considered will be such topics as the nature and justification of moral and value judgments, free will and political liberty, responsibility and punishment and the meaningful-

[9] There had been an earlier effort to introduce general education at the first new British university founded after World War II, — Keele University in North Staffordshire, Against considerable opposition, the vice-chancellor of the university, the late Lord Lindsay of Birker (one-time Master of Balliol and an eminent political theorist), introduced in 1949 a Foundation Year devoted to the bases of Western civilization. But the effort in this direction did not succeed.

[10] A collection of essays, edited by David Daiches, spells out the rationale of the Sussex idea: see *The Idea of a New University* (London, Andre Deutsch, 1964).

ness of religious language. Emphasis will be placed upon the value judgment [in making both social and political decisions], of which both the historical and contemporary accounts will be studied." A second common course is "An Introduction to History." Quoting the prospectus again: "With what problems is the historian concerned and how does he define and investigate them? Why do historians disagree in the answers they give? What is the relationship between the motives and purposes of individuals and sequence of social change? These and related questions will be considered in terms of two historical works: Burckhardt, *The Civilization of the Renaissance in Italy*, and Tawney, *Religion and the Rise of Capitalism*."

Students entering the School of Social Studies take four common courses: one in the "Concepts, Methods, and Values in the Social Sciences"; an option in philosophy; a course in either "International Politics" or "World Population and Resources"; and one entitled "Contemporary Britain." Students then concentrate in one of six subjects: economics, geography, history, philosophy, politics and sociology, or international relations.

All students taking degrees in science take two common courses, "Structure and Properties of Matter" and "Mathematics with Physics," plus an option, then either "Further Mathematics," or "Chemistry." A student then proceeds to the particular subject of his choice: in physics, for example, there are then twelve compulsory courses (from electricity and magnetism to methods of experimental physics).

Students in the arts, after finishing the common first-year courses, take further work in the School of English and American Studies or the School of European Studies. Work in one or the other does not deal exclusively with the area studies. Thus, among the common courses required in the School of English and American Studies, there is one on "The Modern European Mind," divided into Expression ("the ways in which the literary imagination has responded to the problems of modern industrial society") and Diagnosis. In Expression, the students read Dostoevski, Joyce, Lawrence, Kafka, and the like; in Diagnosis, they read Marx, Nietzsche, Kierkegaard, Arnold, Ruskin, Morris, Freud, and Jung. Other common courses in this school are in philosophy, and in history and literature (e.g., "Literature and the Romantic Movement," "The Late Victorian Revolt in Literature, Politics, and Culture"). Students then proceed to a major subject: English literature, history, American studies, or philosophy.

Two things are worth noting about this program. One is the emphasis on the present and the recent past ("history in the making" as the Sussex prospectus puts it) rather than on the classics or the traditions of Western civilization. This, in part, is a reaction to "Oxbridge" and the need, as British educational planners see it, to train individuals for "modern" problems. The second is the early emphasis on analytical and methodological questions, the progression to common or linked subjects, and then the specialization in particular subjects or disciplines.

The concern with general education stems in part from the changed social nature of the student body, which in recent years has been drawn increasingly from the lower middle class and working class, and, in part, from the influence of American experiments in combining various subjects and fields for cross-disciplinary work. It is clear that general education in this British conception does not mean survey courses, or simply a distribution requirement of work in diverse fields, but a genuine effort to "find links between subjects." It is an experiment well worth watching.

Changes at Columbia College

Beginning with the class that entered in 1954, Columbia College abandoned the prevailing "maturity credit" system, which had allowed a student to take a general degree, and instead required all students to complete a "major" or "concentration" in one department.[11] The introduction of the major system, more than any other single element, changed the character of Columbia College in the last decade. While the trends were evident before the introduction of the change, the major system, by encouraging students (in some instances such as the sciences, by requiring them) to begin their majors in their sophomore or even freshman years, has fractured the "unity"

[11] I take as a base line for the discussion of changes the description of the Columbia College program, and the recommendations for change, in *The Educational Future of Columbia University,* Report of the President's Committee (known as the MacMahon Report), 1957.

of the lower college, with its emphasis on a common-core program.[12] The major requirement has been responsible, too, for the creation of a system of multiple tracks in various fields—a crescive innovation that has revolutionary implications for teaching at Columbia College, if not for collegiate education as a whole.

The second most dramatic change in the Columbia College curriculum in the past decade was the decision in 1959 to abandon the common second-year Contemporary Civilization course, and to substitute instead an option of two different terms, or a continuous year's work, in anthropology, economics, geography, government, sociology, Oriental civilization, or the old Contemporary Civilization course, to fulfill the requirement of a second year of work in Contemporary Civilization.

The two-year sequence in Contemporary Civilization and the Humanities had been the core of Columbia's contribution to general education. The decision to break up the sequence seemed to be a step away from the idea of general education as a whole. Certainly, to give up the second-year course after thirty years of *experiment* was a formidable change. Many different elements conjoined to produce this decision. There were, first, evident intellectual difficulties in the formulation of the course. I have used the word *experiment* deliberately. The intention of the course was to provide a year's work in contemporary *social issues,* drawing from the best of the recent work in the social sciences. But throughout the history of the course, there was rarely a continuing consensus about its orientation. The beginning emphasis, reflecting the depression years and the New Deal, was on economic problems and economic policy. In the early 1950s, with the growing interest in anthropology and sociology, the emphasis shifted to the study of culture. Another reorganization, later in the decade, introduced a large section on moral attitudes and added readings from existentialist philosophy and neo-orthodox theology (Sartre, Unamuno, Niebuhr, Tillich, and the like). But no reorganization ever wholly succeeded in erasing the former layers, and the stratigraphic past was evident in the imperfect joinings

---

[12] Thus the catalogue notation for chemistry majors reads; "Most students will need to postpone part of the requirements in humanities and contemporary civilization until after the sophomore year."

of the several layers. Various departments (particularly economics and anthropology) complained that the readings presented were no longer representative or reflective of the newer and best work in their fields. Perhaps the most important objection was that the course skimmed a great many problems, failed to relate them, and required of students an understanding of policy that was impossible inasmuch as the students lacked the necessary training in any of the disciplines concerned. A majority of the committee reviewing the course (headed by Professor David Truman) felt that an acquaintance with a specific discipline, which would treat of general, contemporary problems through its own perspectives while building as explicitly as possible on the materials and themes of Contemporary Civilization A, would be more useful to a student than the loosely quilted patchwork that Contemporary Civilization B had become.

But intellectual difficulties did not altogether account for the decision. There was, second, pressure from the several social science departments for students to begin work in their disciplines in the sophomore year. Under the existing system, a student could begin an introductory course only in his third year (since Contemporary Civilization B was not considered a useful prerequisite to these disciplines), and thus he could not do advanced work until his fourth year. If a student could take his introductory course in the sophomore year, some departments argued, he could do general work in the subject in his third year, and use the senior year for intensive seminar study—readings or research—in the field. The substitution of the social science disciplines for the general course in the second year would allow the departments to build a more useful sequence of advanced work in the subject.[13]

A third and equally compelling factor was the difficulty in staffing

[13] A student using a second-year Contemporary Civilization course to enter his major (as in anthropology, economics, and government, which require their majors to take the Contemporary Civilization course) cannot offer that to satisfy the Contemporary Civilization requirement. He must take yet another Contemporary Civilization course. The practice therefore is to begin one's major course in the second year, and postpone the other Contemporary Civilization course-which acts to further to break up the common-core program—at least in the temporal sense. If one of the intentions of a lower college was to have students share a common experience, which each could relate to the other, then to that extent the intention has been deflected.

the course. Few of the departments wanted to commit their personnel, especially senior people, to the common Contemporary Civilization course when there was considerable need to extend the offerings in the major in the subject. A presentation to the Truman Committee indicated that in a representative year few persons of tenure rank taught the second-year course. The same problem was evident in staffing the introductory course. The existence of the two Contemporary Civilization courses, each with small sections, necessitating the assignment of teachers,to general education rather than departmental courses, strained the resources of a number of departments. The committee therefore felt that if the departments were given direct responsibility for staffing their individual second-year Contemporary Civilization course, with the number of sections determined by the student "market," the administrative problem would be more manageable.[14]

In 1963-64, after three years of experience with the new system, the College decided to maintain the new system of varied options, though a number of the departments concerned (principally economics and anthropology) were asked to relate the course work more directly to the Contemporary Civilization materials, and not to use the occasions to present their second-year Contemporary Civilization courses solely as introductory courses to the discipline. The student market, to the extent that this evidence is relevant, confirmed the decision: of the six hundred or so students taking the second-year courses, fewer than fifty voted to take the old general course, which had been offered along with the new departmental courses. The decision to continue the new system was probably inevitable, since few of the departments wanted to create a new general course.

[14] The college proposal also allowed for acceptable interdepartmental and interdisciplinary courses. These have not appeared, though a modified version of the old Contemporary Civilization B course continues as an option. One can assume that no new interdisciplinary courses appeared for intellectual reasons: the departments felt that none were viable, and wanted to experiment solely with departmental courses. Or, the reasons may have been institutional: the departments were preoccupied with their own course and staffing problems, and since the College lacks a mechanism which brings groups of departments in consultation with each other, no interdisciplinary courses were proposed. Both reasons may have been operative, though if there had been a current of intellectual excitement for interdisciplinary work, as appeared after 1945, the institutional difficulties would have been bridged.

To a considerable extent, the "gestalt" between the first and second year of Contemporary Civilization has been broken, if only because the first year remains a general course, seeking for some unified view of the sweep of Western civilization, while the second year, though focusing on the present, places varied emphases, depending on the course, on the social science disciplines themselves as well as on contemporary problems. The intellectual continuity between the two years remains strong in some instances (especially where the emphasis is on some synoptic view, as in philosophy, in one of the government alternatives and in the first term of sociology) but has become frayed in others, where the emphasis necessarily is more on the discipline.

It may well be that the present arrangement, developing empirically, is the best arrangement, drawing as it does from the strengths of the College and its intellectual and staffing resources; and that some other scheme, more consistent theoretically, or seeking to impose a new unified view, might fail. Yet one can tell only if one is willing to experiment, and to test the experimental process, I present below a new proposal to reorganize the Contemporary Civilization sequence.

The introduction of the major system presented a number of departments with a difficult pedagogical dilemma. This was the varied needs and different levels of preparation of students taking introductory courses in a subject. On the one hand, a number of students wanted to take introductory work in these departments as the beginning of a professional specialization in that field, and for such students a specific pattern of work was necessary. On the other hand, there were students who sought to take introductory courses in these subjects only to fulfill a general requirement (as in the sciences, where a Columbia student has to take two years of a single science, or one year each of two different sciences) but did not intend to proceed further in these subjects. Then, too, there was the case, again in the sciences, of the premedical and engineering students—students who needed introductory work for vocational purposes—whose needs were different from those planning to do professional work in these fields. And finally there was the problem, especially in recent

years as a result of the upgraded work in the secondary schools—
particularly, once again, in the sciences and in languages—of students
entering Columbia with different degrees of preparation, so that for
many of these students the introductory course was too elementary.

In short, the problem has been: how to teach a subject for the general
nonspecialized student, how to teach a "service course" for students
who need it as a tool for other work, and how to teach it as an
introduction to professional work in the field. The device adopted by an
increasing number of departments has been to introduce multiple tracks
to accommodate these diverse needs.

The physics curriculum provides a fascinating example of a department
that has organized *four* different beginning sequences in the subject. One
sequence—called, in the college vernacular, "Physics for Poets"—is a
two-term course for "nonscience" students without laboratory work; it
is not a "survey" of the subject but develops an understanding of the role
of experiment and the nature of theory in physics. The only requirement
is intermediate algebra. Taught by Professor Polykarp Kusch (who
was awarded a Nobel Prize in 1955), and revised in 1964-1965 by
Professor Samuel Devons, the chairman of the university's physics
department, it has become one of the most popular courses in the college.[15]
A second, two-term sequence, which includes laboratory but does not
use calculus, is primarily for premedical and other pre-professional
students. It takes up the study of matter and motion as the foundation
of physics, the development of mechanics in its historical background,
and general topics in the development of physical theory. A third, three-
term sequence, using calculus, is designed for engineering and physical
science majors. It begins with mechanics and heat in the first term,
goes on to electricity and magnetism, combined with quantitative
experiments, in the second term, and proceeds to light and atomic
physics, again combined with experimental work, in the third term. A
fourth, "high-speed" track, designed by Professor Melvin Schwartz, is
for a small, selected group of freshmen who enter with advanced placement in mathematics and physics. This course moves rapidly through

[15] Lest anyone misunderstand, the phrase is not used pejoratively, but was so
designated by Professor Kusch, its innovator, who took it as a challenge to organize
a course which could satisfy a student who has no talent for mathematics, yet is
difficult and demanding as an intellectual exercise.

the elementary phases of physics and is intended to give this special group concentrated work in the more advanced introduction to special problems of physical theory.

The mathematics department, faced with a similar problem, has also organized four different sequences. Students who want to take only one year of mathematics to fulfill the mathematics-science requirement take a general course in the basic concepts of mathematics. For students who plan to begin the study of calculus, there are three different two-term sequences, organized at different levels of purpose and difficulty. The sequence IA-IIA is a standard course devoted to the differential and integral calculus of functions of one variable, and to infinite sequences and series. It is intended for students who need calculus for its application in the natural sciences, but do not have outstanding ability or interest in mathematics itself. It is expected that most of the students who need calculus will take this course. The second sequence, IB-IIB, is devoted to the same topics as IA-IIA, but seeks to develop a deeper understanding of the mathematical concepts involved. This sequence is suitable for students with advanced placement and others who have a sustained interest in mathematics. A third sequence, IC-IIC, covers much the same material as the sequences IA-IIA and IB-IIB, but uses a terminology and style thoroughly consonant with contemporary mathematics, and pays a great deal of attention to the various mathematical structures in their own right. It is intended for students who are exceptionally competent and interested in pure mathematics.

Other sciences have also worked out a multitrack system. Chemistry offers three sequences: a two-term general chemistry course, the laboratory work of which in the second term is designed for nonmajors; a second sequence (for those proceeding with chemistry) that offers more intensive work in qualitative analysis; and a speedier track, a one-term course, for those whose performance on the chemistry placement examination in Freshman Week demonstrates an exceptional qualification in the subject. Zoology offers two beginning sequences, either of which may be offered in fulfillment of the mathematics-science requirement, but one is designed expressly for the nonscience student, the other covers the minimum requirements for the premedical student.

But the process that began primarily in the natural sciences has spread to other fields as well in the last two years. The psychology department now offers "Modern Concepts of Behavior" as a general course for those who do not plan to specialize in psychology. In 1964 the history department, for the first time, divided its program: it offers a general introductory course on the "History of the American Republic," and a more intensive three-part sequence (a year course on the colonial and revolutionary period, a year course on the nineteenth century, and a course on the twentieth century) which, while open to all qualified students, is designed for history majors. The economics department is beginning a two-track system, offering an intensive specialized sequence for those seeking to become economists (and recommending the study of calculus) and a concentration for students interested in learning about economics or business. The English department, in 1962-63, instituted a special course for those freshmen who (through advanced placement examinations) have demonstrated special competence in English. These students, who are excused from the required year's course in freshman composition, take instead a one-term "Introduction to Literary Study," which deals intensively with a single major work. In one instance, Professor Steven Marcus devoted the term to the study of *Hamlet:* the sources of the play, the scholarship of the text, the variant critical interpretations of its meanings, and the styles of performance. For these students—not necessarily English majors—the term becomes an intensive freshman seminar in writing, alongside the regular English course.

The system of multiple tracks was not planned by the administration as college policy, but was an adaptive device, developed by the different departments to meet new problems and diverse needs. It has introduced a great new flexibility in the college curriculum by allowing qualified students to begin work at higher levels (thus it has adjusted to the problem of advanced placement not by excusing students from courses but offering them more intensive work instead). It has separated out the different kinds of introductory courses needed by those majoring in a subject, and those who need or want to study it for general, or related, purposes. From the department's standpoint, it has clarified the *different* functions of the undergraduate and graduate levels. As Professor Lorch has pointed out, "Whereas in the past our mathematics majors naturally gravitated to the graduate program for a considerable portion of their work, they now have at their disposal a complete undergraduate program which will give them an exceedingly thorough education. This has made it possible for us to separate our graduate from the undergraduate studies and thus to raise the level of our graduate program." By creating multiple tracks, the department was also able "to emphasize some of the newer aspects and phases of our subject which has become more important in the past generation."

Yet the innovation of multiple tracks poses some problems for the College. By sorting out special students for advanced work, it emphasizes a "verticality" of college work rather than the common advance a class makes by doing common freshman and sophomore work, and thus breaks down the notion of "common experience" which had been one of the traditional *raisons d'être* of the college community even more. Further, it has placed a greater emphasis on the role of the departments in the college. There are few integrative mechanisms at Columbia for making the several departments aware of each other's work and needs—and it is interesting that, so far as I can learn, the innovation of multiple tracks was made by each department quite independently, rather than by diffusion from one department to another. But the growing insularity of departments, each preoccupied with its own problems, makes it difficult to build into the curriculum the necessary *links* that can provide students with work in common subjects, which are approachable through different disciplines. In this way, too, the college is subjected to centrifugal forces.

A significant feature of Columbia College in the past decade has been the increase in the number of courses offered, despite the limited expansion of the student body—an indication that the College has been seeking to meet its responsibilities to curriculum by offering work in added fields where necessary. An exact count is difficult to make and simply counting courses in the catalogue can be deceptive. For example, the substitution of departmental courses for the old Contemporary Civilization B has meant the introduction of fourteen "new" courses instead of one "old" course with x number of sections, and this is not a real increase. Yet, even so, one can say that, in this instance, there has been a net addition, since some departments, notably government and philosophy, do offer several alternative courses in fulfillment of the requirement, rather than a single option. (The government department offers not only a "regular" Contemporary Civilization course on "Democracy and Dictatorship," but an alternate course on "Politics and Reflections on Politics Since 1914." In one sense, this can be called a "second track" for students.) The introduction of the multiple track system in the sciences and in mathematics has, of course, also greatly expanded the formal number of courses, but in a "functional" sense these varied sequences are all simply equivalents for one older course.

Despite the difficulty of obtaining an exact count, it is clear that the increase has been notable. The most important factor, numerically, has been the expansion of the major program. In 1958, the first full year of the program's operation, seventeen departments offered full majors. In 1965-1966 the number had increased to twenty-six, in some measure because of the reorganization or expansion of departments that had previously offered only sporadic work in the College; this has been true, notably, of sociology, anthropology, and geography.

A second element has been the increased demand for language instruction. In part this has been a response to the new areas of interest to Americans—Russian, Chinese, and Japanese; in part, an expansion of the older language departments as students, arriving with better preparation, seek more literature in the subject rather than advanced grammar.[16]

A third factor has been the development of new programs. One such major innovation has been Oriental Studies and Oriental Civilizations. An interdisciplinary program, Oriental Studies complements

---

[16] Professor Luciano Rebay writes: "Ten years ago the offerings of the Italian department of Columbia College amounted to three courses: one elementary, one intermediate, and one special reading course. The latter was conducted entirely in English and required no knowledge of Italian. . . . In 1964-65 [the Italian department] will offer a total of nine courses: three first- and second-year language courses, three third-year literature courses, one seminar in Italian literature, and two courses in Italian civilization and literature conducted in English."

the general education courses in Humanities and Contemporary Civilization. Oriental Civilizations is one of the alternative options in the Contemporary Civilization sequence. Further, in 1964-65, after a long period of planning, the College introduced a new one-year sequence in the history of science, offered, at the start, as an elective. In addition, there are new programs in astrophysics, linguistics, and the program in the arts which includes work in theater as well as the plastic arts. In all these ways, without a substantial increase in the student body, the College has expanded.

The centrifugal tendencies I have noted in the College curriculum stem in part from intellectual developments, but also from the College structure—i.e., from the concentration of decision-making within the departments, and the inadequacies of the integrative mechanisms of the College itself. This is evident in the uneven relationship between the lower-college program, which is managed jointly by several departments, and the major program, which is handled by the departments alone.

Few of the College departments in the social sciences or in languages and literature build their majors directly on the work in the Contemporary Civilization and Humanities courses. And in the upper college, there have been few links between departments. There have been sporadic and idiosyncratic ventures, such as the cooperation of the English and sociology departments in a joint seminar on "Literature and Society." There now exists, thanks to the creation of a College Committee on Language and Literature, a systematic effort to introduce joint courses between the various language departments which will deal with comparative literature in the several languages concerned. Thus, a joint course in the classics of the Renaissance draws upon the English, French, and Italian departments.[17] And the committee plans to develop a sizable number of similar

[17] A three-term sequence will be offered. The first goes from Petrarch to Tasso, and will concentrate on the Italian background but deal also with related French and English developments; a second term, assuming the Italian background, will deal with Sidney, Spenser, Shakespeare, and related French material; a third term, in Rabelais, Ronsard, and Montaigne, will deal as well with the related Italian and English developments, the discussions will be conducted in English, but all texts are to be read in the original. There is also the joint English-French course on Mallarme and Hopkins.

courses, involving the cooperation of the English and Russian departments, Spanish and French, and the like, in the coming years. But in the social sciences, where one could expect joint programs between, say, the economics and government departments, between government and sociology, and sociology and anthropology, there has been no such effort. And the same is largely true in the sciences. The curriculum at Columbia College, as can be readily seen by comparison with other schools, is still more integrated than it is at most other colleges. The recalcitrance of the problem may lie directly in the structure of knowledge today; and depending on one's point of view, it may or may not be a necessary evil. I do believe that a greater coherence is intellectually necessary and desirable, and this issue of a more unified curriculum—demonstrated at Columbia in the uneven integration of the lower-college and the major programs, and in the problem of intellectual and curricular cooperation between departments in the upper-college program—is the starting point of my own suggestions for the reorganization of the curriculum. It is to this central question that I now turn.

Some Modest Proposals

In this section I shall make some modest proposals for the revision of curriculum. This is not meant in any ironic or Swiftian sense, nor do I want to fight again "the battle of the books." Any institution has a living history, and change, to be meaningful, has to be placed realistically within the framework of the past and the possible. It is much easier to write Utopian proposals, for there is often little prospect of their implementation; the greater difficulty is to change institutions in a direction that is possible and desirable.

My first objective is to reorganize the two years of Contemporary Civilization and to relate those courses to the Humanities so as to provide a more unified lower-college experience; the second, to set forth a program that will integrate the lower-college with the upper-college courses in order to provide for a coherent development of analytical skills and ideas.

The key to this coherence is a scheme that envisages the first year as the acquisition of necessary historical and background knowledge, the second and third years as the training in a discipline and the application of this discipline to diverse subject matters in a field, and the fourth year as a combination of seminar work in the discipline and participation in integrative courses-courses which, in a kind of shorthand, I call the "third-tier" level—in one of the major areas of the sciences, the humanities, and the social sciences.

The third tier—which is the most radical innovation I propose in the curriculum—is not a set of general education or survey courses, or courses of the type called "great issues." Nor are they primarily "interdisciplinary" courses, which give students a passing knowledge of presumably new approaches. Third-tier courses, limited within the triadic division I have used, will give a student a sense of how his major subject can be applied to a problem area, or will demonstrate the broad conceptual foundations of the discipline he has acquired.

I do not propose that all students in their senior year take the same third-tier courses. They will take courses appropriate to the division of field. Thus, for example, I would propose that all students majoring in one of the social sciences take a common third-tier course on the development of new states. In this fashion the nature of economic, political, and social development could be focused upon a set of problems (the creation of an economic infra-structure, the development of a public bureaucracy, the transition from a rural to industrial society) that illuminate the uses, application, and limits of the discipline in which the student has acquired some training. For all students majoring in science, I would propose common third-tier courses in the philosophy of science, which would deal with the conceptual foundations of science, and a course in the sociology of science which would examine the development of science in a social setting, deal with the contexts of research, and the role structure of scientific activity, in order to give the science student a sense of the worldly context in which he will be operating. For students in the humanities, I would propose a third-tier course in the nature of language: the social context and development of language, as exemplified in the older work of Sapir, Bloomfield, and Whorf; the newer classifications put forth in structural linguistics; and problems of meaning, as developed in philosophical analysis.

For the moment, I put these forward as examples. Later in this section I shall give more detailed proposals for a number of courses that can be usefully seen as integrative courses in the senior year. The basic point, however, remains: a student should take integrative or problem area courses after acquiring a proficiency in a specific discipline. In this way, he gains a sense of the foundation or the contextual setting of a discipline. Thus, the application of a discipline is exemplified, and a student learns to use some "tools" for handling these problems.

All of this, further, is integral to the argument that the college, with this sequence, can have a distinctive role that cannot be undertaken either by the secondary school or the graduate school. Equally integral is the argument that the framework of these courses, including those in history, be organized around the analytical modes of conceptual inquiry—the question being always not only what one knows, but how one knows and verifies the knowledge one has.

A NEW RATIONALE

The heart of the Columbia College program has always been the Contemporary Civilization and Humanities courses. For many students, these courses were a "conversion experience," a shock of ideas that gave them a new appreciation of the dimensions of thought and feeling—a conversion, so to speak, to culture. One is told that in the recent years this experience has been attenuated. Some of this derives from a feeling students have—or claim—that they "know" the ideas, if not the specific books. On probing, one finds that these claims do not stand up. But the fact that students think they know the ideas-reflecting often the superficial sweep of the "culture market"—often takes the edge off the confrontation with difficult ideas. In a different way, the lack of any direct relationship *between* the Humanities and Contemporary Civilization readings, contributes, for many students, to a bewilderment about the courses. The great works of the Western mind, which are read in Humanities, arise as singular experiences of individual imaginations, but often the historical or social context which could relate these ideas and changing sensibilities (and modes of expression) to institutional and social developments is lacking. Thus, there is little sense, because of the disparities between the two courses, of a unity of intellectual experience.

This is not to deny the value of the individual courses as they stand at present. For many students there is still a compelling magnetism of ideas, a new wonderment and excitement created by the enduring power of the works themselves. The problem, as I see it, is to provide a context that makes this experience more meaningful as an intellectual whole.

To some extent, the "intellectual capital" of both courses is being used up. This is a process at work in any educational enterprise as the organization of ideas, once novel, becomes common coin or, as new critical views develop, intellectual styles become altered and the analytical conceptions, the organizing principles of the course, become questioned.

The Contemporary Civilization course drew its first great intellectual resource from the "new history" of James Harvey Robinson and Charles Beard. The emphasis of the new history was on social change and the novelty of the times. It was, in effect, the liberal domestication of Darwinian thought. If one looks at Irwin Edman's *Human Traits,* the first book written for use in a session of the Contemporary Civilization course, in 1920, the theme is the social evolution of man, the original continuity with animal nature, the growth of a moral sense, and the triumph of science. James Harvey Robinson's *The Mind in the Making,* one of the great popularizations of thought in the 1920s, saw history as the clash of irrational with rational forces, ending again with the theme of the "indefinite advance" of knowledge. John Herman Randall Jr.'s magisterial *The Making of the Modern Mind,* another book fashioned for the Contemporary Civilization course in one of its early forms, surveyed the broad vista of intellectual history from the standpoint of the Enlightenment. Paralleling these books was the influence of Charles Beard's economic determinism. History was the history of discoverable economic interests, and these underlying forces were the prime movers of change. There was, in effect, a Columbia view of history that can be summed up in the phrase, once popular in the late 1920s but now *démodé*—"history as social process."

The intellectual continuity of the Contemporary Civilization course came from the fact that while in the 1930s the "new history"

—in the Robinsonian sense of the history of ideas—suffered an eclipse, the course was sustained by the infusion of Marxism (through the Beardian back door), which gave it a new ideological premise. By emphasizing the history of institutions, and particularly of economic institutions, Contemporary Civilization was able to continue its synoptic view of social evolution; by treating ideas as a function of, or determined by, material interests, it had a new organizing thread.

These interpretative views, often monistic or overly deterministic, no longer dominate the course. The Contemporary Civilization year is organized along a loose chronological frame, basing itself on the firsthand reading of ideas in the primary texts, rather than paraphrased by commentators, and the use of original documents and source materials. But what was gained by the addition of original material was, in part, offset by the lack of a consistent interpretative framework. Today, the emphasis is on the history of ideas, or islands of ideas, with some reference to institutions. Thus there is a definition to the course, but a narrow one. This is not to argue for some high intellectual adventurism (at the expense of complexity), or for any specific ideological scheme; I plead no *parti pris*. But one can try to place the Contemporary Civilization course in some broader context, for pedagogical purposes, and some more comprehensive methodological framework, for intellectual consistency.

The Humanities course, once past its original "great books" intention to read the classics, was meant to parallel the Contemporary Civilization course: to provide in the realm of ideas and imagination a concurrent sense of the movement of thought with events. It never realized this formal intention. Explicitly, the Humanities course was simply an introduction to great works to be read as *contemporary* works, as enduring masterpieces capable of speaking to each person today; its intention was to make the reader a cultivated man. Implicit was the theme, expressed most directly by Mark Van Doren, of the need to place "culture" against "history." In this view, the reading of the work was not to be a reading in the history of literature or the history of ideas. The work was to be read autonomously, and the purpose of elucidation, in Van Doren's sense, was to educate the imagination as well as the intellect.

The temptation of this approach is that it leads to an extreme "New Criticism," of reading the work *in se,* without reference to any external context. And for certain purposes, this has great value. One can, for example, read Rabelais's *Garganta* and *Pantagruel* as great comic works. But one can also read them with an eye, say, to Lucien Febvre's argument, in his *Le Probleme de l'Incroyance au XVIeme Siecle,* as an instance of the nature of religious belief and disbelief, or of the kind of sensibility (the reliance on touch and smell and the lack of visual metaphors) peculiar to Rabelais's time. One kind of reading need not exclude the other; and the student should be aware of the variant approaches to the work, not simply of his own "naive" response. In short, there is a legitimate approach that takes account of the historical context, relates the work to scholarship, and deals with, the linkage of ideas and the changes in moral temper.

This can be brought about not by wrenching the Humanities course from its present central emphasis on the works themselves, but by bringing it into a closer relationship with the Contemporary Civilization course. It can also be done, as I shall argue at greater length below, by adding a third term to the Humanities sequence which would deal entirely with modern works—the literature of Joyce, Proust, Yeats, Lawrence, and Kafka, Such a course would provide an implicit historical tie with the Humanities sequence. It would deal with the impact on the modern temper of works that have great power and challenge for the student (the question discussed in chapter 4), and it would give the student a sense of how his own standards and categories of appreciation—his presumably "naive" responses—have been shaped by a time that also reinterprets the past.

If the intellectual need of the Humanities course is for historical context, the intellectual need of a Contemporary Civilization course is for "historical explanation." This rationale, often implicit, has to be explicated.

The context of history presupposes a criteria of selection. Events and movements clearly cannot be discussed in chronological sequence alone (though the need for a factual basis is necessary) but as combinations of social forces (the rise of new classes, the influence of technology) and human volitions (a hunger for equality, a desire for domination). Any discussion of historical change—the origins of capitalism, the Puritan Revolution, the French Revolution—should have within its context the logical criteria of a theory of explanation and the specific sociological theories that try to explain the indentifiable social groupings and the-power of ideas at work behind the event.

These "needs" emerge out of a single purpose—that of liberal education. If the purpose of a first-year course was solely to introduce a student to the problems of Humanities, one might want to organize the course about the nature of criticism, the kinds of genre, the qualities appropriate to different kinds of work, a theory of judgment, a history of esthetics, and the like. But the purpose of these courses is essentially liberal education: to give the student a historical grasp of the background and traditions of Western civilization and the movements of ideas and imagination, of social forces and social conflicts within that great stream. And this is why the contexts are necessary.

Intentions have to be realized within an organized structure, and this is the task of curriculum. I cannot, within my competence, describe each course in detail. What I can try to do is to propose an orderly sequence that would allow the more general intentions to be realized.

CONTEMPORARY CIVILIZATION

Under the present system—I am taking the 1964-65 offerings as the basis for discussion—a student is required to take a common course called Contemporary Civilization A and, in the second year, two courses from among twelve offered by the several social science departments.[18]

---

[18] Of the twelve courses a student may take co fulfill the requirement, two are interdepartmental and the remaining ten departmental.

Interdepartmental: CC C1201-C1202, Man in Contemporary Society; V3355-V3356, Oriental Civilizations.

Departmental: Anthropology-CC C1201, Human and cultural evolution; Anthropology-CC C1202, Man, culture, and contemporary societies; Economics-CC C1201, Introduction to economic analysis and public policy; Geography-CC C1202, Problems of developed and underdeveloped areas; Government-CC C1201-C1202, Political institutions and processes in the twentieth century; Government-CC C1203-C1204, Reflections on politics in the past century; Philoso-

The freshman Contemporary Civilization course begins with the medieval period, though this topic is introduced with some readings reflecting the classical and Christian influences, notably selections from Aristotle's *Politics,* Cicero's *The Laws,* the Epistles of Paul, and St. Augustine. In one term, the course moves from the medieval period through the Enlightenment. By the mid-term the student will have covered medieval economic and social foundations, medieval political institutions, medieval scholasticism and mysticism, and Renaissance society, business, and politics. The second half of the first term starts with the Humanist thought of the Renaissance, proceeds to the Reformation, the formation of the modern state, the English revolution, early modern political thought (Hobbes, Locke, and Montesquieu), the development of scientific method (Bacon, Descartes, Galileo, Newton, Pascal), and ends with the problems of knowledge and the nature of God in the Enlightenment (Diderot, Voltaire, Hume, Rousseau). Except for some of the material on the medieval and Renaissance period, the primary readings are largely in the history of ideas. In addition, students read especially prepared chapters in an accompanying text, for background purposes.

The second semester begins with the Age of Enlightenment, dealing largely with new ideals of morality (Kant, Condorcet) and the new proposals of sovereignty (Rousseau). It goes on to cover the democratic revolutions and the Restoration in Europe, the industrial revolution, liberalism and democracy on the continent and in England, science and ethics in the Victorian period, the socialist criticism of liberalism, big business and its critics, politics of the modern national state (including imperialism), and critics of nineteenth-century society and morality (including Burckhardt, Nietzsche, William James, and Bertrand Russell). The major institutional material

phy-CC C1201, Ideology and society; Philosophy-CC C1202, Reason and decision; Sociology-CC C1201, The transformation of society in the nineteenth and twentieth centuries; Sociology-CC C1202, The individual and the social structure.

The history department, which for two years had offered two courses, "Western Civilization in the Twentieth Century" and "An Introduction to Cultural and Intellectual History," dropped these courses in 1963-64, with the reluctant consent of the Committee on Instruction.

The two government courses are offered as year courses. The courses offered by sociology and anthropology are single-term courses though organized as a sequence. The philosophy courses are independent courses, a single term each.

is on the industrial revolution, but most of the readings, once again, are in the history of ideas.

The various second-year options offered by the social science departments are supposed to build directly on the material in Contemporary Civilization A, and to concern themselves with twentieth-century problems through the perspective of the particular discipline. In practice, not all of the courses actually do this. The first sociology-course, the "Transformation of Society in the Nineteenth and Twentieth Centuries," does explicitly continue a historical framework, though it concentrates on the emergence and problems of industrial society. An alternative government sequence, "Reflections on Politics in the past century," is linked most directly, in material and type of reading (Lenin, Mussolini, Freud, E. H. Carr, Collingwood, Franz Neumann) with the first-year Contemporary Civilization course. The geography course concentrates on underdeveloped areas and the Oriental Civilizations course on society in Asia; they are both extremely well worked out, but are not directly linked to the first year. The anthropology and economics courses have been, primarily, introductions to these disciplines, though efforts are made to provide general perspectives—macro-economics in the case of one, and evolutionary theory in the other. The regular government course is largely a comparison of the American and Soviet political systems.[19] The

[19] In 1964, the College Committee on Instruction conducted an intensive review of the syllabi of each course. It indicated "criteria of acceptability," and recommended the continuation of the present structure. Since its findings are relevant to the present discussion, I append below the relevant portions of the committee's report:

The Criteria of Acceptability. In its review of the experimental program the committee has been guided by the minimal conditions of acceptability suggested in the report adopted by the faculty in 1961. The committee feels that these should now be reformulated, as follows:

a. Contemporary Civilization is a two-year program aimed at giving the student a grasp of the changing means by which a society attempts to understand itself and culminating in a study of selected problems of the student's own lifetime, including some of the ideas and concepts offered for understanding and analyzing those problems.

b. The options acceptable in the second year of the program thus must build explicitly on the materials and themes of Contemporary Civilization A.

c. To the extent that they are thus constructed, these options cannot be *merely* introductions to particular disciplines in the social sciences. If they were merely introductions to separate fields, the second year would become only a simple distribution requirement among a number of disciplines.

difficulty has been, and this was foreseen in the Truman report, that the courses sometimes have to serve conflicting, if not incompatible, purposes: to analyze selected problems of contemporary life from the perspective of the discipline, and (of greater necessity in some cases where analytical rigor is more explicit, as in economics) to give the student some sense of the discipline itself.

A persistent problem of the Contemporary Civilization A course is the vast amount of reading, as well as the large number of topics

d. The focus of these options must be upon the twentieth century, its problems, and contending ideas.

e. This focus should include, wherever appropriate, materials and references coming from disciplines other than that of the sponsoring department.

f. Although they are sponsored by particular departments and should meet the standards of rigor appropriate to the sponsoring disciplines, these courses should be aimed at the nonspecialist rather than the prospective major.

The committee is satisfied that eight of the twelve courses currently offered adequately meet these criteria. The remaining four—Anthropology 1201, Anthropology 1202, Economics 1201, and Government 1201-1202—presently fall short. Their chief deficiencies, for the purpose of the Contemporary Civilization program, are that they build inadequately upon the materials of Contemporary Civilization A and that they are too exclusively introductions to the disciplines. These criticisms have been discussed with the departmental representatives, and we anticipate that appropriate changes will be attempted. In particular, we note with approval the agreement of the departmental representative in economics to devote the opening section of its course to a review of the economics materials in Contemporary Civilization A and to the nineteenth-century background of the materials that constitute the main body of Economics 1201. We also welcome the expressed intentions of the anthropology and government departments to revise, respectively, Anthropology 1201 and 1202 and Government 1201-1202.

Recommendations and Statements of Policy. The committee recommends that the experimental program be adopted as the continuing form for the second year of Contemporary Civilization, with the existing restriction upon a student's using any course sponsored by the department of his major (or concentration) to meet the second-year Contemporary Civilization requirement and subject to the criteria specified in *c,* above.

The committee proposes to retain the old Contemporary Civilization B course in essentially its present form as long as the departments and the chairman of Contemporary Civilization are able to secure a suitable staff.

The committee recommends that the history department be requested to reintroduce its courses or to propose one or more new courses suitable to the second year.

The committee recommends that the departments encourage their members to propose interdepartmental courses designed to meet the criteria for the second year. Such courses could be given on an alternating or occasional basis, and they might involve joint instruction by members from two or more departments.

that are covered in a single year. In the 1957 report of the Committee on the Educational Future of Columbia University, this problem was singled out for extensive discussion: "The committee's conclusion is that Contemporary Civilization and Humanities, for all their indubitable merits, are still so burdened with material that they may give some beginning students misleading conceptions of what disciplined intellectual inquiry demands."

The problem remains. Two of the principal members of the Contemporary Civilization staff, Professors Julian Franklin and Orest Ranum, the new chairman of the course, in a memorandum to the Committee on Instruction, pointed to a conflict of purposes in the present organization of readings: "As we see it, the selection of materials required to explain the genesis and relationship of institutions and ideas is in conflict with the principle of selection required for close analysis of particular doctrines or periods. In the first case, what is wanted is a wide variety of excerpts; in the second, few selections in much greater length. In our opinion these two aims, each of them legitimate, cannot be reconciled within the framework of a purely documentary approach supplemented only sketchily by synoptic readings in 'Chapters in Western Civilization.'"

But from the viewpoint of integrating the lower-college experience, the greatest single lack is Greek and Roman history, or selected topics of the classical period. In the Humanities course, the larger part of the first term is devoted to Greek and Roman writers. There are major selections from Herodotus and Thucydides, Plato and Aristotle, Homer, Aeschylus, Sophocles, Euripides, Aristophanes, Lucretius, and Vergil. These are read largely as "contemporary" works with little attention to context. But in the Contemporary Civilization course, there are no readings in this period. Such a lack is startling, especially since students today have little opportunity to read classical history. In the secondary schools today, there is almost no intensive reading in ancient history. In most high schools, students take a course in their junior year called "World History." This begins anywhere from Hammurabi or the Hittites and goes up to World War I. This is the sum total of Western history usually studied in the secondary school.

There are, it seems to me, a number of compelling reasons for beginning with the Greek and Roman period:

1. Such readings would provide a historical context for the Humanities course.

2. The study of such a period shows us societies holding a different view of religion and man, and provides an important basis for the subsequent discussions of the different world views of Christian and Oriental culture.

3. The classical period provides the basis for Western political experience—the idea of democracy and the idea of law.

4. There is a "comparative" value in seeing how these early societies dealt with some of the recurrent sociological problems: the move from tribe to citizenship, the conflict of classes, the relation between polities, the role of force and the military, the meaning of imperialism.

5. The historical distance, and the relatively unified nature of the period, allow for varying interpretations of the experiences of these societies. Thus, I would include not only source material (and instead of "chapters" of background reading) but selections also from major historical interpreters, such as Fustel de Colanges, Glotz, Zimmern, Kitto, Gibbon, Mommsen, Dill, Rostovtzeff, and Ronald Syme. This would introduce the problem of historical explanation.

I would propose, thus, that Contemporary Civilization be reorganized so as to begin with one term in selected topics of Greek and Roman history.

There remains the problem of covering subsequent European history to the present. It is clear that this cannot be done in a single year. The effort to do so in the present Contemporary Civilization A course, beginning with the medieval period, leads to a hop-skip-and-jump process in which some topics are passed over rapidly in class. I would propose, simply, to acknowledge the difficulty of complete coverage, and not try to deal with so much material in a single year. Rather than just select some periods and omit others, I would propose that the same time-span, the medieval period to the present, be kept, but that these be divided into three channels, each concentrating deliberately on one aspect of the history: political history, economic history, and social and intellectual history.

To some extent, this occurs in a rough and haphazard way in the course today, when instructors with different competences (historians, philosophers, economists, and political scientists) emphasize one or another topic in accordance with their own interests and background. The advantage of the formal proposal is that one could cover material in selective detail, although the chronological scheme would make them aware of specific omissions. This would also make the staffing problem somewhat easier, since instructors, particularly young ones, would not have to grapple with material completely unfamiliar to them.

As for the present second-year Contemporary Civilization course, it is clear that many departments, while offering two terms of work, do so with divided intentions. In some instances these are primarily discussions of contemporary issues; in others, they "slide off" into becoming introductions to the discipline.

What I propose, therefore, is the reduction of the second-year options to a single term, recognizing frankly the virtue of introductory courses as necessary components of a liberal education program. These would be single-term courses in economics, government, geography, anthropology, and sociology. The Oriental Civilizations program, brilliant as it is, does not fit into this sequence. It is, however, a valuable third-tier course, offering a comparative view for those who have had a substantial grounding in Western civilization. Similarly, the present government option, "Reflections on Politics in the Past Century," offers a wide-ranging third-tier course, and might become one of the options, open in the senior year, on the compulsory third-tier level.

In sum, what I am proposing is a new four-term sequence in Contemporary Civilization.

First term: A course in Greek and Roman history.

Second and third terms: A year's work in Western history, with an option either in political history, economic history, or social history.

Fourth term: An option of a single term's work in economics, geography, government, anthropology, or sociology.[20]

---

[20] In this organization, philosophy as a separate option is excluded at this point. The two present philosophy options consist of a course in "Ideology and

The advantage of this sequence is that it allows for an orderly progression, following the argument given previously, which would give the student a basic historical background and allow for the introduction of a required discipline, then, in the unfolding of the curriculum, move to more detailed work in a discipline and end, in the fourth year, with seminar work and synoptic third-tier courses that allow for the application of the historical knowledge and the discipline to problems common to a field.

It is not within my charge to write a detailed syllabus for each of the courses or the sequences. The following, therefore, is proposed as *illustrative* of the topics that would be covered.

First Term: The classical period (required of all freshmen):
> From tribal to political units: the emergence of the idea of citizenship (from Homer to Solon and Cleisthenes).
> The Greek city-state (Pericles to the Peloponnesian War).
> The Roman republic (Marius and Sulla to Caesar and Augustus).
> The break-up of the Roman empire (Marcus Aurelius to Constantine).

Second and Third Terms: An option of one of the three sequences:
> *Political history sequence*
> > Medieval political institutions
> > The Renaissance and Reformation
> > The English Revolution
> > The French Revolution
> > The nation-state and imperialism
> > The rise of party systems
> > The Russian Revolution

Society" and "Reason and Decision." Both raise types of questions that are best handled, within the logic of my scheme, at the "third-tier." The "Ideology and Society" course overlaps to a considerable extent with the "Reflections on Politics" course, and the two could be combined. The "Reason and Decision" course raises methodological and analytical questions which are germane to the philosophical underpinnings of the social science third-tier courses and would be absorbed there.

If, for institutional or other reasons, this scheme should not prove practicable, and the present arrangement of one year's work in the social sciences is retained, I would propose (for reasons which are spelled out on page 290) that the second year be an economics-government, or an economics-sociology requirement.

Economic history sequence
  The medieval manor
  The rise of cities
  The origins of capitalism
  The market economy and the price system
  The international economy
  The modern corporation and the Welfare State
Social and Intellectual history sequence [21]
  The estate system of medieval Europe
  The challenge of equality—religious and secular
  Rationalism and empiricism and their social bases
  The industrial revolution and the break-up of traditional soci-
  ety: from status to contract
  Social classes: bourgeoisie and working class
  Critiques of modern society
  Bureaucratization and professionalism
Fourth Term: An option of one of five courses:
  Economics
  Government
  Sociology
  Anthropology
  Geography

In the second and third terms, there would, necessarily, be an overlap of topics and materials in the three history sequences; in face, this would be desirable. The important distinction is that the same chronology is treated from the different perspectives of a political, economic, or sociological approach while, at the same time, the scheme allows for more detailed coverage of particular topics.

This division would also permit the different social science disciplines in the single-term options to deal more analytically with their materials than they can at present, since their focus has to be "contemporary civilization." It would allow the government department to deal more systematically with the nature of political authority and

---

[21] The issue of including elements of the history of science and the history of technology here is an important one; but given the immediate context, almost insuperable. The history of science, here, is allotted to the third tier.

political consensus in its introductory course. It would allow the geography course to stress ecological analysis and patterns in the use of resources. It would allow the economics department to concentrate more usefully on economic analysis, since descriptive material would have been placed in the previous sequence. In sociology, the present first-term course is already the framework of the year's historical sequence, and would allow the department to deal more fully with contemporary sociological theory in the fourth-term course. This would not be a "distribution system," because these courses would still be following two-term sequences which involved economic, political, or sociological emphases.

Is there a danger, in this organization, that early specialization would be encouraged by giving an economics student, for example, three terms in economics rather than one, or a political science student three in politics, and the like? The risk is there but it can be obviated, in part, by making certain that the year sequences are constructed broadly on a historical frame, albeit with the special perspective, and that the present requirement that a student majoring in the social sciences be required to take a term option other than his major be retained. The usefulness of the latter provision, in fact, would be reinforced, in that a social science major would now have a more systematic training in at least two of the disciplines.

Such a proposed organization goes against the tide of the moment in general education, where the emphasis is increasingly on the con-temporary, with the assumption that the concentration on present-day social science knowledge safely parallels the pattern of teaching in the natural sciences, where the history of the field is irrelevant to the teaching of contemporary principles. In my view, this compari-son is wrong. In the social sciences one needs a historical background (if only as a "laboratory") to understand the present. At the same time, it is possible, as I have argued, to treat history in an analytical and conceptual mode, to introduce the problems of the organizing conceptions about a period, the basis of evidence, the relationship of a specific explanation to a general theory, and the like. It seems to me that only in this fashion can one gain the desiderata of a liberal education in the social sciences: an appreciation of the comparative method (e.g., why did economic development take hold in England but not in Spain?); an appreciation of the filiation of ideas (e.g., the social contract in Hobbes and in Rousseau); an awareness of social processes (social mobility, urbanization, revolution); an understanding of the idea of social structure (e.g., the medieval estate system, with its duties and obligations); and appreciation of the relationship of ideas and social setting (e.g., Protestantism and capitalism). In short, a sense of the complex web of society and the processes of social change.

THE HUMANITIES

There is little question that the Humanities A course is one of the great courses in American education. For the past quarter of a century and more, it has been the keystone course of Columbia College. A recent survey of student reaction showed that it still had the power to provoke interest and excite the imagination. The question remains whether in the next decade it can, in its present form, play the same transforming role that it has in the last quarter of a century.

Humanities A is described as a year's course in literature and philosophy. But it is much more: It is a reading of great works of mind and imagination. The first term is devoted largely to the Greeks, with the addition of texts by Vergil, Lucretius, and the Old Testament. The second term begins with the New Testament, goes on to seventeenth- and eighteenth-century authors, and ends with Dostoevski.[22] Two facts are noteworthy. One is that the *format* of

---

[22] Since the course *is* the readings, it is useful to list the books that have been the "depository" of the course. Not all of these are read each year—from time to time some books are added and some are dropped. In the last year, the number of readings has been reduced somewhat to allow more time for discussion. This list, then, is representative of the range of the course.

In the first term; Homer, *The Illiad* and *The Odyssey;* Aeschylus, *The Oresteia;* Sophocles, *Antigone, Oedipus the King, Philoctetes;* Herodotus, *The Persian Wars* (selections); Euripides, *Hippolytus, Iphigenia in Tauris, Bacchae;* Thucydides, *The Peloponnesian War* (selections); Aristophanes, *The Clouds, Lysistrata;* Plato, *Apology, Symposium, Republic* (Books I-X); Aristotle, *Poetics, Ethics, Metaphysics* (Book I); Lucretius, *The Nature of the Universe;* Vergil, *The Aeneid;* the Bible, Genesis, Job.

In the second term: The New Testament, Matthew, John, Romans; St. Augustine, *Confessions;* Dante, *Inferno;* Montaigne, selected essays; Rabelais, *Gargantua and Pantagruel;* Shakespeare, *Henry IV Part I, King Lear;* Cervantes, *Don Quixote;* Milton, *Paradise Lost;* Molière, eight plays; Swift, *Gulliver's*

the course has remained virtually unchanged since its introduction in 1937. Of the authors read in the first term, all have been represented in the course since the start, though at times different plays of Sophocles or different selections from Plato have been required than the ones now read. Of the authors studied in the second term, all except Dostoevski and Nietzsche have been on the reading list since the inception of the course (Dostoevski was added to the canon in 1952; Nietzsche was read twice and then dropped because his work, according to the staff, did not fit in). The second fact is that the Humanities staff has invariably had a high morale, and their vitality has been communicated to the students. The teachers have usually met in weekly luncheons, and discussions of the texts have served to create a small intellectual college within the college itself.

Despite all this, some questions can be raised, not just to play devil's advocate, but to provide an underpinning for some alternative formulations which might be considered by the College faculty.

Humanities A presents, undeniably, a set of great works; but read for what purpose? It is striking that the dean's committee on the review of the Humanities course, headed by Professor Fritz Stern, reported in its final statement, after a year's consideration: "In retrospect it may be considered significant that we found it difficult to define the philosophical or pedagogic ends of the course. We readily agreed that students should read these masterpieces of the past and should even in this rapid manner have to grapple with the timeless themes and ideas inherent in their tradition. We would subscribe to Justus Buchler's forthright dictum 'Humanities was an emancipation from the trivial.' To what end, though, were we committing our students to this path? What was the educational thrust of these courses?"

The committee reported that the answer to these questions, given in the College's past, was "to make whole men," or "cultured gentlemen," or youths of sensibility; and that these answers were "scorned by the committee." Those now teaching the course, the committee reported, felt "almost unanimously that the present goals and

Travels; Voltaire, *Candide, Zadig,* and selected stories; Goethe, *Faust;* Dostoyevsky. *The Idiot;* Nietzsche, *The Birth of Tragedy* and the *Genealogy of Morals.*

present results are something more active and intellectual, and your committee welcomed this emphasis as highly desirable."

What is this "something more active and intellectual" that is the present approach of the course? Professor Robert Belknap, who was a recent chairman, has formulated it this way: "A huge scholarly or technical apparatus enables a modern historian or physicist to see through the data in his chronicle or his bubble chamber and make statements about 'what happened' or 'what is there.' Literary statements, on the other hand, are about something more accessible, a text. There is no real Don Quixote to reconstruct from the evidence of the novel. Most of the data about Shakespeare's life is lost forever, but a student can test his formulation about King Lear's life against *all* the data, cultivating his capacity to devise and test hypotheses with a speed, economy, and intensity which are possible only in such an elegantly limited and opaque realm as a work of literature.

"When teaching Moliére, I do not inform the student that Rousseau considered *The Misanthrope* tragic. I pick the passages on which Rousseau based his opinion and battle the student into formulating it all over again. Then I pick passages supporting contrary formulations and try to extract them from the student. This is what is summed up in the words 'active and intellectual.' "

This is, I think, a brilliant summation of an intention and a practice. But one should note the controlling idea: to take the work as its own "world" and explore the work as an instance of the imagination. And this is a necessary way of seeing a work in its own terms. But a work also exists against its own time and its place in a critical pantheon. And should not the contextual questions be asked as well?

There is a second question. The intention of the course is to present "great" works. But other than "greatness" it is difficult to determine the principle guiding the selection of authors.[23] The first semester has a unity based, in part, on genre (epic, historical, dramatic) and on the nature of the Greek way of life. But in the selection of the authors read in the second term it is difficult to see what

---

[23] Professor Bert Leefmans writes, as a comment: "There is a reason for this: perhaps here alone in the curriculum what is most called for—as is recognized perhaps only by those who have taught the course at some length—is the Keatsian negative capability you mention earlier. You ask about 'greatness'— that is what *is* hard to define and must, as the course does, speak for itself."

progression, in the history of ideas or the nature of styles or any other principle, is at work.

Perhaps the most striking critical formulation of the course was made by Professor Ernest Nagel, who, in his presentation to the Stern Committee, called it "intellectual tourism." There is, he said, too much emphasis on the tourist approach, which requires a tremendous schedule of reading, resulting in an incompatability with the basic objective of giving the students some understanding and responsibility for the subject matter, and its effect on them.

Now "tourism," especially for those who do not know a "city"— and there is a first time for all of us!—may be a necessary prelude for a more intensive explanation of a particular endearing place. But when and where in one's life should the tour take place? Professor Nagel, it seems to me, has put his finger on the heart of the problem. The course is trying to do two things at once: To give the "impressionable" freshman a Cook's tour of Western literature, so that he ends up with *some* notion of who Thucydides, Dante, and Molière were, and what they had to say; and to introduce the student to the practice of thoughtful reading and critical appreciation of complex works. It is difficult to achieve both these goals in a year's course.

The contradiction goes back to the initial reasons for formulating the general education courses in this fashion: the fact that the secondary schools were not doing their job properly. It is compounded by the fact that the secondary schools, in their efforts to upgrade themselves, are doing the wrong job today.

As Professor Charles Kahn has stated: "It is clear that the task of 'wide and superficial' factual coverage is more easily done in the secondary schools (if only because teachers for subtle and advanced work are not generally available). It is equally clear that 'depth' is more alluring, and in fact every high school that I know of that has been trying to do advanced work in literature has imitated the *worst* features of the Humanities course—I mean the features least appropriate to the secondary schools: the excess of critical apparatus ('tragic flaw,' the Christ figure, etc.), the rapid leaps from century to century (from Sophocles to Shakespeare, from Shakespeare to Steinbeck) without a trace of historical or factual background. If the colleges do not step in and advise the high schools on their pre-college program, we will soon have freshmen arriving with a debased and distorted version of our humanities curriculum—and asking for 'advanced placement.'"

The proposal is a sensible one. Since the college is in the best position to know what preparation is desirable for the entering freshman (and could even control this, in part, through its entrance requirements), the task of reorganizing a secondary school humanities curriculum (and that of general education as a whole) should be combined with the planning of a model pre-college curriculum in "general education." Without such a step, our own reorganizations are made in a vacuum, and inevitably will suffer the consequences of such a dereliction. Insofar as the distinction between the preliminary-factual and the advanced-analytic is valid (less so, perhaps, in the sciences, where the "factual" knowledge is much more a function of the conceptual scheme), then there is a proper division of labor between the high schools and the colleges. And nowhere is this more needed than in the humanities.

It may well be that, for the near future—the next decade?—that little can be done to change this state of affairs, that a humanities course is caught in the cleft suck of the need to present the sweep of great works, and to provide time for more intensive exploration of particular works. The fact that a humanities course has been able, remarkably, to achieve much of this dual purpose, and in the process instill a sense of intellectual excitement, is a tribute to the staff. But the intellectual dilemma—and strain—persists as well, especially as more and more students come from secondary schools where some of these tasks will have been mastered. And for such students, an increasing number one hopes, the demand, necessarily, may be for more intensive work with fewer books.

If, as a general principle, the "intellectual tourism" of the course could be reduced so that a larger amount of time can be spent on fewer texts, what, apart from the criteria of "rhetoric" (the problem of how to analyze an argument, the identification of key terms, the distinction between evidence and illustration, and the like), should be the intellectual rationale, or the organizing principle, of the course? One can look at such a humanities course from three perspectives.

1. As illustrative of the history of ideas and ideals, treating of one or another of the great themes or dialogues that have marked the history of human society: e.g., the obligation to "self" as against the obligation to the community; the limits and potentialities of human nature, etc. Or one could take some specific intellectual thread—such as the influence of classical thought on Christian, Renaissance, and Enlightenment thought, or the contrasting histories of Platonism and Aristotelianism upon subsequent philosophical and imaginative developments as the principle of the course.

2. As choosing books that significantly reflect the culture of an age and illuminate its moral temper. Thus, the emphasis might be on specific periods: classical, Christian, medieval, Renaissance, Enlightenment.

3. As intrinsic to the works themselves—in which each work is taken as an inexhaustible well of human imagination and spirit, and can evoke responsive insight in each reader.

It is the consensus, at least among those who teach the Columbia Humanities course, that no single one of these is the controlling one, though emphases may vary, naturally, from teacher to teacher. Nor is there any intention, as I understand it, of saying that there are only fifty, or one hundred, or five hundred and fifty great books. Implicitly, there is the understanding that a book to be chosen speak urgently, or in some insistent way, to our time. It is not the past, or the re-creation of the past, that guides the course but the present. But if this is so, there should be some definition of what it is, in the present, that guides the selections, or the way they are discussed. If, in the next decade, the Humanities readings are to be reduced in order to emphasize "depth" and analysis, what is still needed is some criteria which, beyond "greatness," make the selection of works to be read more explicit.

There is a third dimension that cuts across the problem of the Humanities course: the issue that has unfortunately been tagged "mind" versus "sensibility." In its report, the Stern Committee stated: "The committee felt very strongly that feeding the student's soul or developing his sensibilities was not the proper goal of these courses. This feeling led one member to exclaim: 'I hate sensibility. I hate perceptivity. All I care about is the mind.'"

This attitude brought a powerful riposte from Professor Andrew Chiappe. "There is," he wrote in a memorandum to the dean, "a curious antipathy toward 'sensibility' shown by the committee. There is an apparent reluctance to allow their proper roles to pleasure, displeasure, and the imagination in the experience *and* analysis of works of art. And most of the works in this course are works of art. The easy scorn heaped upon 'affective' responses is strange. . . . Momentarily forgotten is the fact that criticism of a work must begin with affective responses—for example, pity and terror in the case of tragedy, according to Aristotle, who is right. These responses the critic then proceeds analytically (with his 'mind' but always in interplay with his 'sensibility') to justify, or complicate, or revise—even to the point of establishing grounds for a response or responses quite the opposite of the original ones. Always, centrally, there is a complex affective experience ('sensibility')—ideas are 'carried alive into the heart by passion,' This sensibility enters into the criticism itself, and forms part of it, in the work of any critic worth reading."[24]

Seeing this from a different perspective, I feel that both sides are talking past each other. Surely Professor Chiappe is right in asserting that a critical response must be an interplay of mind and sensibility, but is not the fundamental point that *the ways in which both mind and sensibility approach a work* are fashioned by the times. The problem is not one of mind against sensibility, but whether a "naïve" approach to art is actually possible. One attitude which has been prominent in the Humanities courses—in art as well as literature—is that the young should approach the work directly so that they could experience directly the bracing impact of greatness. But what may be necessary *pedagogically* should not be confused with what is the

[24] Professor Chiappe objected, too, to the idea of introducing any intervening "authority" between the work and the student. Is there, he asks, "a *single* essay on Plato, or Shakespeare, or Rousseau, we would wish to enshrine in this way? . . . . Will the introduction of critical authority remedy incompetence? A teacher who can confuse the meaning of Lucretius will be able as easily to confuse the meaning of Santayana's essay on Lucretius. ... Is it only contemporary critics who can be trusted to bring 'mind' to the course? I can easily imagine a situation in which Aristotle's *Ethics* would be bracketed with an essay by Norman Mailer; Spinoza's *Ethics* with a study by Leslie Fiedler ('Grind the Lens good, Baruch!')."

case *intellectually.* While any particular young man may come upon a great work afresh, as an experience for *himself,* the way in which he will respond will be significantly influenced by a general mode or convention of the time. What is true for the history of art, as E. H. Gombrich has pointed out in *Art and Illusion,* is in many ways true for culture as a whole. Styles become "conventions," as perceptual conventions influence style, and what one generation may see as grotesque (e.g., African sculpture) another may accept as authentic art. This is equally the case in the changing acceptance of styles of poetry and of other literary expressions. This is not to deny the obvious point that there are individual differences in response, and that some students are more sensitive than others. But neither could the equally obvious point be neglected that how and what one sees is a function in great measure of convention and context.

In short, one purpose of a confrontation with a great work should be to provoke "self-consciousness," but not only of one's own immediate response, emotionally and intellectually, to a work, but equally the way in which the same work has evoked successively different styles of self-consciousness. The problem for the course is not only to make a student aware of a text, but of the scholarly context in which it arose; not only of his own sensibility, but aware, as well, of the emotions and responses to emotions the work has aroused in others. In sum, the successive histories of mind and sensibility are as integral to the interpretation of a text as the student's (and the instructor's) own "naïve" responses, for these "naïve" responses are to some extent a product of such histories. And it is the function of intellectual understanding to make this explicit.

There are, I think, two ways of accomplishing this end. One is to establish the context of the works that are read. It does not necessarily mean the fatal introduction of historicism to ask that a student understand the world out of which a work of art has emerged as a way of understanding the work itself. Reuben Brower has made the simple point, "Literature is embedded in history, [and] the meaning of the work itself changes when we view it in relation to other works and to the social situation in which it first appeared."

In this regard, one way would be to reorganize the initial Contemporary Civilization course in tandem with the Humanities sequence to allow for a freer interplay of text and historical contexts.

A second way of introducing intellectual sophistication, or an awareness of the way one's own categories of thought are shaped, might be by the introduction of a required third term of Humanities which would deal principally with late nineteenth-century and twentieth-century writers. It may be recalled (see chapter 2) that in 1946, when the Carman Committee reviewed the proposal to extend Humanities A into a third term, it stated that the "merit of the proposal. . .probably calls for no argument." But, as I pointed out, the committee decided that the question had been settled at the start by "recognizing that the readings for Humanities A should be books of established eminence." And they had said, it might be recalled, that "there is for us no question as to the place in the history of European culture of Sophocles, of Dante, or of Voltaire. We have not yet a similar perspective for Carlyle, Nietzsche, or Freud."

Twenty years later, one can say in all fairness that the perspective has changed. Few would dispute the place of Nietzsche and Freud, or of Proust, Joyce, Eliot, and Yeats, the masters of the modern mind in the accepted canon. In fact, of course, the College now offers as an elective Humanities 3-4, a sequel to the initial Humanities course, which concentrates on European and American literature and philosophy of the nineteenth and twentieth centuries.

But the question I raise here is whether or not, as an integral part of the required Humanities sequence, one should not establish a third-term course on "the moderns." Lionel Trilling has called attention to the "insurrectionary character" of all creative disciplines, and it may be that the revolution of the "modern" is now complete; and one can make a case, therefore, for the greater inclusion of the modern masters on the ground that they have passed into "history," But that would be a sorry case. The criterion for a third term of Humanities, or for including any particular writer in such a course, is not "eminence," but the ability to shake us up and make us understand our own time and, as part of such insight, the times of the past. More than that, it is part of a process of comprehending how a revolution in the modes of experiencing and expressing experience has occurred, and how such modes, once "adversary," have become established today.

A third term in the Humanities would also allow us to introduce the graphic arts and music as well as literature. The period from 1890 to 1930, the watershed of modernity, includes as an integral part of the revolution in sensibility (as well as the revolution in mind) analytical cubism and abstraction in art, and "color impressionism" and the break-up of chordal tonality in music as well. To put forth a particular thesis of my own, the nature of modernity, as a social and esthetic movement, is that it represents an "eclipse of distance"—of psychic distance and esthetic distance—between the spectator and the work of art in all the spheres of culture. It involves the destruction (in the ideal-type sense) of rational conceptions—of time as an orderly sequence of events; of space as an ordered composition of figure and background—which had been the dominant mode since the Renaissance, and which had achieved its classic definition of appropriate genre in Lessing's *Laokoon.* Post-modernity, beyond this, breaks up existing genres and traditional distinctions between the arts, and where, in Dewey's phrase, "Art is experience," it seeks to establish all experience, or happenings, without any shaping, as art. And all this, too, conditions our appreciation of the past.[25]

But it is not to support a particular thesis that I propose a third term of Humanities, but to strengthen a viral experiment in liberal education: the argument that a useful and necessary perspective about the present and the past can be gained if such a course becomes the terminus of the Humanities sequence.

If the quite legitimate question is raised of where, in a crowded schedule, room is to be made for one more required course in the college, the answer is, I think, a simple one: abolish English A, the year of freshman composition. It should not be the function of a college to teach composition as a separate course. Students are, of course, required to write papers in different courses and more of this is necessary. But one has the right to assume that by the time a student enters college, he can write clearly enough to make a special course in freshman composition unnecessary.

The course in freshman English today is taught by thirty different members of the English department. A course like English A is

[25] These are themes that I have raised in an essay "The Disjunction of Culture and Social Structure," in *Daedalus* (Winter 1965).

extremely costly to the college, especially at a time when salaries are rising sharply and teaching schedules are being reduced. Given the general upgrading that is taking place in the secondary schools, it is entirely the responsibility of these schools to assure the proficiency of their students in English composition.

One college, no matter how prestigious, cannot enforce such a stipulation. But it would be entirely possible to enforce it if the colleges comprising the Ivy League would, as a group, establish the regulation that any student seeking admission to these colleges must meet a standard of composition set forth in a common college-board type entrance examination. Under certain conditions, a student might he admitted to college with composition as a deficiency. But it would then be *his* obligation, not the college's, to make up this deficiency, either by studying composition in the summertime, at extra cost, or in some form of tutoring outside the college schedule.

There is no reason, however, to delay the introduction of a third-term Humanities course. One could introduce such a course on the third-tier level, as a requirement in the senior year for all students majoring in the Humanities. This would give the College staff sufficient time to experiment with the syllabus of the course in order to see whether or not it should be required of all students in the College as a third-term Humanities course.

There is finally the Humanities sequence in music and in the fine arts. Under the Columbia requirement, a student, on completing the literature humanities in his freshman year, takes a term of music humanities and a term of fine arts humanities in the sophomore year.

The problems of the courses themselves, the staffing and the kinds of reading, have been discussed in detail by the Stern Committee, and there is little point in retreading their suggestions. A few general observations may be in order.

The music and fine arts humanities, more than the literature and philosophy humanities, have as their implicit premise the awakening of a student to esthetic experience by a confrontation with master-pieces. They both assume the student's great ignorance about the "cultural heritage" of music and painting, and seek to remedy it by the study of a dozen or so great works of art, in the case of the fine arts, and an appreciation of the musical styles of various periods, in the case of the music course. There is a question, given the recent deep-seated changes in American culture (at least in the urban professional class from which Columbia draws so many of its students), whether this notion is still valid. Professor Jack Beeson of the music department, in his presentation before the Stern Committee, made the most succinct statement of the case: "If the secondary schools did a better job in music there would be no need for the Music B Course." It may well be that in the next decade this will prove to be true. It certainly indicates that the colleges should take the lead in spurring the secondary schools to do a "better job"

Such a change would be no excuse for the abolition of a music and fine arts sequence from a Humanities course. But it would be an argument for changing the nature of such courses. Words are not the only mode of communication, particularly in our time when painting, cinema, and architecture have become paramount arts, and ours has become so much of a "visual culture." It is an important aspect of a liberal education that the student receive some intensive experience not only in modes of discourse but of visual perception and aural discrimination. And if the art and music "appreciation" work is done in secondary years, then the College courses could turn their attention, in the case of fine arts, to the nature of design and pereepdon—both to the psychological processes by which we create visual images and the understanding of styles against specific contexts; and in the case of music, to a comparative study of the organization of "sounds" and the esthetic principles which underlie the arrangements of sound.

In this respect, one experimental proposal might be in order: that the music and fine arts humanities be extended to a year each, and students be permitted to take one or the other. Those students who demonstrated a competence, say, in music would be allowed to take a year's work in fine arts, the first term of which would be devoted to masterpieces and the second in the broader nature of the visual modes; conversely, a student who, on entering the College, has shown knowledge in the fine arts would be allowed to take a year's work in music, as a means of fulfilling the requirement of a second year in Humanities. Thus, rather than have a student simply "achieve" or place out of one or the other courses on the basis of examination, differentiated alternatives would be available so that a student could take work closer to his interests and competences. In this fashion one could, as in the English department's "Introduction to Literary Study," be more responsive to variations in student achievement, but still remain within the framework of a coherent curriculum.

THE SCIENCE REQUIREMENT

Columbia students today are required, in fulfilling the requirements for the bachelor of arts degree, to take two years of work in mathematics-science. This can be a full-year course in any two sciences or, alternatively, a single two-year course in one of the sciences: astronomy, botany, chemistry, geography-geology, mathematics, physics, psychology, and zoology.

The requirement is a mishmash. It satisfies no logic of general education, other than the nice-sounding statement that the student has had two years of science. Over the last three decades, the College has wrestled with the problem. In 1946, the Carman Committee reported, "Two successive efforts have been made at Columbia to breach this [science requirement] impasse." And in 1957, the MacMahon Committee stated, "For at least twenty years the College has struggled with this part of its program." As one administrator ruefully remarked, "our situation is no worse than anybody else's." That is true. The existence of a "distribution requirement" (i.e., an open choice of any option) is a common one. But it is a condition in need of remedy.

In 1934 the College established a general science sequence for students who did not intend to specialize in science. It was a cooperative, rather than an interdisciplinary, course, with an instructor in physics teaching the physics term, an instructor in geology the geology portion, etc.[26] There was also, from 1924 on, Frederick

---

[26] As a curio, these were the principal readings in the two-year sequence in 1934: Science AI: *Matter, Energy, and Radiation,* by Dunning and Paxton; Science AII: syllabus and laboratory manual (prepared by the staff); Science BI: *Stars and Planets,* by D. H. Menzel; *Outlines of Geology,* by Longwell, Knopf, Flint, et al., *The Earth in Space,* Panorama of Physiographic Types,

Barry's elective lecture course in the history of science. But the general science sequence, which was looked on with disfavor by the science departments, vanished during the war. Professor Barry's course, which had met with considerable appreciation, ended with his death in 1943.

After the war, a committee headed by Professor Ernest Nagel submitted a report calling for a science sequence to complement the ones in Contemporary Civilization and Humanities. In 1948 the faculty of the College formally approved a proposal (which differed somewhat from the recommendations of the Nagel Committee) for a new interdepartmental course aimed at the general student. The course, however, never materialized, owing, in part, to a lack of enthusiasm on the part of the science departments, and, more, to the inability of the College to find the necessary space and staff.

What motivated the opposition by the science departments was less the wish to preserve vested interests than the intellectual conviction that a general sequence, even a two-year one, touching on physics, chemistry, astronomy, geology, climate, biology, and physiology could not be integrated, and that staffing it would be insuperable.

In retrospect, the science departments were correct. Many persons had uncritically applied the general education idea—of either a survey of the many sciences, or an interdisciplinary course that would relate common concepts to the sciences—without realizing that the development of knowledge in the sciences differs considerably from that of the humanities and the social sciences.

After the war, too, in the flush of enthusiasm for the necessity of teaching science in a new way, there was another approach, the idea of teaching science through the "history of science." But this too was repudiated. For what the history of sciences courses tended to do was to present science as part of intellectual history—to deal with the impact of science on cosmology, philosophy, the poetic imagination, and the like—all of which was very valuable, and indeed an integral part of general education, but it did not give the student

by A. K. Lobeck; *Climates of the World,* by G. T. Trewartha; Science BII: *The Machinery of the Body* by Carlson and Johnson; textbook in zoology by Curtis and Guthrie.

the sense of what science as an enterprise did, or the logic and substance of science itself.

The rationale for the requirement of science in a general education program has been well stated by Professor Jerome Bruner: "Science represents one of man's principal avenues of knowledge. Its mode of access to nature, the analytical methods it employs to achieve an economy of description and understanding, the techniques it invents for rendering concrete observation into systematic theory, its powerful logic of verification, the deep philosophical dilemmas that it has recently posed—all of these are matters of enormous cultural and human relevance."

In short, science is to be taught not only for its subject matter, but because its mode of inquiry illustrates intellectual, cultural, and creative aspects which give the scientific imagination a claim in liberal education coeval with the literary and other human imaginations.

In place of the older general education idea of an interdisciplinary science course, or science taught through the history of science, has come a new formulation. If one is to study any science itself, not its history, philosophy, or sociology, one must study how a particular discipline goes about its business, what its methods and fundamental principles are. The roles of hypothesis, experiment, observation, conceptual foundation, and interpretive schemes must be understood through the substantive elements of a science, not as statements to be considered in the abstract. This is what is appropriate to the understanding of what science is; and this is the way the best courses are taught.

If such is the case, then what is the best way of fulfilling a mathematics-science requirement? Columbia's present "distribution" requirement follows no principle other than that of exposing the student to a science. This *ad hoc* arrangement has left it to the science departments to determine what to do. Some give a survey course, some have made such courses a straight introduction to their disciplines, some introduce a student to the discipline, though providing variation for the nonscience student. The best arrangement, as typified by the physics and mathematics departments, has been the creation of "multiple tracks," in which the same rigor in presentation of principles is maintained in all the introductory courses, but the coverage of topics differs in extent and in depth of explanation, according to the interests and needs of the different students.

There are, it seems to me, two different ways of dealing with a science requirement: one is to require a course in the history of science; the other is to focus on a science sequence that can best realize the aim of illustrating the methods and principles of science.

The argument *against* a history of science requirement, *as a means of teaching science,* is, it seems to me, a persuasive one. In teaching the history of science, one can present it "internally" as the successive corrections of inadequate theories; or one can approach it "culturally," as the impact of various scientific ideas (e.g., the mechanistic image of the universe) on philosophical and social thought. The first method is useful and interesting for a student who wilt be specializing in science; but neither for him nor the general student is it an adequate way of showing how science or scientists, rather, reason and comprehend. The second one is extraordinarily important, but largely as part of general intellectual history. Moreover, one can appreciate the impact of science on other areas of human thought best, perhaps after one has first learned what science itself is. The history of science is, in fact, a perfect third-tier course because of the integrative qualities inherent to it.

The best method is to teach science by requiring the student to learn a particular discipline, modifying the material to give him some knowledge of the conceptual basis of the discipline. But if one is to teach science in an orderly sequence, then the present "distribution" system should be restricted, particularly since not all of the courses now open to the student teach science as conceptual inquiry, but simply give him a "rhetoric of conclusions" or some dogmatic statement about what is known, at present, in that field. Such an experience is worse than none at all, for the student assumes that he is acquiring a fixed body of knowledge, when he is in fact learning some conclusions that may be outdated ten years hence. He has learned little about the process of science as inquiry.

In place of the present system, I would propose a limited choice between two two-year sequences: a mathematics-physics sequence, or a mathematics-biology sequence.

Central to this proposal is the requirement of a year's work in mathematics for all students. This needs little justification. As a practical fact, a knowledge of mathematics (calculus, probability, matrix analysis, and differential equations) is today a basic requirement not only in the sciences but in the social sciences as well. No competent student in psychology, economics, and sociology (and even in such aspects of political science as organization theory) can get along without a "reading" knowledge of mathematics. Even a student of history and politics who wants to keep abreast of work in the other social sciences must be familiar with the ideas expressed in mathematical language.[27] Further, the impact of what I have called the new "intellectual technology" (model construction, simulation, information theory) is such that no graduate student in the future will be able to continue in any of the social sciences without some knowledge of mathematics—and, along with it, of computer programming.

One cannot overestimate the importance of the computer for the development of intellectual work. Two citations, one from economics, the other from physics, may be relevant here.

About economics, Oskar Morgenstern has written: "The electronic computer . . . puts into the hands of the mathematical economists a practical device such as could not be dreamed of even a single generation ago. The nonmathematical economist is helpless vis-a-vis this tool. He either has to acquire the necessary skills or

---

[27] For a comprehensive discussion of this problem, see *Mathematics and the Social Sciences,* ed. by James C. Charlesworth (Philadelphia, American Academy of Political and Social Science, June, 1963).

As Oliver G. Benson writes, apropos of the use of mathematics in political science: "For some the use of mathematics is anathema; for others a coveted arcanum. Some idealists identify esthetically with the individual digit, seeing it as a symbol of human individuality, vested with an eternal right not to be averaged, have its square root taken, or to be namelessly merged into a sum of squared deviations. Others are overly enthusiastic and see in mathematics the answer to all social problems. A point not always fully grasped is that mathematical models can never incorporate all factors in the real world, nor can they ever supply precise or definite answers to nonmathematical questions. They can merely simulate what are thought to be the salient concepts of reality-physical or behavioral—and their usefulness must he judged by the adequacy of their results. If the results do not agree with further observation, the model must he discarded for another—a process which has been repeated over and over again in every field of mathematical applications." *Ibid.,* pp. 32-33.

he must learn how to cooperate with his mathematically trained colleagues. Both procedures are difficult, but both are necessary. This merely repeats the development in physics where the experimentalist must be able to talk to the mathematical physicist though he need not match him in all his skills and vice versa. In economics, the computer will also obliterate the artificial borders between historical and statistical research, because time-series are of the essence; but, being statistical series, they require delicate mathematical-statistical series in order to yield their information. In short we see that mathematics penetrates more and more aspects of economics and that no limits are in sight where this process may stop."[28]

The way in which the computer is transforming experimentation in physics has been vividly described by Leon Lederman in his testimony before the Joint Committee on Atomic Energy on developments in high energy physics research.[29] The Columbia Synchrocyclotron Laboratory at Nevis has, for more than twenty years, conducted experiments in particle physics. One problem has been to follow the decay of the muon and to chart the resulting spectrum

---

[28] Professor Morgenstern cites a host of new problems which the joint application of mathematics and the computer has posed to economics. "For example, this happens in routine numerical operations to which economists would now no longer object. Such are the solving of large systems of equations arising, say, from application of linear programming to a concrete case. There one question is whether the hundreds of thousands of numerical steps, cheerfully carried out by the computer, produce a significant set of numbers in the answers or mainly 'noise,' due to the repeated rounding off of numbers which inevitably has to be done. This is a deep problem, still much neglected, which raises a host of new questions. Though they are not particular to economics, the economist has to face up to them and is thus pushed into an additional area of mathematical considerations.

"No one writing before the advent of computers could have foreseen this situation and the need for economists (and all theoretical scientists) to occupy themselves with these intricate problems," Professor Morgenstern concludes. "Indeed there was no need to worry about it in pure mathematics either. The two developments went hand in hand and this, in a minor way again proves the point of the interaction of man's exploration of the physical world and the development of mathematics. Just as mathematics has profited from having been tied so closely to the physical sciences, mathematics will benefit from becoming deeply involved with the problems of the social world." Oskar Morgenstern, "Limits to the Use of Mathematics in Economics," in Charlesworth, pp. 28-29.

[29] The examples are taken from the statement by Professor Lederman before the Subcommittee on Research, Development, and Radiation of the Joint Committee on Atomic Energy 89th Cong., 1st sess. (March 2, 3, 4 and 5, 1965), pp. 314-15.

of electrons. A bubble chamber experiment in 1960 collected 10,000 events and obtained a number 0.78 ± .022. The theorists insisted this number must be 0.750. In 1962 a Columbia group, under Professor Allen Sachs, devised a series of sonic spark chambers embedded in a magnetic field, which was coupled to a small computer. In a ten-day run they collected 10 million events, and got a number 0.747 ± .005, which made the theorists happy.

But it is more than mammoth data processing which makes the computer so valuable. It is its ability to disclose new possibilities. Lederman has described, for example, one such use in particle physics. Particles arrive from the accelerator into a target and the observer seeks to measure the reaction products which emerge: the angles of emission, the velocities of the fragments, the masses, charges, etc, "In the old-fashioned day of last year," said Lederman, "the emissions in the spark chambers would be pulsed on film, the film would be developed, and the measurements processed on a computer. Today, the scintillation logic is processed directly by a computing machine, online with the experiment. The results can be displayed before the experimenter both to verify his procedures and to advise him as to how to best proceed. In more sophisticated systems, a feedback loop can automatically modify the exposure to optimize the data collection."

As Lederman summed it up: "The growing awareness of computer capabilities is shaping the development of the non-bubble chamber particle detectors. . . . The time spent by my generation [he is 43] in learning arts and skills of plumbing and electronics will give way to acquiring greater familiarity with programing and computer science."[30]

Besides these "theoretical" considerations, there is the important

----

[30] The difficulties for Professor Lederman's generation, in this regard, may be best illustrated by the following colloquy between Professor Lederman and Congressman Holifield:

Chairman Holifield: Would any physicist be capable of programing or does it take a specialist?
Dr. Lederman: I find it is like learning a language. Young students take to programing very, very quickly. The older professors have the hard time. They have to work at it.
Chairman Holifield: Is this what you might call a natural ability or capability of an individual or is it a science that can be learned, can be taught and learned on regular principles.

fact that in field after field, the computer has become an indispensible tool not only for research but for practical activity. In medicine, computer programs are becoming an important adjunct in diagnosis —particularly in cardiac cases where cardiograms can now be "matched" against thousands of similar tracings, by computers, to make a reading more accurate. In business firms, computer programs are a necessary tool not only for data processing, but for the making of day-to-day business decisions.

But more important than the "practical" requirement, crucial as it is, is the fact that the general study of "axiomatic systems," or postulational theories, is one of the major modes of explanation in science and the social sciences, and as part of a general education all students should be aware of the nature of this type of hypothetical-deductive thought.[31] The foundation of this thought is mathematics.

The rationale for concentrating on physics or biology, rather than any of the other sciences, seems to me to be equally clear. Physics

---

Dr. Lederman: IBM at Columbia gives a course called the Fool-proof 3-Day Course in Computing, and I failed.
Chairman Holifield; Maybe you needed an extra day.
Ibid., p. 318

[31] "The mathematical development of any science culminates in the axiomatic formulation of its contents. The modern axiomatic method has achieved superb success in mathematics itself ever since David Hilbert first axiomatized geometry in the 1890s. . . .

"The axiomatic method consists of formulating a set of propositions which must fulfill certain conditions. They must, in particular, be free of contradictions, and the deductions derived from them must contain our knowledge of the field and, beyond this, hopefully, lead to new insights. If a part of mathematics is axiomated, the axioms will be mathematical propositions—for example, through two points in a plane there passes only one straight line, and so on. If one is dealing with an empirical field, the axioms will be statements about some part of the real world— for example, one may say that the speed of light is constant. In no case have the axioms any superior truth value to that of their implications as these are brought to light in the deductions which can be based on the axioms. The latter are chosen for reasons of convenience, because they are intuitively acceptable and express in agreeable and perhaps esthetically satisfying form some basic knowledge of the field in question. But they are not self-evident truths as the old and now completely superseded view of an 'axiom' stated. The axiomatic method is simply a superb technique for summarizing our knowledge in a given field and for finding further knowledge deductively. This involves inevitably logico-mathematical operations, sometimes of great complexity. If the state of axiomatization of an empirical field has been reached, which is a state of some perfection, mathematics is indispensable." Morgenstern, pp. 23-24.

and biology exemplify orderly theoretical structures formulated in conceptual paradigms[32] that are themselves open to change as new principles of inquiry or new perspectives create new theoretical solutions or challenges.

Physics is the foundation of our inquiries in a wide range of sciences, from cosmology to biology. It shapes to a considerable extent our philosophical outlooks as well as our practical activities. In biology, the current "clash" between classical biology, with its emphasis on observation and experiments with living organisms, organs, and cells, and "molecular biology," with its assumption that chemical constituents separated from the cell can become the unit of study, affords a fascinating example for the present-day student of the "paradigmatic revolution" in a science that promises to create as much change in biology in the next two decades as the theory of relativity or quantum mechanics created in physics in the first two decades of this century.[33]

In this respect, I have been strongly persuaded by the essay by

[32] I follow here the formulations of Thomas Kuhn. A paradigm consists of a "strong network of commitments—conceptual, theoretical, instrumental, and methodological . . . which for a time provide model problems and solutions to a community of practitioners." From paradigms "spring particular coherent traditions of scientific research" which Kuhn calls "normal science."

Scientific change, for Kuhn, is not simply the cumulative, or self-corrective, growth of a body of knowledge but a succession of paradigms. A scientific revolution is taken to be "those noncumulative developmental episodes in which an older paradigm is replaced in whole or in part by an incompatible new one." Thomas Kuhn, *The Structure of Scientific Revolution.*

[33] Professor Barry Commoner has described the conflict in these terms: "Anyone who has learned biology by dissecting a frog must find the reports of present-day biological research strange and unfamiliar: molecules that reproduce themselves; a molecular 'code' that tells an egg whether it should turn into a turtle or a tiger; efforts to create 'life' in a test tube of chemicals.

"These new ideas seem to clash with long-familiar principles of biology. If a molecule possesses the essential property of life—self-reproduction—then the cell theory, which states that the attributes of life reside in the whole cell and not in any smallest part must be wrong. . . The present conflict in biology reflects uncertainty about the most profound attributes of life; for that reason, it will, when resolved, have a far-reaching effect on what we know about the living world and what we can do about it.

"The two antagonists, classical and 'molecular' biology, represent conflicting concepts of the nature of life. Classical biology is built upon observations and experiments with actually living organisms, organs, and cells. Classical biology insists upon studying these complex systems because no simpler ones are alive; it assumes that life is inherently associated with the complexity of at least the cell.

John R. Platt, the biophysicist, on "strong inference,"[34] which appeared in 1964 in *Science*. For Professor Platt some fields in science are more rapid moving than others, in part because "a particular method of doing scientific research is systematically used and taught, an accumulate method of inductive inference that is so effective [as to] be given the name of 'strong inference.'"

The principle of "strong inference" seeks to formalize a method of inductive reasoning based largely on the procedures of devising alternative hypotheses for any problem, devising crucial experiments, each of which would, as nearly as possible, exclude one or more hypotheses, recycling the procedure to make subhypotheses or sequential hypotheses, and, when the "branching points" are identified, to carry the same steps further in a "logical tree." As George Polya has defined it: the hypothesis, experiment outcome, and exclusion have to be related in a rigorous syllogism.[35]

In one sense, this is little more than the scientific method itself. But as Professor Platt points out, many scientists have almost forgotten it: "How many of us write down our alternatives and crucial experiments every day, focusing on the *exclusion* of a hypothesis. . . . We fail to teach our students how to sharpen up their inductive inferences. And we do not realize the added power that the regular and explicit use of alternative hypotheses and sharp exclusions could give us at every step of our research."

"On the other hand, the approach which we now call 'molecular biology' assumes that chemical constituents, separated from the cell and studied with sufficient subtlety and detail, will be found to possess some lifelike properties. It assumes that life could reside in a cellular constituent and permits the notion of a 'living molecule.'

"We are sometimes told that molecular biology is a modern science, while classical biology is a surviving relic of nineteenth-century science. This view casts the conflict into a familiar pattern; old-fashioned classical biology doggedly resisting inevitable replacement by the up-to-date molecular variety. Despite its convenient simplicity, this view is inaccurate, for both classical and molecular biology have long and intimately connected histories. They represent two paths which, although far apart when they began nearly 200 years ago, have steadily converged toward their present collision." Barry Commoner, "Biology Today," *NEA Journal* (March, 1964).

[34] John R. Platt, "Strong Inference," *Science, CXLVI,* No, 3642 (October 16, 1964), 347-53.

[35] See George Polya, *Mathematics and Plausible Reasoning* (2 vols.; Princeton, NJ, Princeton University Press, 1954).

The new molecular biology, Professor Platt argues, is a field where this systematic method of inference has become widespread and effective. The logical structure shows in a chain of experiments. In 1953, James Watson and Francis Crick suggested that the DNA molecule—the "hereditary substance" in a cell—had a long, two-stranded helix shape. This posed a number of alternatives for crucial test: do the two strands of the helix stay together when a cell divides, or do they separate? Meselson and Stahl showed that they separate. Further experiments showed that the DNA helix can have two strands or three (as atomic models suggested) depending on the ionic concentration.

Crucial experiments of this kind can be found, of course, in every field, but as Professor Platt points out, "The real difference in molecular biology is that formal inductive inference is so systematically practiced and taught."[36]

This analytical thinking is by no means restricted to the new biology. High-energy physics is another field where the logic of exclusions is obvious as, for example, in the famous experiments (by Professors Wu, Lederman, and Garwin among others) which answered the questions about the "parity principle" which had been asked by T. D. Lee and C. N. Yang.

The emphasis on "strong inference" in biology and physics is due in part, Professor Platt believes, to the kind of scientists who have taken the lead in these fields, but equally to the nature of the fields themselves. "Biology, with its vast informational detail and complexity, is a 'high-in formation' field, where years and decades can

[36] As Professor Platt points out further: "The strong inference attitude is evident just in the style and language in which the papers are written. For example, in analyzing theories of antibody formation, Joshua Lederberg gives a list of nine propositions 'subject to denial,' discussing which ones would be 'most vulnerable to experimental test.'

"The papers of the French leaders Francois Jacob and Jacques Monod [who shared the Nobel Prize in 1965] are also celebrated for their high 'logical density,' with paragraph after paragraph of linked 'inductive syllogisms.' But the style is widespread. Start with the first paper in the *Journal of Molecular Biology* for 1964, and you immediately find: 'Our conclusions . . . might be invalid if . . . (i) . . . (ii) . . . or (iii). . . . We shall describe experiments which eliminate these alternatives.' The average physicist or chemist or scientist in any field accustomed to less closely reasoned articles and less sharply stated inferences will find it a salutary experience to dip into that journal almost at random." Platt, p. 348.

easily be wasted on the usual type of 'low-information' observations or experiments if one does not think carefully in advance about what the most important and conclusive experiments would be. And in high-energy physics, both the 'information flux' of particles from the new accelerators and the million-dollar costs of operation have forced a similar analytical approach."

The argument for the establishment of biology as one of the two required courses in science need not rest solely on the rigor and so-phisticated methodology of "molecular biology." Almost as striking have been the developments—at the other end of the scale, so to speak—in physical anthropology, which has been transformed from a specialized, largely historical discipline dealing with bones and skull measurements to a major science of human biology, and in ethology, which, in its observation of social behavior in animals, has laid some new foundations for the study of human behavior.

In human biology, work in evolution, human genetics and biological variation in modern populations, research data on growth patterns and constitutional types of individuals as well as populations, and the striking advances in human ecology (the effects of nutrition, climate, disease, and demographic pressure on human variation) all add up to a body of knowledge that is increasingly central to work in medicine, psychology, and sociology.[37]

The detailed observation of animals in natural environments, as against the older studies of animals living under abnormal conditions in zoos and laboratories, has given us a new and broader understand-ing of social behavior, including, for example, the limited and specific nature of aggression among animals of the same species, as against the diffuse and ferocious nature of aggression in man. The careful observational techniques in "animal sociology" provide a model of recording, inference, and generalization that provides the student with yet another dimension of the scientific enterprise in its manifold forms. Moreover, the strikingly different advances in biology, from molecular biology to ethology, raise fundamental questions about

[37] For a magisterial work in this field, see *Human Biology,* by G. A. Harrison, J. S. Weiner, J. M. Tanner, and N. A. Barnicot (Oxford University Press, 1964.) For an overview on recent work in genetics to the social sciences, see Gardner Lindzey, Social Science Research Council, *Items,* September, 1964.

modes of explanation, bring back questions about the nature of "emergence" and "function," and pose central questions about the nature of complex organization at the most minute and at the gross levels of life.[38]

This does not mean, therefore, that one should begin the study of biology with the problem of the molecule or the smallest cell and its more than a quarter of a million protein molecules engaged in coordinated activity to sustain life; or that high-energy physics or quantum physics (with its nonmedium and multidimensional non-space) should predominate over classical physics (with its ordered world of time and space) in the physics courses. It may well be that in biology the "tensions" between molecular and classical biology, and in physics the successive paradigms, should be the focus of a course. These are matters for the biologists and physicists to decide. Yet physics and biology today represents two of the most successful and elegant formulations of knowledge that have been created by the human mind. And for these reasons, the coherence of theoretical structures, the sophistication of methods, the significance for other sciences, and the exemplification of conceptual innovations—which are indeed compelling ones—the choice of physics or biology, along with mathematics, seems to me to be the desirable requirement in a liberal arts program.

These sequences should be required of all nonscience students in Columbia. For a science student, however, such a requirement makes little sense. A science student will necessarily have at least one and possibly two years of calculus. In most cases, even if he is a chemistry or biology major, he will be taking physics. If the purpose of the science requirement is to exemplify how a science is constructed, he will find this out in his own specialized courses—though the emphasis in some of the courses is often upon the acquisition of detail and attention to conceptual foundations is neglected. What a science stu-

---

[38] For a useful introduction to ethological studies, see N. Tinbergen, *Social Behaviour in Animals* (New York, Wiley, 1962). A book which examines the links between animal and human behavior is *The Natural History of Aggression,* ed. by J. D. McCarthy and F. J. Ebling (London, Academic Press, 1965).

A book which reopens a host of philosophical questions about the significance of the recent work in ethology is Adolf Portman's *New Paths in Biology* (New York, Harper and Row, 1964).

dent often lacks is a knowledge of the history of science and, more often, an awareness of the theoretical problems posed by the philosophy of science. Few scientists today are "metaphysicists," and it is striking to observe the indifference and even disdain of many working scientists for the philosophical aspects of their own modes of inquiry. When such questions are raised, they profess a crude "operationalism," and argue flatly that science is what science does. Yet the general rules of theory construction, the problems of verifiability and falsifiability, the import of scientific positions for philosophical thinking, are all legitimate and important dimensions of a scientist's work. Equally relevant is a knowledge of the social contexts of science: the social norms of science, the organizational contexts in which science operates, the social consequences of science, etc. What I propose, therefore, is that a science major, in lieu of the two-year "math-science" requirement, be obligated to take a two-term sequence in the history of science, philosophy of science, methodology of the sciences, and the sociology of science. These are legitimate and necessary third-tier courses.

THE MAJOR SYSTEM

Columbia's introduction of the major system in 1954 was influenced by the trend toward specialization; yet it had the pedagogic virtue, especially in a college like Columbia where more than half the graduates go into the professions rather than graduate school, of giving students a firm grounding in a specific discipline, rather than the amorphous experience of educating the "whole man."

Within the past decade most of the departments have expended much of their intellectual energies in working out the sequences of a major's program, except in the sciences where worked-out programs already existed. But as each department has extended its major program, it has increased the number of points required, in some cases so enormously, as in some of the sciences, as to take up almost the entire time of the student, leaving no room for electives outside the specialization and its related field. Such requirements may be necessary for a program designed to prepare the student for graduate work or some professional qualification, but given the advanced preparation now being done in the secondary schools, it should be possible to reduce somewhat the concentration of work in college, so as to allow the science major for example some breathing space for other courses.

In 1965, the College, realizing that disproportions existed, took steps to correct the situation. Case studies of students with a large number of points in their major departments revealed that in some instances a student had taken all of his courses in the major department except for those, such as Contemporary Civilization or Humanities, which were required for the degree, and that students with highly specialized programs often ranked relatively low in the class. The Committee on Instruction concluded from these studies that some of the Columbia students were doing excessive work in their major department to the detriment of their intellectual growth and in contradiction of the commitment of the College to liberal education. Feeling that some restraint was warranted, the Committee proposed, and the faculty approved, a resolution that no student could take more than ten credits in excess of the minimum points prescribed in the department of his major.

But the resolute action of the College does raise a more general question: What is the function of the major? Most departments would reply: to provide a basic minimum of specialization and coverage in a field. But to what end? As a direct stepping-stone to graduate work in the field; to provide some knowledge of a particular discipline or subject as the background for professional or related work (e.g., in law or medicine); or what?

It may be useful at this point to consider the distribution of majors in Columbia College and the career plans of the undergraduates. In the class of 1963, six departments out of thirty-one accounted for more than two-thirds of all majors in the College. These were: history, economics, government, English, chemistry, and zoology. (Physics and mathematics followed closely behind.)

The students' career plans showed how these subjects were used in their graduate intentions. Of 457 students who indicated that they would pursue advanced work, 57.5 per cent intended to go into the professions, the single largest groups being medicine (almost 30 percent) and law (more than 15 percent).

In the sciences (particularly physics and chemistry) a considerable number of the majors in these subjects had determined to go on to graduate study in the fields. But in history and English—the departments with the largest number of majors in the College, accounting in some years for about 20 to even 25 percent of all students in a class—less than a fourth or so of the majors in those departments intend to go on to graduate study in that subject. The question then is, for what reasons does a student take a major—for background purposes or for subsequent specialized use? Clearly, other than the sciences, both reasons are operative.

Most departments, it would seem, have planned their major in order to give a student the basic amount of work necessary to give a student a specializing knowledge of the field, on the assumption that he would go on to graduate work and become a professional in that field. The introduction of "multitracks" in the elementary courses showed that the departments were aware of the different kinds of "introductory" work for students with differing needs. But it may well be that there is a need for "multitracks" in the major programs as well, in order to satisfy the varying needs of majors as well. In these instances, one might ask the departments to scrutinize their major programs with an eye to the different purposes they might serve, rather than the single purpose of professional training in the subject. This is particularly true of the three social science departments—history, government, and economics—which comprise nearly 35 percent of all college majors, and whose students seek preparation for graduate work, a background for law school, training for business, for government service, and the like. The question of multipurpose can be suggested to the science departments as well. Dean Truman, for example, has raised the question of whether the physical sciences might be able to organize a concentration for a student who would not go into physics but into law, in order to deal with public or legal problems in science policy, and would therefore need some detailed scientific training.

A second problem about the major program is the ambiguity, in almost all instances except the science programs, of the "related courses" stipulation. In the College catalogue one finds, in the listing of requirements for a major, statements calling for twelve or so credits in a "related field." But these courses are rarely specified, and, in practice, a departmental representative or consultant will often accept *any* grouping of courses in a roughly related field as fulfilling the requirement.

This is more than an administrative deficiency. It indicates that a department has not thought through what a student should know in related fields in order to do adequate work in a major. The lack is especially glaring in the social sciences, the more so since, as I have argued earlier, the acquisition of knowledge in the social sciences depends on a set of "linkages" between fields to make problems intelligible. Thus, the government department requires twelve points of upper-level courses, but makes no requirement in sociology or economics, though the newer analytical concepts and models of political science draw heavily from both of these related disciplines. Similarly, the economics department carefully indicates various sequences open to students with different plans for using the major, but requires no work in government or history, though these are necessary as contextual subjects for the discipline.

The problem exists in the Humanities as well. A student majoring in English literature, for example, will take a carefully worked out sequence of six courses, covering the major writers and trends in English literature from 1616 to 1900, but he is not required to take any English history at all.

Some of these deficiencies arise from intellectual insularity, some from the failure of the College to provide the mechanisms that, in a detailed way, could create coherent programs of intellectual work, both for the student and for the discipline. One of the important tasks of each department, it seems to me, should therefore be to spell out, with the attendant intellectual rationales, the kind of related courses necessary for the different configurations of a major program.

One simple step in this direction would be a requirement that each department publish a syllabus or reading list for each course in its major and elective program. At present the only guides a student has to the scope and content of a course are the brief and often ambiguous statements in the College catalogue, the vague description volunteered by a College adviser, or the hearsay of fellow-students. The publication of syllabi and reading lists would give the student a clearer idea of the contents of a course in relation to his own needs and purposes, would help the advisers in guiding a student who is uncertain of the utility of a course, and would allow departments to see how much overlapping or repetition there is within and between the departments. Even a brief review of reading lists in the social science courses reveals a tremendous duplication of material. While Marx, Weber, Durkheim, et al., can be read, of course, from many different perspectives, one finds, especially in comparing sociology and government courses, and government and history, repetitions due to a lack of coordination or discussion between departments.

The discussion of multipurposes in the major programs, and the specification of related courses, raises a more general problem that will confront the College with increasing urgency in the coming years, particularly as various subjects begin to require multidisciplinary competences. This is the problem of a department that offers advanced work in its own specialty and must also be a "service" department on an elementary level for other departments as well. The situation is particularly compelling in mathematics. This department includes some of the most eminent mathematicians in the world, whose chief devotion, understandably, is to their own advanced, speculative work, and whose interest in the College derives from the pleasure of finding brilliant young mathematicians and giving them superlative training. It is difficult to invite an eminent mathematician to give an elementary course in calculus or some work in probability or matrix algebra although one finds Nobel-prize physicists interested and willing to teach introductory physics. Yet these needs are growing, particularly, as I indicated earlier, since the social sciences and allied fields have begun to use mathematical models (e.g., mathematical models of kinship in anthropology, set theory in linguistics, finite mathematics in sociology and political behavior, and so on). For obvious reasons, the department does not want to give tenure or promotion to men who are simply "superior schoolmasters" and who do little research or creative work on their own. How does one deal with this? The problem has already begun to confront other fields as well: in physics, where special courses are necessary for biologists who want to deal with biophysical problems; in biology, where the new needs of psychology require special "service"; and the like. (In physics and chemistry the needs have been met in part by providing men who teach *some* service courses, but who are not merely service-course men.)

In the past the College faced the "service" problem largely through the departments' relation to the general education courses. Now the problem must be faced "across the board" as well, and it involves administrative and institutional policy, as much as intellectual inquiry.

The relationship of "action program" or "work programs," run by the College, to the departments is a different type of dilemma. Columbia has not been, in the modish sense of the word, an "experimental" college in which work outside the departmental courses has been integral to the courses themselves. Yet in the past ten years there has been a significant development in College educational policy, through the expansion of the Citizenship Council. Today, more than 400 students are involved in community service programs of one sort or another. A number of these are useful projects in which a student donates his time (a reading program for disadvantaged children, a remedial program for dropouts) primarily as a community service. But many other projects—internships in government, summer work in political campaigns, or reform work in local communities—relate directly to the social science departments, and are invaluable as laboratory and research training. At present there is little or no attempt made (except in the case of a student intending to go directly into government service), by the dean's office and the departments to coordinate these programs. The question can be raised whether these activities might be related more directly to course work or not. There are arguments, understandably, pro and con, that one can advance. But the question has not been discussed actually with the departments.

One further question about the major program is the failure of most departments to set forth an honors program. Fifty years ago, Dean Keppel, in his book on Columbia, called for an honors program. ("The honors courses seem to furnish a clew to the possibility of maintaining in a university, no matter how large and overcrowded, a place for earnest undergraduates, not grinds, but boys with red blood, of real intellectual curiosity and promise.") In the 1957 report on "The Educational Future of Columbia University," the Mac-

Mahon Committee noted that "implicit in the emergence of Columbia College's 'major-concentration' program is the opportunity to develop a 'Senior Honors' program." The Committee indicated the variety of special work—including a senior thesis, individual research and study, a comprehensive examination—that might be required of a student in order to graduate "with honors."

The function of an honors program is obviously not just honorific. It is an opportunity for the qualified student to do more intensive study, independent study, and tutorial work with a departmental member. In a number of universities (Chicago, Princeton, Harvard) an honors or a senior thesis program has produced notable work by students. If one of the developing threads of the College, as exemplified in the *ad hoc* introduction of "multiple-track" courses, is the differentiation of programs to meet the individual aims of the students, then the development of a coherent honors program is a question that should be debated and decided directly.[39]

Finally, there is the problem of how and where new disciplines, or significant advances in a field, are to be introduced into the College curriculum. Columbia College, as I have indicated at a number of points, not only lacks a working integrative mechanism between departments; it lacks, as well, an adaptive mechanism for the introduction of new subjects, fields, or disciplines into the curriculum. At present, these initiatives are almost entirely in the hands of the departments. But in a number of cases, partly because of the inchoate nature of the field, or for parochial reasons, some departments may reflect one special "school of thought" rather than another, and the question of what is to be taught and what new subjects admitted is interpreted from the special vantage point of that "school." In phys-

---

[39] The College now has a number of unrelated programs that could be grouped into an honors sequence. Thus, in cooperation with four other colleges, Columbia selects about four students in their junior year to spend a summer in Europe doing research. This is developed during the student's senior year as an important paper, which can give him four to eight points of credit in a department. The College now offers three to four Kellett fellowships for study at Oxford and Cambridge, plus a number of other fellowships for graduate work in the United States. At present these fellowships are awarded through departmental nominations, yet they do form, together with the summer-study fellowships, the nucleus of an honors program in which the fellowships become an award for outstanding senior theses and individual study projects.

ics, there are no formal "schools" and there is general agreement on what constitutes the frontiers of thought and research in the field. But in philosophy, psychology, sociology, linguistics, anthropology, English and the Humanities and, to some extent, in economics, such "schools" and established interests often prevail. It is difficult, of course, for "outsiders" to challenge a department's decision about what is relevant or necessary to a field. Yet some continuing mechanism of inquiry may be necessary in order to keep the College, and the university, abreast of new developments.

This is part of a more general question. In a previous chapter I alluded to the new "intellectual technology" that is a feature of the newer developments of analysis. These include decision theory, information theory, simulation, model construction, gaming, and so on. Some of these (e.g., political gaming and simulation) are heuristic techniques. Some of these (e.g., information theory) may have applications in a particular field, or promise to become disciplines in their own right. Dominating these advances in analysis is the computer, which, as an intellectual tool, promises to revolutionize work in some fields (e.g., genetics and molecular biology) the way calculus changed the study of physics.[40]

In many instances there is still a question whether the more general claims of a new intellectual conception to be itself a new discipline (e.g., cybernetics as an extension of information theory) will hold. Yet there ought to be some overall body of review in the College—and in the university as a whole—which assesses such developments and can make suggestions about the introduction of these materials or disciplines into the curriculum.

THE THIRD TIER

The very conception of an intellectual discipline implies a method of analysis and a logical framework of concepts at high levels of generality and, indeed, of abstraction. The heart of a college education today is mastering a discipline (not acquiring a specialization, which

[40] It is quite likely, in the next few years, that work on a computer, for the student in physics and biology, if not in other fields, will become part of the routine "lab" requirement. Like any lab, this not only would be a mechanical exercise but a genuine intellectual opportunity to see new avenues of work and new combinations as a result of acquiring a new technique and a new tool.

is a fixed knowledge of a small piece of subject matter through the use of a discipline). But within a liberal arts framework, mastering a discipline gains a significant dimension only if that mastery is placed within a proper sequence of understanding. What I have been proposing is such an orderly sequence. The idea of the "third tier" is that it would apply for each field, or set into appropriate context, the knowledge previously acquired. The College curriculum would thus be organized on these four "steps":

1. History and Tradition. The first step is a detailed discovery, through the Contemporary Civilization and Humanities program, of the history and traditions of Western civilization, the awareness of the great works of moral imagination and science, the basic processes of social change, the great intellectual movements of self-conscious reflection and ideas on the events of change.

2. Introduction to a Discipline. The second step is the introduction to a discipline. Through the proposed "math-science" courses, the nonscientist will have a detailed sense of how a specific science acquires, utilizes, and revises its basic concepts. Through the proposed social science options, all students will have the opportunity of learning how at least one social science organizes its perspective on society; and in the case of the social science major, he will have an introduction to a discipline other than his own.

3. The Extension of the Discipline to Subjects. The organization of the major program is essentially the application of the discipline to different subject matters in the field, and this would be the heart of the third year and the upper-college courses.

4. The Third Tier. The third tier is a synoptic program, at the senior level, whose purpose is twofold: to deal with the methodological and philosophical (and, in the case of the social sciences, historical) presuppositions of a field; to show the application of the discipline to general problems, or to issues requiring a multidisciplinary approach, in order to test the operation of the discipline in a wider context. These contexts, almost invariably in the social sciences, and increasingly in the biological sciences, involve issues of value or of moral choice; and the explication of the value problems involved would be an added purpose of these courses.

So defined, the third-tier courses become a distinctive contribution to general education. They seek to explore interrelated issues between disciplines, to try to create a philosophical sophistication about the foundations of the fields, and to raise, where possible, value problems in the application of the discipline. These third-tier courses differ from earlier kinds of general education courses—such as Contemporary Civilization B at Columbia or Social Science 2 at Chicago—which were either introductory courses implying the existence of an interdisciplinary set of logically related concepts (as at Chicago), or courses focused mainly on great historical topics (such as industrialization) or large-scale policy choices (such as planning versus laissez-faire) to which the student brought no previous work in at least one discipline in order to appreciate either method or materials. The present proposal differs further in that the same third-tier, or synoptic, courses would not be required of *all* students in the College: each division—the social sciences, the humanities, and the sciences—would have third-tier courses appropriate to the particular problems of each field, and each student within a divisional area would be required, in his senior year, to take a specified number of these third-tier courses.[41]

In principle, there would be *four* kinds of courses in the third tier. These would be courses in:

1) the historical foundations of the intellectual disciplines in the field;

2) the methodological and philosophical presuppositions of the disciplines;

3) the extension of the various disciplines to applied problems;

4) comparative studies, particularly of non-Western cultures.

The last point requires some clarification. The requirement that a student take some courses in non-Western cultures seems to be almost axiomatic today. There is the general intellectual rationale that such a set of courses would be one important way of overcoming the parochialism of students who know only Western (in this instance, European and North American) civilization. There is the sociological reason that such knowledge is immensely valuable for under-

---

[41] While these would be required for students within each division, there is no reason why they should not be open to qualified students who would want to take some third-tier courses in fields other than their own.

standing political currents and for testing generalizations about literature or social processes that have emerged out of Western experience and the Western moral temper. For reasons that I will elaborate later, I would propose that all students majoring in the humanities be required to take a year of Oriental Humanities, and that all students majoring in the social sciences be required to take a year of Oriental Civilizations.

As to the practical problem of fitting these courses into the student's schedule, there is a simple pointer to a solution: since almost all departments usually require "related courses" as part of the major program—courses amounting usually to twelve credits, or four courses—the third tier, if accepted by the College, would become the "related courses" in the major requirement of the departments. Such a procedure would not necessarily cut unduly into the number of free electives available to a student. Since the requirement of "related courses" is itself presumably a limitation on what the student can offer a department in work for his major, the third-tier courses, including as they inevitably will, a number of options, become the arena of elective choice.

To exemplify the kinds of third-tier courses I have in mind, I will make here a number of specific proposals. These are not, as in the case of the courses proposed for the Contemporary Civilization program or lower-college courses, outlines of syllabi, but illustrations that attempt to show the range of possibilities open in this area. (Most of the courses I shall propose are in the social sciences, since this is the area in which I have the greatest experience; it may well be that some colleagues in the humanities and the sciences will be able, on the basis of their own competence, to propose some detailed courses in these areas.)

The Social Sciences. I shall here illustrate an historical course, a methodological course, and two synoptic courses which require several different social science disciplines to be brought to bear on the subject.

1. "The Historical Emergence of the Social Sciences in the Nineteenth Century." More than other fields—at least at this stage of their development—the social sciences can be understood only

in part as historical disciplines. The problems posed for each discipline are still rooted in their histories; the differences in points of view are still derived from conflicting schools of thought. In most of the social sciences we are still only two or, at most, three intellectual generations away from the masters—Marshall, Walras, Keynes; Weber and Durkheim; Wundt, Freud, Pavlov, Tolman, and Hull; Tyler, Frazer, Boas, Malinowski, Radcliffe-Brown, and Kroeber; Pareto, Mosca, Bentley, and Dewey.

The course would cover the emergence of economics, political science, sociology, psychology, and anthropology as separate disciplines out of philosophy and general political thought. Thus, the study of economics would begin with Petty and Child, and the effort to ascertain, through "political arithmetik," the actual effects of mercantilist trade policies; the efforts of Smith and Ricardo to create economics as an analytical discipline independent of historical contexts, the formalization of supply-and-demand theory through the price mechanism in Marshall; the idea of general equilibrium: and the emergence of macro-economics in the twentieth century.[42]

The rise of political science, as against political theory or political thought, would begin with the emergence of the idea of "public opinion" and the active role of masses of people in political affairs. While only a few systematic political observations are possible, one could begin with Tocqueville and Bryce, as commentators who introduced the idea of direct political observation; Ostrogorski, Michels, Mosca, and Pareto, who made comparative studies of party systems, and, in the instance of the last two, sought general laws of

---

[42] It is surprising to note how long it took economics to become established in the universities. In 1878, Professor J. K. Ingram took the occasion of his Presidential Address delivered to Section F (Economic Science and Statistics) of the British Association for the Advancement of Science to speak "On the Defense of Economics Against its Elimination from the B. A." Professor Ingram wrote: ". . . an Oxford professor of political economy has recently disputed the possibility, or at least the utility, of a scientific handling of economic questions. According to him, ordinary people are right in believing that they can arrive at truth on these questions by aid of their natural lights, by their untrained sagacity—that they can take a shorter and far clearer path through their own observations, than through what he calls the 'tangled jungle of scientific refinements.' In plain terms, he is in favour of relegating the study of economic phenomena to the domain of empiricism—to what is called the common sense of practical man." *Advancement of Science* (March, 1963), pp. 524-32.

political behavior; and writers like Bentley and Dewey, who introduced a broad perspective about the nature of the public and the political process in general.[43]

The study of sociology would deal with four streams of thought: Marxism and German idealism, French "collectivism" (Saint-Simon, Comte, Durkheim), British empiricism (the social survey of Booth, et al.), and the tradition of statistical inquiry into human affairs (Le Play, Quetelet, Pearson, and Galton). Central to the emergence of sociology is the problem posed by the French Revolution: if a society can be "torn up" by its roots and new principles of legitimacy introduced, then what is "society"? What are the kinds of norms and socially regulative mechanisms that hold societies together, and what are the conditions for conflict, change, and consensus?

The study of psychology offers a particularly striking example of the specific differentiation of a field from philosophy. Kant's question, "What is perception?", which was posed in order to deal with the *a priori* basis of sense impressions, was given an experimental answer in the researches of Weber and Fechner on the diminishing and appreciative intensities of light, and the formulation of a psycho-physical law. Mill's effort to deal with "association" as the basis of idea was analyzed subsequently in Wundt's laboratory experiments on word and idea associations and Titchener's on introspection. Such

[43] Dewey has remarked, in this connection: "It is not accidental that the rise of interest in human nature coincided in time with the assertion in political matters of the rights of the people as a whole, over against the rights of a class supposedly ordained by God or Nature to exercise rule. The full scope and depth of the connection between assertion of democracy in government and new consciousness of human nature cannot be presented without going into an opposite historic background, in which social arrangements and political forms were taken to be an expression of Nature—but most decidedly not of *human* nature. . . .

"The story of this development and of the shift, in the eighteenth century, from Natural Law to Natural Rights is one of the most important chapters in the intellectual and moral history of mankind. . . . I must content myself then with emphatic reassertion of the statement that regard for *human* nature as the source of legitimate political arrangements is comparatively late in European history; that when it arose it marked an almost revolutionary departure from previous theories about the basis of political rule and citizenship and subjection—so much so that the fundamental difference between even ancient republican and modern democratic governments has its source in the substitution of human nature for cosmic nature as the foundation of politics." John Dewey, *Freedom and Culture* (New York, Putnam, 1939).

examples illuminate the basic efforts to provide laboratory and experimental foundations for questions that were (and to some extent
still are) philosophical.[44]

Anthropology, too, has its roots in philosophy, in the Kantian phi-
losophical-anthropological question, "What is man," and found its
scientific development in evolutionary theory, the discovery of the
"primitive," the idea that primitive customs are survivals of the earliest
forms of behavior of pre-civilized man, and the sophisticated realization,
beginning with the introduction of field work by Malinowski, that small-
scale societies by virtue of their size provide a fundamental laboratory
for comparative generalizations about human nature.

The purpose of such a course would be threefold: to review the
original problems that led to the creation of the field; to illustrate the
general process of the formation of a discipline in its differentiation from
a larger and more inclusive field; and to provide an intellectual history
of the nineteenth century as the immediate background for present-day
problems.

2. "The Logic of the Social Sciences." Several models for this
course already exist in the College curriculum. One is Professor Mor-
genbesser's course in the "Philosophy of Social Scientific Inquiry";
the other is William Martin's sociology course in the "Logic of Social
Research." The purpose of each course is to demonstrate the methodological and philosophical underpinnings of the several social sciences. The proposed third-tier course would deal with the nature of
concepts, variables, and theory construction. It would deal with evi-

---

[44] Alfred Kroeber, the distinguished anthropologist, has written a charming
memoir of his first encounter with psychology, "The very lateness of recognition of psychology as an autonomous science is notorious. . .In my undergraduate days in the middle 1890s experimental psychology had just been
recognized as a field by Columbia University and installed in an attic above the
president and bursar on Forty-ninth Street. James McKeen Cattell, surrounded
by instruments brought over from Wundt, lectured there to a class consisting
of a woman (women were very rare as students), a Japanese (equally rare),
and Kroeber (soon to leave comparative literature for anthropology). In belated
peripheries at Berkeley in California, psychology remained within the department of philosophy until after World War I." Alfred Kroeber, "Integration of
the Knowledge of Man," in *The Unity of Knowledge,* ed. by Lewis Leary,
Columbia University Bicentennial Conference (New York, Doubleday, 1953),
p. 117.

dence and inference. (The question is often raised in the sociology course: "No one has ever seen a 'custom': how is it inferred?") It would raise the question of the types of models that are appropriate to the different kinds of theories. Thus, Malthus' law of population—that food supply tends to increase arithmetically as human population tends to increase geometrically—is based on what was then the presumably "ideal" circumstance; the situation in the United States at the time when land was unrestricted. The theory is not an inductive empirical one, based on many diverse studies, but a postulational one derived from a stipulated "optimal" circumstance. Is this type of model appropriate to this type of problem? Or can one point out that most social system models—those of organizations, for example—imply a homeostatic equilibrium theory in which changes in one section of the organization create counterefforts to restore the balance of the system? But under what circumstances would one say that equilibrium theory or some form of developmental theory would be the more adequate?

A course in the logic of the social sciences would deal with this root question: In what ways do the social sciences differ from the natural sciences, if any, with regard to criteria of adequate explanation, the nature of causation, and the meaning of determinism? It would differentiate between historical and analytical disciplines and show the limitations of generalizations in each case. The course would explore the nature of fact statements and value statements, and discuss the nature of valuation and evaluation (in Dewey's sense of *prizing* and *appraising,* or Nagel's distinction between "characterizing value judgments" and "appraising value judgments") of social issues. In short, the course would provide a "meta-language" to deal with the foundations of social science inquiry.

3. "The New Nations: Problems of Development." This course, which I have briefly mentioned before, would allow for a useful application of the social science disciplines to a set of problems that illustrate the need for a multidisciplinary approach. The questions of how a new nation establishes itself, how it builds a national identity, how it creates political stability, how it begins the process of economic development, how it institutionalizes change, involve at every point the insights of sociology, economics, political science, anthro-

pology, and social psychology. We know now, without being able to spell it out fully, that there are some "functional requisites" for development. But the economic requisites (e.g., an "infra-structure" of roads and communications, a steady process of investment) are dependent upon certain political conditions (the legitimacy of the regime, the development of a competent bureaucracy, a regularized process for recruiting leaders, etc.), and these in turn may be dependent more broadly on certain sociological conditions (open mobility in the society rather than fixed or inherited positions, a "modernizing" attitude, an adequate educational system, and the like).

A course of this kind would be a general education course in the best sense of the term, for it involves the study and understanding of fundamental social processes that occur in the creation of institutions and adaptive social change. The only question is whether our social science knowledge is adequate to the pedagogical, let alone the actual historical, task. But even the demonstration of our deficiencies—assuming, in humility, that we know them—is an important advance in being able to show students the right questions, if not the right answers.

4. "Urban Planning: The Character of the City." Such a course, employing the skills of the geographer, economist, sociologist, and political scientist, also involves the application of the social science disciplines to a problem central to our lives. One could begin, as Paul and Percival Goodman so perceptively do in their book *Communitas,* with the question, What kind of style of life does one prefer and why, and then proceed to the study of how such objectives can be achieved, at what social cost, and with what sacrifices of other objectives? Or one could begin analytically. The study of urban society involves a theory of economic location (why is there no heavy manufacturing in the City of New York?), of the ecological layouts of the different sections of a city, the kinds of communities and associations that arise in cities, and the local political processes that shape the allocation of social resources in cities. Either approach calls upon the different disciplines, and value assumptions, relevant to the problem.

The Sciences. I shall not attempt to spell out the third-tier courses in the sciences. I can only indicate, in line with my criteria, the types of courses I think suitable.

It seems to me fairly clear that a science major should, in his senior year, take a number of general courses that discuss the role of science in human affairs. There should be, as one requirement, a course in the history of science that would give the student an appreciation of the range and scope of scientific thought in the past. This would deal with the continuities and discontinuities in the growth of science.

A second course would deal with the philosophy of science: the relation of science to common sense, the meaning of a "law" in science, the relation of an observation and experiment to theory construction, the epistemological problems involving operationalism, positivism, rationalism, the cosmological questions posed by new concepts of space and time.

A third course, as I indicated earlier, would deal with the sociology of science. This would cover both the internal structure of the "republic of science" as well as the relation of science to society.

A fourth course would deal with what Gerald Holton has called "Physics and Culture."[45] Such a course, modeled on the one Professor Holton gives at Harvard, would deal with the effect, on other systems of thought, of science as an intellectual enterprise. Thus, one topic would be the impact of the Newtonian world view, with its impetus to search for natural laws of regularity, on social philosophy (the mechanism of La Mettrie), economics (the self-regulating mechanisms of Adam Smith), politics (the hierarchial world order of Saint-Simon), literature (the sense of order in Alexander Pope and the reaction to the Newtonian synthesis in Blake and Wordsworth). There could be similar topics on the intellectual and cultural impact of the theories of evolution and relativity.

In the last year, the College has taken some important steps to expand the discussion of science in relation to society. Professor I. I. Rabi, the distinguished Nobel laureate, is offering in 1965-66, a College course on the "Philosophical and Social Implications of Twentieth-Century Physics." Professor Daniel Greenberg has organ-

---

[45] "Physics and Culture," the keynote paper of the International Conference on Physics in General Education, Rio de Janeiro, July, 1963.

ized a one-year course in the History of Science which treats of the origins of science in the ancient world; the development of the two key physical concepts, matter and energy; and the relation of science to technology, intellectual, and moral developments in the West. Mr. Christopher Wright has offered several courses on the relationship of science to public policy, and in 1965-1966 is giving a comparative course on the relationship of government to science in the United States, the United Kingdom, and the USSR.

All of these are, in their ways, examples of "third-tier" courses, and the experiences of these instructors are relevant to the question of formalizing these courses into some integrated procedures.

The Humanities. Using the same criteria for a third-tier general education course, I would propose courses of the following kind for majors in the Humanities:

1. A course in the history of criticism. All literature courses, and to some extent all philosophy courses, are exercises in criticism: the explication of the underlying structure of a work, and the principles that separate one type of work from another. It would be useful for a student working in the Humanities to have a systematic course in the history of criticism. He begins now with Aristotle's *Poetics*. Much would be gained if he then went on to Horace (and understood the history of the phrase, *ut pictura poesia*), Longinus, Johnson, Lessing, Coleridge, Arnold, the nineteenth-century French critics (Sainte-Beuve, Taine, Renan), and the moderns. Such a course would not be primarily a course in esthetics (the rules distinguishing the principles of the arts), but in the methods different critics have employed to read a work and establish standards of judgment.

2. A course in modern literature. I have dealt at length with the case for the modern. I would argue further that such a course should be a requirement for all students in the College. Failing that, it can serve as an integrative course for all students in the Humanities—in the different literature and language departments and in the art history and music departments. The singular characteristic of modernity is its syncretism, and a study of Joyce, Proust, Yeats, Eliot, Kafka, and Mann involves not only an awareness of national traditions, but of the unique sensibility of modern life.

3. A course in the nature of language. Central to the humanities is the nature of "meaning," and this requires some background in the nature of language. A student majoring in literature, it seems to me, should take a course dealing with the nature of signs and symbols, the social contexts of language, the problems of syntactical analysis, giving him some familiarity with work in structural linguistics, and the modern philosophers of language and linguistic rules.

The question of "language" is so important that the question may be raised whether or not in coming years that a course in *language*— dealing with the nature of symbolism, communication theory, psycho-linguistics (and computer languages), structural linguistics–should be a basic course, required of *all* students, as the foundation for many different lines of study. The striking advances in linguistics—as it has developed in psychology, anthropology, and technical linguistics itself—raises this as an important question.

4. A literature course in a foreign language. Students in the Humanities should be required to take a literature course in a foreign language, conducted in a language other than their own. This, too, would be an important means not only of "broadening" a student, but of giving him a firsthand acquaintance with the problems of grappling with a foreign text in the original, and with learning criticism in a language other than his own.

Non-Western Civilizations. There is little point in repeating here the reasons that, within a liberal arts program, students should be required to take work in non-Western civilizations. It is a necessary window onto a way of life that in some measure, particularly through the influence of technology and its imperatives, has taken on some of the coloration of Western life; yet equally these are civilizations that have gathered enormous wisdom and a reflective way of life of their own.

I make the implicit assumption that the courses for study for the Columbia program should be Oriental studies. Other colleges, in representing non-Western studies, offer sequences in Russian civilization, African history, Latin American civilization, and so on. But I think there are compelling intellectual and institutional reasons why Columbia should restrict itself to Oriental studies.

The intellectual fact is that other than Oriental (and Islamic) studies, the non-Western "fields" do not offer the scope or unified knowledge necessary for a comparative course. Russian history has its unique blend of Byzantine culture and Western thought, but after the eighteenth century it is the Western elements that predominate and merge into the general study of European society. I cannot argue whether Africa does or does not have a history, but this history has, since the eighteenth century, been so interlocked with the history of colonialism and imperialism that the greater value of studying the African past would come in the course on the new states, rather than in a whole sequence on a non-Western civilization. As for Latin American society, whose political history in span of time parallels that of the United States, the blend of Hispanic culture and indigenous politics makes it an interesting comparison with U.S. society, but this is a different value from one designed to acquaint the student with a long tradition and historical civilization quite distinct from his own.

The institutional fact is Columbia's good fortune in having on its campus one of the most distinguished groups of scholars in Asian civilization. The anthologies *Sources of Indian Tradition, Sources of Chinese Tradition,* and *Sources of Japanese Tradition,* edited by Professor Wm. Theodore de Bary and his colleagues, have had wide national use in hundreds of other colleges across the country. The courses in Oriental Civilizations and Oriental Humanities have served as models for similar courses in dozens of other schools.[46] In Columbia College, a large number of students take these courses each year. Part of this increase can be attributed to the inclusion of Oriental Civilizations as a second-year Contemporary Civilization B option, but the growth of the Oriental Humanities colloquium (there are now four sections), without that "advantage," has proved the attraction of these courses.

Oriental Studies today is divided into two parts. The Oriental Civilizations course (in two semesters) deals with China, Japan,

[46] See, *Asian Studies in Liberal Education: The Teaching of Asian History and Civilization to Undergraduates,* edited by Eugene P. Boardman (Washington, D.C., Association of American Colleges, 1959).

India, and Pakistan.[47] It examines the pervasive problems of the ancient agrarian civilizations and the institutions that gave them such long stability and durability, and places them within the framework of the major religious and philosophical traditions—Hindu, Buddhist, Islamic, and Confucianist—as well as the lesser ones. The course avoids a purely topical arrangement of subject matter, which would involve skipping back and forth from one civilization to another.

As Professor de Bary describes it: "In our first semester we take up the traditional civilizations of India, China, and Japan separately and in that order. Indeed, we discourage the making of any comparative judgments until the year is well along and the student has some understanding of each civilization as a living, growing thing. In the second semester the order is not so neat. Modern India is presented first, since Western power and influence were exerted there first and most fully. But then Meiji Japan is taken up, as the first example of resurgent nationalism and modernization in Asia, before examining the long process of disintegration in the Manchu empire and the unsuccessful efforts to constitute a stable social and political order before the outbreak of full hostilities between China and Japan in 1937. At this point we turn back to Japan, to the struggle between divergent forces in Japanese national life from the first world war to the present. Finally we take up the collapse of Nationalist China and Chinese Communism."

The Oriental Civilizations course, in line with the parallel intention of the original Contemporary Civilization course, is organized primarily along historical lines, though there is every effort to consider broad social processes along with the sequences of events. The Oriental Humanities course, parallel in its own way to the Western Humanities course, considers works of art and thought not for their historical importance but for their intrinsic value to man. This course, also in two semesters, involves the reading and discussion of works in literature, philosophy, and religion, including canonical texts like the Koran, the Upanishads, the Bhagavad-Gita, Shankara,

---

[47] I am following here Professor de Bary's lucid exposition of the program in *Asian Studies in Liberal Education.*

the Analects, and also such works as the Ramayana, the Scheherezade, and the writings of Ibn Khaldun, Tagore, and Gandhi.

I do not believe that the Oriental Civilizations course should be included as an option in the second year of the Contemporary Civilization sequence. Within the program I have outlined, which provides an orderly sequence from the history of the classical period, through Western European history in one of three channels, to the introduction to a discipline, an alternative option of Oriental Civilizations in the second year has no logic. But there is considerable logic in making such courses required in the senior year. The organization of these courses, as they now stand, make them ideal third-tier courses, allowing students who already have some detailed knowledge of the Western tradition and of a discipline to deal with a non-Western area, and students who have worked at a Western literature to study a non-Western culture.

The proposal I would make is that each student in the social sciences be required to take a year's course in Oriental Civilizations in his senior year, and that each student in the Humanities be required to take a year's work in Oriental Humanities in his senior year.[48]

A Course in Values and Rights. Is there a place for a required course on "Values and Rights" in the curriculum? In a society where social control is constantly becoming, of necessity, direct and "visible," bureaucratic and formal rather than customary and informal, the decisions that restrict the rights of one group in order to enhance another's must increasingly be formulated consciously. The right of managers to manage is restricted in order to give workers some voice in decisions about work. The right of individuals to make rules about their private property is curtailed in favor of public accommodation. More and more we are moving into social situations where questions of rights will be debated openly. In a different sense, values and conscious choice come to the fore with the

---

[48] I do not mean, of course, to restrict the Oriental studies program to this third-tier role. For many students, Oriental studies would be a major or a concentration that they would begin in their second or third year. Students in the sciences might well want to elect Oriental studies as cultural courses. I mean here only to propose a required set of courses in Oriental studies for majors in the social sciences and humanities in their senior year.

increasing power of science. Science, enlarging the possibilities of controlling phenomena (from weather to genetics) raises more and more problems. (Should one experiment with human beings? In artificial insemination, what factors should determine the choosing of donors? If we can control the genetic code, which decisions belong to public authority?)

Certainly, if one of the aims of a liberal education is the translation of values into practice, is there not a crucial rote for a course in values and a central place for the social sciences and philosophy in explicating the nature of values? It is remarkable to note how easily we all agree on abstract ends, yet divide so sharply on means, priorities, what one is willing to forego in one sphere to enhance another.

Should such questions be handled in a single course, or should one seek to make them components of various relevant courses? Should there be a course that tries to show the modes of reconciliation of ideas and the various meanings of rationality, or should such questions be assigned to a single substantive course (as in the present Contemporary Civilization option on "Reason and Decision")?

A single course, like the one on "Reason and Decision," could deal with the logical and sociological problems involved: the types of rationality, the interplay of upbringing and vested interests, the way in which the consequences of value statements can be tested. And yet, if a single course on "Values and Rights" is to be offered, my preference would be for dealing with such matters not formally and abstractly, but in a course such as the one on United States Constitutional history. Such a course takes crucial constitutional decisions and examines them in their historical settings, the legal reasoning employed, the values implied, the changing definition of rights, and the like. Supreme Court decisions offer a superb case study of the interplay of continuity and change within a contextual framework, and allow us (in the post-Civil War cases on contract and state regulation, the New Deal cases, the civil rights issues) to deal with large socio-philosophical and moral problems within a specific cultural tradition.

But I am not altogether certain whether such a single course is the best way to deal with the issue, and whether such a course should be required. I leave this as an open question.

I have not considered the "practical" problem of counting points and reckoning how many extra points are to be added to the student's schedule (nor the problem of staffing, which I consider briefly in the next chapter). For one thing, I was trying to explicate the rationale for a proposed new organization and sequence of courses. But in practical terms, if one considers the proposals, little more has been added in the way of requirements than exists now. The proposed reorganizations of the Contemporary Civilization, Humanities, and math-science courses involve no additional courses for the student, other than a third term of humanities, which would be gained at the expense of the English composition courses.

The third-tier courses would consist of four to five single-term courses, of a total of eight or nine, which are taken in the senior year. In the social sciences this would consist at most of five courses: the historical emergence of the discipline, the methodology of the social sciences, the application of the social sciences, and a year of non-Western civilization. In the sciences this would consist of four courses: the history, philosophy, and sociology of science, and the relation of science to culture. The Humanities would consist initially of five courses: the history of criticism, a course in language, one in modern literature, and a year of Oriental Humanities. But most departments, as I pointed out, usually require twelve or so credits (four courses) of related work. What I am proposing is that these courses might well be considered the "related work" for the major.

The real change is not in the addition of more points to heavy schedules but in the substitution of a new sequence for a restricted set of electives now open to the student. The real point, then, is whether this proposal for prescribed third-tier courses, viewed as a form of synoptic general education courses, is to be preferred to the present system, whereby students can freely follow their wishes— and I make no invidious judgments in this respect, since there is a good case to be made for allowing a student to take whatever courses he feels will fit his needs—in filling out his program in the senior year.

All this involves a fundamental pedagogical issue: whether the interests of the student are best served by a kind of planning, or whether the student should be quite free to pick and choose. The ideal solution would be for the College, if it found these proposals meritorious, to offer the third-tier simply as additional electives, open to those students who wish to take them. But the constraint is one of resources. The College cannot do both; and it has to choose. One of the choices is for Columbia College, in the next several years, to begin an experimental program in which a selected proportion of the student body would go through a curriculum such as I have outlined. Such a program could take a hundred students through the new Contemporary Civilization, Humanities and third-tier sequences for a period of four years and allow for a testing of the proposals as well as the feasibility of the program on an intellectual and institutional basis. The tradition of Columbia College has been one of "continuing inquiry." It has been in that spirit that this essay and this program has been written.

Chapter Six

A REPRISE,

WITH SOME NOTES ON THE FUTURE

Every new book verbalizes some new concept, which becomes important in proportion to the use that can be made of it. Different universes of thought thus arise, with specific sorts of relation among their ingredients. The world of common-sense "things"; the world of material tasks to be done; the mathematical world of pure forms; the world of ethical propositions; the worlds of logic, of music, etc., all abstracted and generalized from long forgotten perceptual instances, from which they have as it were flowered out, return and merge themselves again in the particulars of our present and future perception. By those *whats* we apperceive all our *thises.* Percepts and concepts interpenetrate and melt together, impregnate and fertilize each other. Neither, taken alone knows reality in its completeness. We need them both, as we need both our legs to walk with.

William James, "Percept and Concept," in
Some Problems of Philosophy

This book is entitled *The Reforming of General Education.* The work *reforming,* in this context, may have an awkward sound. Why not simply *reform?* Why the gerund? Because education is not just a set of new structures, but a continuing experience that reworks the thought of the past and is a self-conscious scrutiny of one's own practice. The reforms proposed here, apart from their particular application to Columbia College, are not meant as a new enlightenment or new general truths. They build upon a tradition and are intended to adapt that tradition to fresh circumstances—and also to bend some of those circumstances to the necessary needs of a continuing tradition.

What is, then, new and distinctive about the present that has called the old practices into question? For the purposes of this reprise, I shall identify briefly some of those elements.

1. The college is no longer the place of the elect. Today about 40 percent of the eighteen to twenty-one age group (as a total figure, although not all proceed ahead immediately) attend college; at present, even though, only little more than half these students complete the four-year course and obtain a degree. The rapid growth of the two-year junior and community college has tended to blur the once distinct "break" between secondary school and college, and this fact, along with the failure of many students to complete their work for a bachelor's degree, is creating new social and intellectual distinctions—not, as before, between those who have attended college and those who have not, but between the graduates of "elite" colleges and those of "mass" or of "second-rank" colleges.

2. The pressure for admission to the elite colleges will probably increase. But the number of talented young people has not risen in proportion to the number now seeking admission to college. According to figures compiled by George Keller, only about 80,000 male students (of 86,300 total) scored 550 or higher in the College Boards last year.[1] As more and more schools work to maintain or improve their intellectual standing, the competition among the elite colleges to recruit a superior student body will become more intense.

3. The graduate school has become central within the university. In 1936, when Robert Mayard Hutchins first proposed his plan for general education at Chicago, and less than a decade later, when the Harvard proposals were set forth in the Redbook, it was assumed that only a small proportion of undergraduates would proceed to graduate school. The reverse is true today. The graduate school has tended to enhance research rather than teaching within the university. It has encouraged the trend toward intensive specialization in the undergraduate colleges. It has drained away teachers from the colleges and

[1] The perfect score in these examinations is 800. The median score of the entering Columbia College freshmen was 664 in the verbal aptitude and 683 in the mathematic portions of the examination.

reinforced a status distinction between those who teach in the graduate school and those who teach only in the college. Because relatively few students are admitted to the elite graduate schools, the competition for superior grades in the colleges has increased, as has the undergraduates' sense of pressure about the future.

4. The scope of the college as a place for intellectual exploration, or, in Erik Erikson's phrase, as a "psycho-social moratorium" for testing one's interests or finding oneself, has shrunk. This loss be comes expressed, in the voiced and unvoiced dissatisfactions of the students, as a protest against the impersonality of a university, its rushed and dispersive quality, and the lack of "encounter" between student and faculty—not just personally, but in a moral and intellectual sense. The student comes to a college and expects to find a "community." Instead he finds a "society."

5. Education in the United States today takes place within a radical new political, economic, and intellectual setting. The fact of war and the state of protracted ideological conflict have given a new mold to American society in the past twenty-five years. The new role of the United States as the great power in the world, along with the extension of our political commitments around the globe, has made us sharply aware of non-Western, societies and cultures. The emergence of half a hundred new states has enlarged our area of political and intellectual inquiry and created a vast new "laboratory" for the comparative study of nation-building, economic and political development, rapid social and psychological change, and the like.

The conditions of the cold war have created a new "mobilized polity." For the first time we have developed a large-scale permanent military establishment. For the first time, too, the federal government has begun to spend huge sums of money on research and development, and to give systematic support to science and research. Large new laboratories and research centers in the physical sciences, life sciences (biology and medicine), and social sciences (particularly "area studies") have been built with government support. The relationship between the government and the intellectuals is now, clearly, permanent.

6. The growth of knowledge and the process of "branching," whereby new discoveries give rise to distinct new sub-specializations

and fields, have multiplied the number of subjects a university is now called upon to teach. The emergence of such new intellectual conceptions as game theory, cybernetics, and information theory, and their application to such techniques and procedures as simulation, systems analysis, linear programing, and operations research, raise the question of where and how they are to be taught in the colleges. (I use the awkward word *conceptions* for game theory and the like, because these are not yet formal disciplines or substantive theories but new conceptual schemes that redefine or extend certain intellectual problems—the meaning of rationality, the nature of conflict and bargaining, the formalization of utilities and choices, the cognitive aspects of learning, etc.) Many of these conceptions have already made their mark on economics, psychology, and linguistics, and to a lesser extent on sociology; but as conceptions they transcend the boundaries of existing disciplines. The rise of these new "intellectual technologies" gives mathematics, as a subject—and the computer, as a tool—an essential role in research (in the social sciences as well as in the sciences) and a crucial place in the curriculum.

7. The university now occupies a central position in the society. Formerly its chief function was that of conserving and transmitting the intellectual traditions and cultural values of society. Now the university serves more as the center for research and innovation. Though the university once reflected the status system of the society, it now determines status. Its ties with government have become more complex. The university is the training center for specialists; the best of the professors now move easily in and out of policy-making and advisory positions in the government.

More so than ever before in American life, the university has become a public service institution, its resources increasingly used by government, industry, and the local communities, At the same time, because of its vastly increased financial needs, the university has itself become a "constituency," a significant claimant on the monetary powers of government. The scientific, technical, and literary intelligentsia, most of whom are now housed in the university, has become a significant social stratum, amounting almost to a new class of society.

Traditionally, the university has been a collegium; it is now becoming a bureaucracy. A complex administrative superstructure is built above the academic, research, and business parts of the university. Functions once inseparable from a school's identity (admissions, for example) have been taken over by specialized and professional personnel without faculty status and often, outside faculty control. The activity of teaching—the heart of the tradition of the university as a free community of self-governing scholars—has been diminished as a function of the university.

The intellectual direction and emphasis of the university—the elements that define its character—are influenced more and more by outside forces. Thus a university's expansion into new fields is often less the product of a long-range intellectual plan than it is a response to pressures from the foundations and the government, both of which have taken over in considerable measure the defining of the society's needs in relation to new intellectual, social, and political areas. The multiplication of nonteaching research centers, institutes, and laboratories, each with its own hierarchy and professional employees, not all of whom have faculty status, brings more strain and stress into the university. To work out new structural forms appropriate to its tasks, and still maintain its self-directing and self-governing autonomy in intellectual affairs, will be one of the great problems of the university in the years ahead.

The "Idea of the College"

Only a little more than a decade ago, Lionel Trilling could write: "Within recent years it has come to seem that the American undergraduate college has established itself at the very heart of our culture." From any intellectual point of view, this is no longer true. Sociologically, Professor Trilling's statement acquires a new dimension in 1966, for the rise of mass higher education has given the college an importance in our culture—as the place where intellectual values can be "imprinted"—that is greater than any it has ever had in our history.

Yet at this same time the "idea of the college"—the idea represented by the liberal arts tradition—is being attacked. It has been suggested that a liberal arts education has lost its force; that because of the recent curricular reforms the secondary school already covers, or will soon do so, the "general education" features of the college are mere repetition; and that the requirements of early specialization are in the process of transforming the college into a pre-professional school. In short, it has been stated that because the college is no longer the terminal educational experience, it has lost its distinctive function and is becoming simply a corridor between the secondary and the graduate schools. These were, in fact, the statements that prompted this investigation.

In the course of this inquiry, these arguments have been rejected. The proposition about the secondary schools; to the extent that it can be answered empirically, finds little proof to back it up. At least at Columbia, the introductory liberal arts courses—Contemporary Civilization and Humanities—still have a "transforming power," and provide a new kind of experience for college youths. There is much truth in what is said about specialization, but its consequences are misinterpreted. Specialization *can* lead to a narrowing of vision and an overconcern with vocation, but if that specialized knowledge is acquired in a context of inquiry, rich in philosophical and methodological presuppositions, and if a student learns not "received doctrine" but the modes of conceptual innovation, then special learning can be as liberalizing (i.e., in inducing a critical spirit and an independent temper) as the study of the humanities.

The most important claim, perhaps, is that the college would become a way station between the secondary and graduate schools— a statement that, even if it is made in a tone of resignation, denies the students' need for a period of unforced maturation and overlooks the distinct function many of the better colleges perform, of making their students self-conscious about the grounds of their knowledge and of their values.

But in all this, a misconception has been responsible for a mis-placed anxiety. To accept the diminished status of the college is to be stampeded by transient considerations—the graduate schools' sense of urgency about accelerating work in the colleges in order to reduce the time it now takes to earn a Ph.D., and thus increasing the supply of teachers. For one thing, such considerations are mindless of history. It is useful to remember that forty or so years ago the professional schools (principally medicine and law), with a similar sense of urgency, began admitting students after two or three years of college—in some cases this practice was not abandoned until after World War II—only to realize that the broadening scope of present-day knowledge made a full four-year college preparation altogether necessary. But ironically, and this is the second point, even the jeremiad about the prospective shortage of teachers and the lag in the number of Ph.D.'s may turn out to be groundless. Allan M. Cartter, the vice-president of the American Council on Education, has pointed out that before 1960 there was a good deal of pessimism about the future supply of Ph.D.'s. In 1957, the President's Committee on Education Beyond the High School stated that, even thinking optimistically, "there may be only one new Ph.D. available for every 4 or 5 new college teachers needed between now and 1970." A "distinguished Committee of Fifteen" reported to the Ford Fund for the Advancement of Education that the expectation "that by 1970 the proportion of college teachers holding the Ph.D. degree will have declined from the present 40 percent to 20 percent is not statistical hysteria but grassroots arithmetic." And even as late as 1964 college presidents were reminded by one of their distinguished colleagues, John W. Nason (speaking to the Fifty-First Annual Meeting of the Association of American Colleges), of the "frightening figures for the prospective shortage of teachers. . . . I repeat with all the urgency I can command that our traditional and conventional doctoral programs will simply not produce the number of teachers with doctor's degrees our educational system demands."

Mr. Cartter asks: Can so many presumably knowledgeable observers be wrong? "The answer seems to be 'Yes.' In fact, the situation has improved nearly every year over the last decade, and it has improved for every category of institution—large and small, public and private, liberal arts college and university."

How did we come to believe these dire prophecies? "The reason appears to be that both educational researchers and responsible government agencies have collected wrong information for many years and drawn hasty conclusions from imperfect data."[2]

Why these estimates were wrong is an interesting question, but it would take us far afield. (To take one error of judgment: the number of earned doctorates had been consistently underestimated in the various projection series. But the estimates themselves may have induced a "self-defeating prophecy": since a crisis was predicted if strong measures were not taken, such a measure was taken in the passage of the National Defense Education Act. Another important error occurred in the estimates of future demand.) But the singular point is that because of these dire prophecies, it was urged that the college years be compressed, that more college work ought to be taken over by the secondary schools, that the four-year college B.A. ought to be combined with an accelerated M.A. program, and that specialization should begin at a much earlier period in the college itself. Many of these proposals were made with little attention to pedagogical and intellectual questions (for example, what kind of college-level subjects the secondary school could teach). Many were mindless of the nature of the college itself.

A New Rationale

To say this is not to claim that there is no need for intellectual and institutional questions about the college. But the wrong questions were being asked. Returning to my principal interest, the character of general education today, I am forced to conclude from my inquiry

---

[2] Allan M. Cartter, "A New Look at the Supply of College Teachers," *The Educational Record* (Summer 1965).

One of the *few* who took a relatively sanguine view, it might be noted, was Bernard Berelson, who, in his report to the Carnegie Corporation in 1960, concluded: "We have a good chance to increase the present rate of doctorates in the classrooms of higher education by 1970, not lower it. . . . I conclude that the sense of crisis that makes discussions of graduate education sound shrill these days is unwarranted and misleading. There is a problem, to be sure, but not one of the magnitude now commonly accepted." Bernard Berelson, *Graduate Education in the United States* (New York, McGraw-Hill, 1960), p. 79.

There is, it should be noted, a real concern about the prospective shortage of medical personnel in the light of increased demands that may be generated by Medicare and other government legislation; and this concern will lead to a demand to reduce the time required to train doctors which now, from entry into college to the completion of Boards, averages about fourteen years. Yet such needs can be met by the training of para-medical technicians, who can take over the routine functions of physicians, and the reduction in the teaching time in medical school (e.g., in anatomy) because of the upgraded work in the colleges.

that, for reasons largely different from the ones given by the initial critics of the college,[3] the rationale for general education (however much one sympathizes with its original civilizing intentions) has become enfeebled and the intellectual *structure* (despite the value of individual courses) has lost its coherence.

General education, in the main, had three broad aims:

1. To provide a "common learning";
2. To give the student a comprehensive understanding of the Western tradition;
3. To combat intellectual fragmentation with interdisciplinary courses.

The idea of a common learning was an attempt to recapture the humanist ideal of an age when, as Douglas Bush put it, all educated men had more or less the same kind of classical education and read, spoke, and wrote the same language, literarily or metaphorically or both. But the effort to create a common language froze into one dogma that a common learning had to be a specific number of "great books." Or it settled on the notion that isolated masterpieces could be approached, apart from their time and context, as works that spoke so directly to the individual that the common reading of such works would provide a common experience. Or the humanist goal was obscured by the claim that a tradition consisted only in the reading of the works of the past.

The trouble with these approaches lies in the idea that a few works can define the central range of human issues and experiences, and that if individuals are exploring great emotional and imaginative themes in order to achieve a common ground of discourse, they all have to read the same works.[4] What may be more important than a

---

[3] Let me emphasize here, to avoid misunderstanding, that in using the phrase "the college" I am not speaking specifically of Columbia College. (My criticisms of the Columbia program are explicit in chapter 5.) I am speaking here more broadly of the rationale of general education, as theory and practice, in the past several decades.

[4] As the historian Stephen Graubard has written: "The notion that [in the nineteenth century] intellectuals met on the basis of shared intellectual com petences would be difficult to demonstrate. . . .The philologist cannot have expected the political economist to know his work, neither can he have looked to the botanist for particular intellectual insights. They met on another basis which had little to do with specific learning, but involved a shared set of values, attitudes and experiences. . . . If they learned from each other, it was not be-

single tradition and a single past (for there are many traditions and many different pasts) is to have the student accept *the idea* of tradition (and become part of its continuity) and *the idea* of the past (and relate himself to it). Nor can the humanities assume that there exists only an "eternal present" in which sensibilities are awakened anew with each encounter; without history the humanities are only myth and commentary. An intellectual community is not necessarily defined by similar readings and a common fund of allusions (though this makes discourse easier) but rather by common standards and values that permit the interchange of judgments and opinions on diverse matters of experience.

The second purpose of general education, a comprehensive understanding of the Western tradition, has, particularly in the last ten years, come to seem parochial. The study of other civilizations as rich and complex as Western culture has contributed to this parochialism, along with the growing syncretism (particularly in the arts and to some extent in religion) that tends to mingle diverse traditions into a *musée imaginaire*. As a result, a number of schools have been perplexed by the question whether the Western tradition means the study of "Western civilization" (e.g., an effort to combine ideas, arts, and religions into a succession of "periods" or "styles"— Gothic, Renaissance, Baroque, etc.), or, more simply, the study of "Western history," in which the chronology of events and "islands of ideas" build up a loosely patterned background to the present. The question has been unresolved.

The interdisciplinary aim has suffered the most and has indeed all but disappeared from many general education curriculums. Institutional factors in part account for this failure: in many colleges the departments preferred to concentrate on the disciplinary sequences and directed their students to the specific research problems of their subject, instead of attempting the more difficult task of searching out a conceptual language common to several fields (there is still no

cause they were involved in inquiries less complex than those which presently engage us, but that the pace of life permitted a certain sort of communication which is now difficult to achieve, and also, that their number was small enough for them to form fairly compact societies. . . . The values of the society militated against an individual defining himself wholly by what he did." Unpublished planning paper for *Daedalus* issue on "Science and Culture" (Winter 1965).

agreement between anthropologists and sociologists on the scope of the term "culture"). Even more telling were the intellectual difficulties inherent in interdisciplinary studies. To some scholars such studies meant a new holistic approach that would fuse diverse disciplines (e.g., the study of "culture and personality" or of "national character" would combine anthropology and psychology, or psychology, or psychology and history), but this early enthusiasm did not materialize into a continuing body of work.[5] To others it meant the study of policy problems, bringing the resources of different disciplines to bear on specific issues. (A favorite chestnut has been Planning versus the Market.) But students were often asked to consider complicated topics when they had no training in any of the disciplines necessary for intelligent judgments about the dispute. Criticism of such topics was airily dismissed with the argument that these topics were primarily "value problems" or "moral issues," as if a discussion of goals required no technical knowledge at all.

As I have said earlier, my objection to interdisciplinary courses is not to the idea itself, but to the place they occupied in the general education sequences. I shall come back to this once again in discussing the proposed third-tier courses.

The disenchantment of many colleges—I do not mean Columbia, Chicago, or Harvard—with the idea of general education, and their difficulties in recruiting teachers for the courses, have led a number of them simply to substitute "distribution" requirements for the general education sequences; and this has brought them back to the very disorder that had prompted the widespread adoption of general education in the mid-1940s and the 1950s.[6]

[5] The idea of interdisciplinary studies, as used here, should not be confused with the emergence of such new combining specializations as *psycholinguistics.* Psychologists have long sought to deal with linguistic symbols as a necessary condition of understanding cognitive processes; linguists have always admitted that some kind of psychosocial motor moves the machinery of language and grammar; the result is psycholinguistics. In similar fashion, but much less advanced as a field, is sociolinguistics, the study of how language is shaped in diverse social settings, and how the structure of language itself changes over time in response to different media and group usages.

[6] In particular fairness to the three colleges I have studied, and which I admire, few of their *epigoni* ever made the rigorous intellectual (and institutional) efforts of Columbia, Chicago, and Harvard to maintain viable general education courses. Some colleges simply copied (in drastically shortened form) the syllabi of the original courses; this in itself defeated the purposes of the courses. Other

A "distribution" requirement means that a student has a free option in the number of courses outside his major subject or concentration. Thus a science major might be required to take at least two social science and two humanities courses. No specific courses are stipulated or prescribed. Nor is there any ordered sequence or arrangement of courses. It is simply assumed that a student's education is broadened by some courses in other fields than his own. Ironically, a number of educational "radicals," once fiercely opposed to what they called the "cafeteria system," are now enthusiastically in favor of this laissez-faire arrangement on the grounds that students should be encouraged to prowl around on their own, taking any courses that intrigue them, and that a distribution requirement is as good a way as any of shaking up the creaking system because it shows the faculty what the students really want.

The return to a distribution requirement is, I believe, an admission of intellectual defeat. At worst, it serves up a mishmash of courses that are only superficially connected. At the very worst, it stimulates a modishness that caters to the immediate and the sensational, or that looks for esoteric or gnostic links because the ordinary canons of intellectual order are too repressive. Pascal once said that law without power is anarchy (and power without law is tyranny). One may extend the apothegm by saying that anarchy without intellectual order is perversity (and intellectual order without freedom is dogmatism).

I have tried in these pages to formulate a new intellectual structure for general education. Despite its emphasis on the explication of underlying conceptual foundations of knowledge as essential to the purposes of a college course, the proposal is not a radical break with tradition; in many respects, as a careful reading will show, it is even recensional. Its main intention is to undercut the distinction between general education and specialism. The justifiable fear that the colleges are turning out trained technologists who have no acquaintance with the humanist tradition reinforces the need for required humanities courses. But such courses, necessary as they are, merely provide

colleges took an even easier way out by organizing loose "survey" courses that were then labeled "general education."

an "overlay" and do not deal with the character of specialization itself. The question is, of course, what one means by specialization. The Literae Humaniores, or "Greats," the most celebrated of the arts courses at Oxford, which in one sense is the inspirer of the general education ideal, is not simply a reading of classical authors for the sake of learning about a tradition. "Greats" is itself a specialization and training in the way to read texts, in order to produce a distinctive mind. As two Oxford dons characterize the course, perhaps a bit smugly: "The effect of Literae Humaniores on its students is to develop thought and speech and a keen and critical intellect. It is deficient in providing knowledge of the modern world, and history and economics will remain a closed book unless the student, as often indeed happens, makes himself well informed by his own efforts and intelligent general reading. But it is said to produce men who are unrivalled as expositors and judges of any situation or set of facts placed before them."[7]

If the task of the college is to broaden the context of specialism, it will not be accomplished by literary poultices. It *can* be achieved, perhaps, by making the intellectual specialist knowledgeable about

---

[7] J. L. Brierly and H. V. Hodson, "Literae Humaniores," in the *Handbook to the University of Oxford, 1962* (London, Oxford University Press, 1962), pp. 149-50.

In effect, "Greats" is a combined school of classical history and philosophy. A knowledge of both Greek and Latin is required and the First Public Examination, at the end of the second year, includes translation from Latin and Greek into English and the rendering of passages of English prose (verse is optional) into Latin or Greek in the style of the classical authors or orators. The school covers three centuries of Greek history and a somewhat longer period of Roman history, ending with the death of the Emperor Trajan in 117 A.D. The study of philosophy is based on Plato's *Republic* and Aristotle's *Ethics*, to which is added modern philosophy from Descartes.

One always risks claiming too much for a single educational program as *the* formative reason for an intellectual elite. A simple sociological point must be remembered: that the best students take "Greats." As Mr. Brierly and Mr. Hodson write: "Much of the deserved fame of Literae Humaniores at Oxford is due to the fact that for over a century a veritable *elite* from the best schools in England has prepared itself for classical scholarship and proceeded to Oxford after intensive competitive examination. The students and teachers in this Honour School of Literae Humaniores have been, and probably still remain, the most naturally gifted and the most severely disciplined elements in the University, and to a greater or lesser degree the rest of us are a little bit afraid of them. It is probably true to say that no single definite curriculum of study in any one university in modern times has produced so many famous men in public life, in learning and letters."

the logic of inquiry and the philosophical presuppositions of a subject. "The intellectual life of man," William James once wrote, "consists almost wholly in his substitution of a conceptual order for the perceptual order in which his experiences originally come."[8] The effort of sophistication, the beginning (but not the end) of self-consciousness, is the effort to uncover the underlying intellectual structure in which one's work is embedded. In this way, the context of specialism can be enlarged, and becomes an aspect of the liberal education itself.

But to deal with concepts alone would mean choosing an arid intellectualism that would dry up our senses and leave us only with the shadows in the cave. Concepts are "maps of relations," but by their nature they are "forever inadequate to the fullness of the reality to be shown." Reality, James insisted, "consists of existential particulars" of which "we become aware only in the perceptual flux."[9]

The forest life of Natty Bumppo, the world of craft and lore, was a natural world in which the encounter with wind and cloud, animal and tree, sharpened the senses and gave one an immediacy of place (though not of time), just as, in different fashion, the earlier arts of manual skill, and the apprenticeship to a craft, gave a youth a feeling for material, and of the recalcitrance of things, which an education

[8] William James, *Some Problems of Philosophy* (New York, Longmans, 1940), p. 51.

James developed the point with his characteristically poetic wealth of ideas: "The substitution of concepts and their connections, of a whole conceptual order, in short, for the immediate perceptual flow, thus widens enormously our mental panorama. Had we no concepts we should live simply by 'getting' each successive moment of experience, as the sessile sea-anemone on its rock receives whatever nourishment the wash of the waves may bring. With concepts we go in quest of the absent, meet the remote, actively turn this way or that, bend our experience, and make it tell us whither it is bound. We change its order, run it backwards, bring far bits together and separate near bits, jump about over its surface instead of ploughing through its continuity, string its Items on as many ideal diagrams as our mind can frame. All these are ways of *handling* the perceptual flux and *meeting* distant parts of it; and as far as this primary function of conception goes, we can only conclude it to be what I began by calling it, a faculty superadded to our barely perceptual consciousness for its use in practically adapting us to a larger environment than that of which brutes take account. We *harness* perceptual reality in concepts in order to drive it better to our ends." *Ibid.*, p. 64; italics in the original.

[9] *Ibid.*, p. 78.

more abstracted and dependent on symbolic skills may lack. That world of "natural experience" may be gone, but there is, then, all the more the urgent need to find those modes of learning that plunge students into experiences which provide esthetic rewards, intellectual play, and a disciplined apprenticeship in work. If the world is double-storied, a factual order and a logical order imposed upon it, then a curriculum cannot sacrifice the one for the other. It has to be drawn from the stuff of events. The rationale for the study of history is that it gives the student the particularities and the differences, an imaginative involvement in the varieties of circumstance wherein ideals and passion, visions and hopes, play out their ambitions in the arenas of conflict, just as the rationale for the humanities is that they combine "fixed reason and wayward spirit," the flight from one's daemon, and the search for an epiphany, the restless effort to transform the mundane self.

Yet each of these embodiments of the "perceptual flux" must necessarily be caught in a net of meanings if we are to come to terms with it—history as governed by the logic of explanation; humanities as disciplined, finally, by the order of art. Each of these modes is part of the common stuff of the conceptual inquiry.

For some, such a rationale is disturbing. They may feel that it implies a wholly instrumental approach to education. An ordered curriculum, it is argued, must have a set of substantive ends rooted in some moral definition of man or some ultimate picture of nature. But those who posit virtue or reason as the ends of education, or of society, put too much faith in their resounding abstractions. To say that the purpose of education is the rational pursuit of knowledge, or a love of truth, is not to state an end, for these are the necessary conditions of any intellectual life.[10] Those who speak of the need for fixed ends usually mean a fixed set of books or a fixed set of ideas that for them exemplifies truth or a specific notion of obligation. But such a conception would lead only to the circumscription of truth and the creation of a closed system of dogmatic and even

---

[10] "Truths are as plentiful as falsehoods, since each falsehood admits of a negation which is true. But scientific activity is not the indiscriminate amassing of truths; science is selective and seeks the truths that count for most, either in point of intrinsic interest or as instruments for coping with the world." Willard Van Quine, *Methods of Logic* (New York, Holt, 1950).

tyrannical knowledge (even though the tyrant may have a philosopher as his adviser).

"Le bon sens," Montesquieu wrote, *"consiste beaucoup à connaître les nuances des choses."*[11] The nature of individual differences, of individual experiences, and of individual ends is an element to be respected as much as different natures of societies and institutions (including colleges), each developing in its own way. A respect for truth or the rational pursuit of knowledge can come from contemplation, or from a grounding in the processes of inquiry through which one learns to define standards, to question them, apply them, and redefine them, and thus be true to the nature of the intellectual enterprise itself. The ends of education are many: to instill an awareness of the diversity of human societies and desires; to be responsive to great philosophers and imaginative writers who have given thought to the predicaments that have tried and tested men; to acquaint a student with the limits of ambition and the reaches of humility; to realize that no general principle or moral absolute, however strongly it may be rooted in a philosophical tradition, can give an infallible answer to any particular dilemma.

The Proposals in Review

Writing a curriculum, like cooking, can be the prototype of the complete moral act. There is perfect free will. One can put in whatever one wishes, in whatever combination. Yet in order to know what one has, one has to taste the consequences. And as in all such acts, there is an ambiguity for evil, in that others who did not share in the original pleasures may have to taste the consequences. In sum, it is the moral of a cautionary tale.

Every argument has its key terms within a master structure. To the extent that a structure has been articulated for the present argument, the key terms would, I think, be *conceptualization* and *coherence*. Yet such nouns make the approach sound unduly abstract, and

---

[11] "He speaks," Isaiah Berlin writes of Montesquieu, "with contempt and hostility of the *Décisionnaire universel* (a term he invented) who is never assailed by doubts, because societies [and curriculums] organized by such persons, however well ordered and enlightened, are necessarily tyrannous." In *Montesquieu,* by Isaiah Berlin; from the Proceedings of the British Academy (19 October 1955), Vol. XLI (London, Oxford University Press).

this would be far from my intention. The curriculum presented here is organized along a number of dimensions, of which the emphasis on the centrality of method is but one. Other equally important aims are to reduce the intellectual provincialism bred by specialization and to demonstrate the philosophical presuppositions and values that underlie all inquiry. The emphasis on history and the humanities is as integral to these proposals as the concern with conceptual innovation. The unity of the scheme derives from the efforts to link the necessary historical and humanities sequences with training in a discipline, and to relate one's own discipline not only to a number of other subjects but to broader intellectual problems as well. To recapitulate the proposals:

1. The Contemporary Civilization A course would be reorganized and extended to a year and a half instead of the year it is now allotted. All students would be required to take the three-term sequence. The first term would deal with Greek and Roman history, in an effort to provide specific historical contexts for the readings in the Humanities course. The second and third terms would cover the period from the Middle Ages to the present, but they would be organized along three tracks, one devoted primarily to economic, a second to political, and a third to social and intellectual topics. Students would have a choice of one of the three sequences.

2. Following the year and a half work in history, each student would be required to take a one-term course in one of the following: economics, sociology, government, anthropology, or geography. These courses would be organized not as Contemporary Civilization courses, but as introductions to disciplines, so that students would acquire a competent understanding of at least one social science subject. Ideally, each course would have two tracks—one for a student beginning his major in that subject, the other for students who would prefer to study the discipline in a broader social science context.

If the three-term introductory historical sequence should prove to be impractical, and the present requirement of two years' work in Contemporary Civilization is retained, I would propose, in place of the present second year (paralleling my proposed math-physics, math-biology requirement), an economics-government, economics-sociology sequence. More and more, it seems to me, that economics is becoming the central discipline of the social sciences. Not only does it have a more complete intellectual structure than the other social sciences, but its subject matter is crucial in contemporary society. Each student, to be an adequately informed citizen, should have some knowledge of economics; equally significant is the fact that many of the basic analytical concepts and techniques of economics (optimizing, programing, rationality, utility preference) are permeating the other social sciences. Given these developments, I would argue that economics can be linked most fruitfully with a course in government or a course in sociology, to provide a coherent unit for the study of contemporary society.

3. The Humanities course is organized on the principle of having a student confront a literary or philosophical masterpiece directly, so that his reading will be as fresh an experience as possible. The Humanities staff has for this reason consistently opposed the use of secondary or critical writing about the work that is being read. While one may want the individual student to experience a "shock of recognition," I have argued that it is faulty esthetic or social reasoning to assume that a wholly naive approach is possible. As E. H. Gombrich has said, "the innocent eye sees nothing." Esthetic experience is in great measure conventional; it can be understood only within the specific context of the tradition that produced it and the historically available alternatives open to the original artists working from that tradition. I have proposed that the Humanities course add more critical and historical reading in order to give the student a sense of how an imaginative work relates to its own time and how its enduring qualities transcend that time.

I have also proposed that a third term be added to the Humanities year; it would introduce modern and contemporary art into the course in order to extend the student's sense of the historical continuity of literature.

4. The music and fine arts Humanities courses, even more than the first-year course, are organized on the premise that a student is best initiated in esthetic experience by confronting him with masterpieces from our cultural heritage. I have suggested that because students in the secondary schools are now so greatly exposed to

culture both in school and through the mass media, these Humanities courses should be examined with a view to devoting more attention to the nature of visual forms in the arts and new forms of sound in music. It was proposed further that since some freshmen can be expected to show proficiency in music or art, those who could be exempted from, say, the music course be allowed to devote a year to the visual arts, and a student exempted from fine arts to spend a year in music.

5. The English composition course has come to be more and more of a financial and organizational strain on the College. To staff this course, the English department has increasingly had to rely on preceptors, who then become employed in teaching the Humanities courses as well. I have suggested that Columbia College, in conjunction with the other Ivy League colleges, take steps to eliminate such courses by requiring applicants to demonstrate competence in English composition as a prerequisite for entrance. Students lacking such proficiency would be required to have made up for it, on their own, by the start of the second year.

6. The present distribution requirement in science seems unsatisfactory. I have proposed that all students be required to take a two-year mathematics-physics or mathematics-biology sequence, for these reasons: mathematics is a necessary tool (as well as a style of thought) for work in almost all fields except the humanities; and physics and biology, by virtue of their successive logical "paradigms," can best exemplify the conceptual order of science.

7. The system of majors, which has become increasingly important in Columbia College, should be reexamined with two problems in mind: first, the possibility of creating a "double track" in each major as a whole (not just in the introductory courses); second, being more specific about the necessary "related courses" for each major.

At present, each department sees its major mainly as a preparation for graduate work in that subject. Yet an analysis of career plans indicates that, except for physics and chemistry, a sizable number of students do not intend to remain permanently in their field of major study but plan either to cross over into other disciplines or, more often, to enter one of the professions—law, medicine, etc. In this light, a number of departments might review their courses with an eye to creating a "double track" for those who want, not detailed preparation in a discipline for graduate work, but a broad background. This is especially relevant in the social sciences, where more work in crosshatching can be established. Thus a sociology undergraduate major can be a preparation for graduate work in government or history, just as an undergraduate history or economics major would be a useful background for sociology. The problem of the different purposes of students merges into the second problem— the failure of the separate departments to consult each other and work out combined sequences that would be helpful to students going into law or government, or teaching and who are often vague about required related courses.[12]

8. A third-tier scheme is proposed wherein each student in his senior year would take a number of courses that would "brake" the drive toward specialization by trying to generalize his experiences in his discipline. There would be, in principle, four kinds of third-tier courses: one in the historical foundations of the intellectual disciplines in a common field; one in the methodological and philosophical presuppositions of the disciplines in a common field; another in the application of several disciplines to common problems; and still another in comparative studies, particularly of non-Western cultures. The kind of course would differ with different fields—the social sciences, the humanities, and the sciences would each have third-tier courses appropriate to its particular problems. By exploring interrelationships, by aiming at philosophical sophistication about the foundations of a field, and by pointing out the possible value prob-

[12] Professor Edward Shils has pointed out a related issue: "Only exceptional students discover their real interests before their third year, largely, I think, because they have not been pressed or inspired to dig into any subject with an intensity sufficient to arouse their curiosity or to give them a sense of achievement. Consequently, many students who develop an interest in a subject late in their undergraduate years decide to become graduate students in order to learn more about their subject which has interested them. Many of them do not wish to make careers in research or even to be trained in research techniques, but since this is a condition of their further penetration into the subject of their belated interest, they are pushed willy-nilly in this direction. The multiplication of research students is thus, in part at least, a consequence of the neglect of the intellectual side of undergraduate education and contributes to its further neglect." Edward A. Shils, "Observations on the American University," *Universities Quarterly* (March 1963).

lems that might be encountered in applying a discipline, such courses would make a distinctive contribution to general education.

Two final points are in order about the subject of curriculum. First, the emphasis on conceptual inquiry thar has been raised so often in this book comes from the conviction that learning is not simply a matter of empiricism or of conditioning but a skill that derives from our unique ability to deal with the world symbolically. It is dependent on a rational faculty, on mind. One can observe this process in the primary skill one has to acquire—that of learning and using language. As George A. Miller has pointed out, in individual speech a person uses, on the average, about ten words in a grammatical and meaningful combination at one time. A simple English sentence can easily run to a length of twenty words, so that there are about 10^{20} such sentences that an English-speaking person must know how to deal with. "Putting it differently," Miller writes, "it would take 100,000,000,000 centuries (one thousand times the estimated age of the earth) to utter all the admissible twenty-word sentences in English. Thus, the probability that you might have heard any particular twenty-word sentence before is negligible. Unless it is a cliche, every sentence must come to you as a novel combination of morphemes. Yet you can interpret it at once if you know the English language."

But knowing the English language is not a matter of learning sentences from parents or teachers who have pronounced each one, and explained what it means. What one learns "are not particular strings of words but *rules* for generating admissible strings of words." Rules enable us to locate a pattern and identify particulars. Rules allow us to handle novel situations and relate meanings.[13]

The nature of rules has been a central concern of modern philosophy. Wittgenstein, who has had a great influence on the analysis of rules, has remarked about "rule-governed behavior" that while a person may not be able to formulate the rules explicitly, he knows a mistake when he hears it. And such rules, since they involve con-

---

[13] George A. Miller, "The Psycholinguists," *Encounter* (July 1964). Miller's work in cognitive theory offers, I believe, high promise in the creation of a "learning theory," based on learning rules, that will go beyond the mechanistic stimulus-response approach that has governed most present-day psychology.

cepts of right and wrong usage, necessarily introduce a normative element in the social sciences. A concern with conceptual inquiry is a concern with the formation and operation of rules as they govern the meaning of statements and the behavior of human beings.

Second, I have attempted to repair a serious deficiency, for in the excessive preoccupation with the cognitive elements of thought (concepts, paradigms, intellectual structures) one neglects the esthetic element that is present for some people in the elegance of intellectual solutions, the fidelity to intellectual craftsmanship, and the pleasure, even the sensuous beauty, of a well-wrought theory, as in the contemplation of a Grecian urn. Intellectual work has, or should have, its esthetic, as well as its practical, satisfactions, and a curriculum must take them into account.

The Institutional Realities

The revisions of the curriculum that I have proposed have been made with an awareness of the Columbia context and the hope of continuing the tradition of general education. But the implementation of a revision depends, in great measure, on the adaptability of the institution to the proposed changes. While the question of institutional realities lies outside the scope of these proposals, a few, necessary words are in order.

In any large institution there are always shifts in the center of gravity, the point which exercises the greatest pull and attraction. At times the reasons for shifts may be idiosyncratic (e.g., the presence of some truly distinguished minds in a few fields); but more often these changes are in response to underlying processes in the society.

In Columbia University, the center of gravity from 1858 to 1880 lay in the College, from 1880 to 1900 in the graduate faculty of political science, after the turn of the century in the professional schools (particularly medicine), and in the 1920s, owing principally to a great faculty in English, philosophy, and history, once again in Columbia College.

Since the end of World War II, and particularly since the 1950s, the center of gravity at Columbia, as at almost all major universities, has been the graduate schools. The expanding college population has required more Ph.D.'s for college teaching; the new emphasis and prestige of research, particularly in the physical sciences, has given the graduate schools an added impetus; the new needs of government, particularly in the development of foreign-area specialists, has brought about the development of a wholly new field of graduate education, that of area studies.

If the College had grown proportionately, it would have fewer problems today. But the fact is that Columbia, like most universities, has rarely done balanced planning. University expansion has resulted largely from the power of its individual parts (engineering, business, law, and area studies) to raise their own funds, rather than from a centralized university policy. Clearly no university can control the wishes of a generous donor who, for personal reasons, prefers to endow a school, or a purpose, of his choice. Nor can it affect directly the decisions of government and foundations as to which areas should be most heavily subsidized. In consequence, however, the College, lacking the leverage of other university schools, has suffered somewhat in staff and facilities.

The structure of Columbia University creates an additional burden on the College. Within Columbia, a man's primary tie is not to his faculty but to his department. For the senior professor, the various burdens created by the expansion of the graduate school militate, even when he has the best of intentions, against his devoting too much time to college teaching. The work load of a Columbia professor, compared to that of professors in other major universities, is high. Usually, he teaches three courses, directs a number of Ph.D. dissertations, participates in Ph.D. thesis "defenses" in his own department as well as in others, sits in on Ph.D. "orals," is a member of a number of university committees, and sees countless students seeking advice about careers or aid in preparing papers—all of this while he is trying to do research and writing of his own. If his chief responsibility is in the graduate school, he will probably give a research seminar, a lecture course, and, if possible, one College course. In the College, he can teach a senior seminar, an upper-level lecture course, an introductory departmental course, or a lower-level general-education course. Since teaching Contemporary Civilization or Humanities requires considerable preparation, he rarely chooses to teach one of these courses.[14]

The problem is not one of good will, for much of this already exists. More flexible cooperation between the College and the graduate schools would inevitably benefit the upper-level college courses. The problem lies in reducing the pressure on the faculty—the scope of which is beyond the range of this inquiry.[15]

[14] This is the general situation. It varies considerably, from department to department. In the sciences, a gratifying proportion of senior men, including some of the most eminent figures in their fields, teach regularly in the College. For one reason, there are fewer graduate students in the sciences than in the humanities and the social sciences, fewer graduate courses, and consequently a higher professor-to-student ratio than in the other fields. In the sciences, graduate work involves more time doing research as an "apprentice" to a professor, then taking formal courses, while the large amount of research money allows the university to "stockpile" a greater number of professors. Thus, even though many science professors teach only two courses, a high proportion of them are available for courses in the College. In addition, teaching in the College does not, for these men, involve a reduction in prestige as is sometimes felt to be the case in the social sciences.

In the humanities, while the College and graduate staffs are often distinct, the College has been able to retain the services of some of the most eminent men in the university. Scholarship in the humanities is still, largely, an individual affair, and there are few prerequisites (e.g., research assistants or research money) in the graduate school. At the same time, the College tradition, embedded largely as it is in the humanities, has been able to enlist the continuing loyalty of senior persons.

In the social sciences, a distinction once fairly fixed between the College and the graduate school has come to be, in recent years, somewhat softened. The difficulty in getting senior personnel to teach in the College is due largely, today, to the competing pressures of heavy graduate enrollments and the drive to do research.

[15] Dean Keppel's comment, fifty years ago, is strikingly relevant: "The Columbia faculty is a producing community and is less affected than is commonly the case by the current claptrap as to the capricious sanctity of research. . . .

"The University Bibliography is printed each year and gives thirty or more closely printed pages to the individual contributions of officers. Of course some of these records are padded—there is one case of a man whose mere list of titles for a single year covered nearly four pages—but the record as a whole is one of which the University may well be proud. The fact that each year several publications by our colleagues are translated into foreign languages, Oriental as well as European, is particularly pleasant. It is refreshing to see how reluctant our academic cobblers are to slick to their lasts. We find engineers, architects, and psychiatrists writing poetry, a zoologist who writes authoritatively on medieval armor, a classicist on current American politics, an experimental psychologist on radical democracy, a mathematician discussing Swedenborg. . . .

There remain the vexing problems of staff for the Contemporary Civilization and the Humanities courses. The problems, as they have existed for the past dozen years, are twofold: a high turnover; a low proportion of senior men teaching these courses. (The difficulties have been more acute for the Contemporary Civilization courses than for the Humanities. In the social sciences, career lines have opened more rapidly than in the humanities, so that younger men who already have their doctorates are under greater pressure to do research and publish in order to get ahead.)

In and of itself the presence of a large number of young instructors in the Contemporary Civilization and Humanities course is no drawback. These courses are best given by younger men of enthusiasm who want to broaden their background. But because these are staff courses, some proportion of older men is necessary to provide experience and leadership.

If the Contemporary Civilization and Humanities courses are to be viable as staff courses, the College, it seems to me, has to find a new orientation toward them. It may be that what is needed are the "superior schoolmasters" that John Burgess talked about, and a staff should be selected on this basis. There are, I think, two sources of teachers for such courses. One—and this is a system in part already developed in the Humanities courses—is to search out young men who have already completed their doctorates, who would want to spend up to five years teaching at Columbia, benefiting from the association with the university, before going on to teach, rather than concentrate on research, in smaller liberal arts colleges in the country, This does not preclude accepting qualified instructors interested also

"For a time it looked as though these multitudinous activities were crowding out, or turning over to beginners, the more prosaic duties of undergraduate teaching, but the pendulum is swinging today in the other direction, and the words of Solomon, although addressed to the student rather than to the teacher, express fairly enough the present attitude of our faculties: 'Take fast hold of instruction, let her not go; keep her, for she is thy life.' In official words: 'We are trying by increasing the compensation of the undergraduate teachers, by adding to their dignity and prestige in various ways, to make it clear that we put as high a value upon first-class teaching as we do upon research and investigation. We hold that the two things are different, but we hesitate to subordinate either to the other.' Appointments to the undergraduate faculties are not of short tenure, to the end that the men who actually control the College will always be the men who do the college work." Frederick Keppel, *Columbia* (London, Oxford University Press, 1914), pp. 158-61.

in research who are willing to take their chances for promotion to a tenure position at Columbia. But the major emphasis should be on establishing definite career lines in teaching, by making arrangements with independent liberal arts colleges so that young men know that there is a future for them, and by using the superior resources of Columbia to recruit such a faculty.

A second and untapped, yet superior, resource is the professor about to retire. Columbia University has a compulsory retirement age of sixty-eight, and in the past a number of superior teachers have retired who were able, physically and mentally, to teach for many more years. There is the sound sociological reason (summed up in the classic Pareto phrase "circulation of the elites") for retirement of professors, since it opens up the way for younger men. Yet the wisdom, knowledge, and vast experience of the retiring professor can be suitably realized for the general education courses. I would envisage an arrangement such as this: with selected professors, the university would enter into an agreement whereby, at the age of sixty-two, a professor would be given a contract to remain at the university until he reached, say, age seventy-two. From the age of sixty-two to sixty-seven, the professor would "taper off" his obligations in the graduate school by reducing the number of graduate courses and dissertations he is responsible for, and teach one general education course in the College. From sixty-seven until he reached seventy-two, the professor would teach two full general education courses in the College in conjunction with younger men.

The benefits, it seems to me, would be reciprocal. For the College, the gain would be the addition of some superior men of distinction who could stimulate and direct the younger faculty as well as coming into firsthand contact with the freshman students.[16] For the professor there is the double gain of added income and fruitful activity in his later years, as well as the opportunity, in general education courses, to examine the grounds of his own knowledge after many years of specialized research.

---

[16] I leave aside, for the moment, the concrete organization of such courses. However, if the system, say, of triple channels is introduced into the Contemporary Civilization sequence, it would be easier to introduce a modified lecture system into the course, whereby the senior professors would share lecture assignments with the younger men, as well as teach discussion sections.

The costs of such a staff organization would undoubtedly be considerably higher than at present.[17] Yet the existing tendencies are such that, unless they are reversed, the College may find itself forced to rely more and more on preceptors, or on itinerant and part-time personnel, with a corresponding fragmentation of the College faculty. The present suggestions, though difficult to implement, would stabilize the amount of turnover, and would add to a staff superior teachers who would give the courses further élan.

Finally, there is the question of the size of Columbia College. Although the College population has expanded hugely in the past twenty years, there are still few schools in the United States where one can find the unique blend of a highly qualified intellectual student body with the resources of an eminent faculty. Many state universities have an eminent faculty, but are forced by public regulation to admit all students who meet minimal standards in the state high schools. A number of small liberal arts colleges, by providing individual attention, attract a highly qualified student body, but often lack the broad resources that a major university provides. Columbia College, with its intellectual traditions, diverse faculty, and selected student body, plays a central role in the constellation of American colleges.

There is a compelling case to be made for the expansion of Columbia College—as both the Everett Committee in 1956 and the Buchler Committee in 1960 have already made clear. The College today has about 2,700 students. It could expand to 4,000 without losing its intimacy, or diluting the eminence of its faculty. Societal obligations provide one rationale for expansion: the College has

[17] A third source, which the College has rarely explored, is the availibility of men in fields other than the Contemporary Civilization and Humanities courses to teach in these programs. In the course of this inquiry, for example, I encountered a distinguished physicist who said that he wanted very much to teach in the Contemporary Civilization course, but felt that he was "unqualified." It is true that he had not "specialized" in history, yet his own talents, intelligence, and enthusiasm were such that he would be a gifted and inspiring teacher for the course. In other instances, I have encountered scientists and social scientists who, to "educate themselves," would like to teach in Humanities for a year or more. In these instances, one is able to tap the best kind of teaching, for a man earnestly seeking to "educate himself" is bound to educate his students as well.

turned away many qualified applicants who could have brought added vigor to the College community. The institutional reasons cited by the Buchler Committee are also impressive: the unchanging size of the College has placed it at a disadvantage in relation to other sections of the university.

But beyond these persuasions, there is a reason that increases in importance: the need for experimentation with and the diversification of the curriculum which can be accomplished only within a larger student body. In 1960, the Buchler Committee observed tartly that the failure of the university to act on expansion, while "widespread experimentation and self-appraisal by American colleges of standing" goes on, makes it difficult to escape the impression that Columbia College is threatening to smother in its own piety. In consequence, said the Committee, "it cannot really apply in fresh and important ways its time-honored principles of 'intelligent flexibility.'" There must be room, it said, to test, vary, and compare ideas, and this can be done only by the expansion of budget, plant, faculty, and student body.

The situation is even more urgent today. At a time when the "idea of the college" has been called into question, Columbia College which, in the past, because of its traditions and university resources, was able to lead the way in so many fresh innovations, must now resolve its role or lose its leadership in the educational scheme. Expansion is a necessary condition for new experimentation. It is also the premise for the survival of Columbia College as a first-rank school.

A Coda—about the Future

Is it *hubris,* perhaps, to say that if one were to look back at the present from the year 2000—which, after all, is less than thirty-five years away—one could already discern in the second half of the twentieth century the transformation of the university into the primary institution of the emerging post-industrial society, just as the business firm had been the most important institution in the previous century and a half? The business firm had become paramount because, through its creation of new products, it was the center of innovation. But a change has taken place in the character of change, for it is not knowledge alone, but *theoretical* knowledge, that has become the necessary condition for innovation and the conscious direction of change, and the university—the place where such knowledge is codified and tested—has inevitably begun to move to the center of the stage.

One can see this in the changing relation between science and technology. In the nineteenth and early twentieth centuries, the great inventions were the work of inspired and talented tinkerers, many of whom, like Thomas Alva Edison, were largely ignorant of or even indifferent to the fundamental laws of science. Yet, beginning with the organization of the chemical industry, theoretical knowledge increasingly determined the areas of inquiry and the direction of research in the creation of new products. Similarly, the operation of a modern economy is no longer left to impersonal market forces, but is managed consciously by political technicians who rely upon theoretical economic knowledge and sophisticated economic techniques. And it is in the university that this fundamental knowledge is amassed and debated.

Sociologically, too, the university has assumed a new role in our time. Before the mid-twentieth century, a serious person went to college to acquire learning in the humanities, but except for the professions, his basic vocational skills were obtained "on the job," through experience. But the nature of training that requires theoretical knowledge has changed. The function of theory is to "reduce" empirical experience (i.e., trial and error) and to provide principles of explanation that can be applied to a wide variety of situations. Hence the growth, particularly after the end of World War II, of engineering, business administration, and graduate schools, in which specializations are acquired, not on the job, but as a condition of being hired for a job. In this way, too, the university has become a determinant of the emerging new stratification system based on education.

Because it concentrates such a wealth of intellectual and cultural resources, the university has also become the home of a powerful new stratum, the scientific and cultural intelligentsia, whose growth in numbers and influence makes it a distinct social class with status and power of its own. Members of this class, of course, are to be

found outside the university, in many institutions—research corpora-
dons, laboratories, planning institutes, academies, museums, and
the commercial satellites such as the publishing, entertainment, and
information-processing media. But in all this activity the university
is central.

It is, then, at a stage of increasing power and status unprecedented in
its history. And this new role carries with it a number of problems that
the university must solve before it can cope with the new responsibilities
that have been thrust upon it. In this coda, let me single out the four
problems I consider to be the most important and difficult.

1. *The question of organizational and intellectual flexibility.*

The structure of contemporary knowledge makes invalid the idea
of an education as a "fixed" body of thought and technique that one
acquires in four or eight years of study. To begin with, the college
years—undergraduate and graduate education—must be reorganized to
deal with "how one learns" rather than "what one learns." But the newest
and greatest need is for continuing postgraduate education. Within
the existing intellectual system, it may be that such postgraduate and
research institutions as Rockefeller University in New York (in the
biological sciences) and recently formed research institutes devoted
to forecasting the policy formulation will become the leading centers
of intellectual work. (The RAND Corporation could have been the
prototype for such institutes, but it has been working too exclusively,
especially in recent years, for a single sponsor, the Air Force.)

The sufficiently rapid introduction of new disciplines and techniques, even in the graduate schools, may be too difficult for the
ponderous structure of the University, with its many different departments, to handle.[18] One result is that much significant work in

---

[18] Professor Paul Lazarsfeld has provided an instructive account of how
difficult it has been to introduce applied mathematics into the Columbia curriculum. Even though much of the work in decision-pioneering theory, for
example, was initiated at Columbia (by Abraham Wald in the 1930s, and by
the sociology department in the 1950s, sponsoring the exploratory work by
Luce and Raiffa), the university has let this work go by default. There are
only three one-term courses that teach mathematics with special reference to

programing, mathematical learning theory, communication theory, and the like may be concentrated in a few research institutes; inevitably there is a dangerous lag before the new work is introduced into the regular graduate curriculum. Few universities have bothered to organize interdisciplinary committees that survey new fields and decide which should be introduced into the university curriculum, and where.

The question of university structure itself is highly complex. The universities have usually grown without any plan. Many with fifty-and hundred-million-dollar annual budgets still retain a degree of centralized operations control that would be unthinkable in a modern corporation. Presidents and provosts are expected to deal with trivial administrative details (individual research leaves, salary increases) that, in the organizational theory taught in the business and public administration schools on the same campuses, should be handled by subordinates or integrated into policy. Taken alone, such incongruity would have little significance. But it does show that the university has not yet solved the problem of bureaucratization nor defined the scope of the *collegium*. The relation between democracy and bureaucracy, which will be an increasingly urgent matter for *all* organizations by the end of the century, will have its most important trial in the university.

2. *The limited amount of talent.*

In the post-industrial society, the scarcest resource will be "human capital." Modern economics has taught us how to raise financial capital. (The principle is simple, the politics difficult: restrict consumption and use the savings for investment.) But the husbanding of human capital—recognizing talent at an early age, instilling and

---

subject matter. A number of pertinent areas such as mathematical learning theory are ignored completely, information theory, despite its broad application to the social sciences, is listed in the catalogue only under Electrical Engineering, and *few* outside that department are aware of it. Operations research, though extensively offered in the Department of Industrial Engineering, comes to the attention of economics students, but of few others. Neither the government department nor the anthropology department offers anything on recent mathematical work in these fields. Paul F. Lazarsfeld, "The Seminars and Graduate Education," in Frank Tannenbaum, editor, *A Community of Scholars* (New York, Praeger, 1965).

maintaining motivation, providing adequate guidance, and preventing good students from dropping out—is a long and arduous process. Planning for human capital means planning over a span of fifteen years or, in the case of intensive professional careers such as medicine, of twenty-five. Our schools, particularly the primary and secondary, are not at all equipped for such long-range planning. Career counseling in the secondary schools, to take a single instance, is often left to teachers close to retirement, or to a crony of the principal who is tired of teaching, and is rarely done with professional competence. The secondary schools themselves, as I pointed out in chapter 3, do not provide an intellectual atmosphere that encourages independence of mind or of decision.

Beyond this, there is a more perplexing question that so far has no answer: whether the genetic distribution of intelligence slows down scientific and economic progress by imposing a natural limit to the number of talented persons who can fill the scientific and professional positions in our society. Until recently, few doubted the doctrine of a fixed intelligence based on genetic inheritance—a doctrine worked out largely by Darwin's cousin, Sir Francis Galton. The I.Q. has been an immovable tyranny in American education, determining where a child is "placed" in school. But psychologists now question the idea of a fixed intelligence, and believe that even intelligence itself is "learned." It is now asserted that half the learning potential of a person is developed between the ages of two and five, so that the cultural influences on a child during that period are crucial to his later abilities.[19] If man is indeed alloplastic (i.e., molded by his environment), then large-scale efforts must be made to enrich the cultural environment in which very young children grow.

3. *The university as a political institution.*

As a new seat of power, as a source of technical and policy-making advice for those with political power, and as one of the chief means

---

[19] As Charles Silberman has recalled (in an unpublished study, "Education and the New Role of Knowledge"), John B. Watson, the father of behaviorism, argued in his book on *The Psychological Care of Infant and Child*, published in 1928, that since the child can learn nothing useful until he has matured sufficiently, the pre-school years are unimportant.

of obtaining place and preferment in other occupational sectors of
society, the university will not be able to escape involvement, despite its
ancient rank as a realm of disinterested truth, in political storms and
political wars. One can see this in two ways.

1. The university has become a major claimant of public funds,
and is thus in political competition with other elements of society
for public money. Further, the increasing interdependence of university research endeavors and economic development (even research itself is a big business with enormous employment) has made
the university a political arm of regional interests, both public and
private. This was recently demonstrated in the Midwest's protest
that research contracts were unfairly concentrated in East Coast and
West Coast schools, and in the demand for a "just share" of the
money allocated to universities. Among universities there is now
intense political competition for research apparatus (as in the present
tug-of-war over the location of the costly high-energy particle
accelerators), since a university's future is dependent on obtaining
such installations.

2. The university has become primarily a public service institution. As such, it serves public needs that are defined by government
agencies or foundations (e.g., training students in area studies, under
taking secret defense research). And its leading faculty move in and
out of government as policymakers and policy advisers. The political
system and the university system have become inextricably meshed,
but as a result, the university has become more vulnerable. It is wide
open to the resentments of the left, which deplores the university as
part of the new Establishment; it becomes the target of a rancorous
right, which reviles the university as the initiator of fundamental
social change that is dispossessing the older power groups of their
place and privilege.[20] At the same time, since the university is so
much a part of "liberal" culture, various groups within the university
begin to question its involvement with the government and seek to
detach themselves from such a relationship. Yet the institutional
relationship between government and higher education is irrevo-

---

[20] This theme is explored in my essay, "The Dispossessed," in *The Radical
Right* (New York, Doubleday, 1963).

cable; and it will become an increasing source of strain and tension among groups within the university.

4. *The disjunction of culture and social structure.*

In a more profound intellectual sense, what strikes most cruelly at the university as the social institution that joins knowledge and culture is the radical disjunction between social structure and culture, a disjunction expressed most directly in the two major orientations towards the future that divide the intelligentsia today—the technocratic and the apocalyptic. This issue, I submit, will be the source of a serious intellectual crisis in the university.

The technocratic view distrusts ideology; emphasizes the discipline of mind and the discipline of fact; is oriented to problem-solving; and employs an increasingly powerful armory of intellectual techniques to enlarge the means for controlling nature and to sharpen the definition of the rational conduct of men. Its vocational meaning is summed up in the word *professionalism.* To be a professional means to belong to a guild dedicated to the advancement of the certified knowledge—and competence—that has been tested and accumulated over a great span of time. Necessarily, professionalism erodes the world of opinion, a world where each man can pass judgment on any issue by invoking, at best, the canons of taste. (Robert M. Solow informs me that a contemporary of Newton, reviewing the *Principia,* complained bitterly that Newton's ridiculous calculus was just an attempt to remove gravitation from the list of subjects any English gentleman could talk about.) The new world is one shaped increasingly by engineers and economists, the riders of technology and rationality—a one-dimensional world, in Herbert Marcuse's phrase—if left unchecked.

The alienation that is invoked so often these days represents the "dispossession" of the young intellectuals whose forebears lived so vividly in nineteenth-century Russian novels (the word *intelligentzia* was first used in the 1860s by one P. D. Boborykin; ironically, the root of his name, *boboryk,* means to talk endlessly) and who take their own sensibility and experiences, rather than reason or tradition, as the touchstone of truth. They abhor the remoteness and coldness of "social engineering" and prefer to create worlds of "participation" and "community." In the end, however, they lack the technical knowledge, or even the willingness to acquire it, that could test their abstractions against a social reality.

But it is not "alienated youth" that tells the whole story, for they live, sadly, in a halfway house. There is a deeper current of nihilism at work today, with new radical features, that is embattled against the technocratic society.

One vital strain of modern literature has always been in opposition to the direction of rationalist history. It emphasizes the subjective self as against everything outside its ken—against mind and against society. Its roots go back to the theme, vividly expressed in *Rameau's Nephew,* that art alone, but art infused by passion, speaks the truth. For the Romantics only the experiences of the artist is truth. But as the distance between the self and the world increased, the retreat into self became a radical nihilism, invoking terror and the daemonic in an effort to transform the world. "Only if the nihilism latent in our culture would appear as nihilism would it be possible to go beyond it by understanding it" writes J. Hillis Miller in a recent book.[21] But "this is a course which our civilization has not yet chosen, or had chosen for it."

But the extraordinary fact is that in the recent years—in the works of Genet, of Burroughs, of the Beat poets, and of that new prophet of the apocalypse, Norman O. Brown, who has had a vast influence on the young—nihilism has begun to attack the very core of culture and to proclaim a way of life that is really a withdrawal from society, a retreat into the "interior distance," a new gnostic mode which beats against all the historic, psychological taboos of civilization.

Perhaps we are too close in time to these new styles, and mistake

---

[21] J. Hillis Miller, *Poets of Reality* (Cambridge, Harvard University Press, 1965), p. 5. This is a brilliant and exciting study of six twentieth-century figures —Conrad, Yeats, Eliot, Dylan Thomas, Wallace Stevens, and William Carlos Williams—as writers who confronted nihilism. "Each begins with an experience of nihilism or its concomitants, and each in his own way enters the new reality." In Conrad, "the nihilism covertly dominant in modern culture is brought to the surface and shown for what it is." Yeats transcended nihilism by "his affirmation of the infinite richness of the finite moment; Eliot by his discovery that the Incarnation is here and now; Thomas by an acceptance of death which makes the poet an ark rescuing all things; Stevens by his identification of imagination and reality in the poetry of being; Williams by his plunge into the 'filthy Passaic.'" *Ibid.,* p. 11.

what may be a passing fad for a rupture in moral temper. But I think not. The crucial line of difference is that the older modern writers, no matter how daring, constrained their imagination with the order of art. The post-modern sensibility seeks to abolish constraint by substituting experience for art, sensation for judgment. And it wants to impose that sensibility of undifferentiated experience upon all realms of culture.

The older cultivated sensibility was contemptuous of mass culture because it was produced only to be consumed. The "only authentic criterion for works of culture," Hannah Arendt wrote five years ago, "is, of course, their relative permanence and even their ultimate immortality," The chief difference between genteel society and mass society, Miss Arendt pointed out, is that the former "wanted culture and devaluated cultural things into social commodities but did not 'consume' them. Mass society, on the contrary, wants not culture but entertainment, and the wares offered by the entertainment industry are indeed consumed by society just as are any other consumer goods."[22]

Now in the present-day attacks on all culture, it is asserted that ideas are only decor, not explanation; that the "truly" modern arts, like cinema or Happenings, are "consumed on the premises"; and that experiences in the environments of passive immediacy and erotic envelopment are not to be interpreted, but must exist untranslated, to suffice as presences, "not as statements or an answer to a question." What, then, of judgment? A truly critical value, we are told by Susan Sontag, is "a sensibility based on indiscriminateness, without ideas [and] beyond negation."[23]

If this were only arty hugger-mugger, one could see it, perhaps, as an oneiromantic version of *dandyisme* (with the coldness of feeling of Lautréamont becoming the nonchalance of Andy Warhol, and the name-calling invective of Rimbaud becoming the campy prose of Tom Wolfe). But this new sensibility is linked to an ethic whose pronounced intention is to celebrate the "resurrected body," not of Christian theology but of the "polymorph perverse" narcissism

[22] Hannah Arendt, "Society and Culture," in Norman Jacobs, editor, *Culture for The Millions* (Princeton, D. Van Nostrand, 1961), p. 47.

[23] *The Nation,* April L3, 1964. Reprinted in *Against Interpretation* (New York, Farrar, Straus and Giroux, 1966).

of the savage but noble child. "The modern secular humanist intellectuals," according to Norman O. Brown, "have in the main
followed Plato and Descartes over the abyss into the insane delusion that
the true essence of man lies in disembodied mental activity. The pattern
of normal adult sexuality," he writes further, "can be no clue to the
essential nature of the erotic desires of mankind." The root of man is
"the desire of the immortal child in us for pure polymorphous play,"
the recapture of the primal narcissism that the reality principle has
forced us to surrender.[24]

Lionel Trilling, with his acute sensitivity to moral nuance, sees
modernism as having led us, "beyond culture." But Professor Trilling
still feels an allegiance to its liberating potential, and he has sought in
his recent essays to rescue the modern from the status of an ideology
by hoping that the "rational intellect," if it comes into play in this
situation, "may be found [to work] in the interests of experience."[25]

But it is probably too late. The formal control of the conscious
mind, the idea that the ego should remain master in the house of art,
will not do, Norman O. Brown writes in rejecting Trilling's view
of Freud, "The path of instinctual renunciation is the path of sickness
and self-destruction."[26]

In one sense, of course, the implicit libertinism is hardly novel.
One can find it in the gnostic sects of the second century A.D., in the
Brethren of the Free Spirits of the thirteenth century, in the
Ranters of the seventeenth century, and the bohemians of the nineteenth. What is new is the full turn of the wheel regarding an attitude to work and nature. The basic tradition of modern society,
from Protestantism through Marx, was one of active striving to
conquer nature, and to assert man's primacy and control over the
material world. It is this activity principle—expressed in Freudian
terms as delayed gratification, control of instinctual impulses, sharply
defined male and female sexuality expressed in genital terms—which
is being repudiated as a cultural mode. Such world views, too, have

---

[24] Norman O. Brown, *Life Against Death* (Middletown, Wesleyan University
Press, 1959), pp. 29, 34, 40.
[25] Lionel Trilling, *Beyond Culture* (New York, Viking, 1965), p. xviii.
[26] Brown, pp. 56-57.

also cropped up in the past, but they have been expressed in disguised, mystical terms or practiced by sects or esoteric groups in private. The new dimension is the public call and the response already apparent in that small cultural world that sets the tone and style others copy in a vulgarized and more raucous form.

For in the relationship of cultural styles to broader audiences— particularly in the way "high" cultural *modes* are produced and consumed—three new dimensions have recently appeared, and they add up to something new in the history of moral temper. One is the heavy anti-institutional and even antinomian bias of the dominant literary culture. Few novels speak up for society or equate a social order with a moral order—even as a Utopian possibility. Second, the receptive cultural media, eager for sensation, feed these ideas, albeit in vulgarized form, to a new and widening middle-class market for "culture." Third, the radical ideas, though recurrent, trace a "widening gyre" so that at each successive turn more and more restraints crumble, all areas of the imagination are brought into explorable, sensible reality, and, in the hunger for experience, *anything* is possible.

The tension between the technocratic and apocalyptic modes will be expressed most sharply in the university. The university is today increasingly committed to a technocratic orientation: in its devotion to professionalism, in its emphasis on specialization, in its expanded roie as a public service institution training students for the society. The university, too, is devoted to *humanitas,* but the sense of tradition and of the past that could be one anchorage against such tides is being eroded by formal pieties or is in danger of being swept away by the swift-running currents of the post-modern moods. The confrontation between these two modes, I would predict, will be the most urgent cultural problem of the university in the future.

The ellipsis that I noted in chapter 4 has now been made explicit. A great and troubling double task remains—to humanize technocracy and to "tame" the apocalypse. It will be easier to do the first than the second. Even for the technocrat, a well-developed skill has an intrinsic esthetic and a well-constructed theory an inner beauty; and these could be made manifest. But to show that order has virtue is more difficult when the appeals to instinct and irrationality, bound up in the coil of pleasure, begin to weave their lure. Yet, if experience and pleasure are the goals, the thread of redemption may emerge from the reassertion of an older kind of pleasure—the pleasure of achievement and of making, of imposing a sense of self upon the recalcitrant materials, physical and intellectual, of the world. For in the process of making and achieving, one learns that it is not the business of art to use chaos to express chaos, nor is it the character of experience to be entirely unreflective. This is the traditional wisdom of maturity.

The liberal arts, which this book affirms, have their own hard and difficult place, which is too often easily surrendered when a university seeks too freely to please those who rule, be it elite or mass. A liberal spirit, it should be noted, is not always a democratic one, for it is not *who* rules but *how* one rules that counts. The liberal spirit is not an opposition to orthodoxy, but to its enforcement; not against virtue, but against its imposition, whether Jacobin or Platonist. The liberal arts must have as an end, when confronting the young, both self-consciousness and self-transcendence. One lives, thus, in the tension between the universal and the particular, and often in that painful alienation which is the continuing knowledge of doubt, not of certainty. And yet this, too, is a state of grace, for as Dante said, "Doubting pleases me no less than knowing."

INDEX

The terms "Chicago," "Harvard," and "Columbia" refer to the colleges of those universities, unless "university" is so specified.